BEYOND THE DIGITAL DIVIDE: CONTEXTUALIZING THE INFORMATION SOCIETY

BEYOND THE DIGITAL DIVIDE: CONTEXTUALIZING THE INFORMATION SOCIETY

PETR LUPAČ

Charles University, Czech Republic

emerald
PUBLISHING

United Kingdom – North America – Japan – India – Malaysia – China

Emerald Publishing Limited
Howard House, Wagon Lane, Bingley BD16 1WA, UK

First edition 2018

Reprints and permissions service
Contact: permissions@emeraldinsight.com

British Library Cataloguing in Publication Data
A catalogue record for this book is available from the British Library

ISBN: 978-1-78756-548-7 (Print)
ISBN: 978-1-78756-547-0 (Online)
ISBN: 978-1-78756-549-4 (Epub)

Printed and bound by CPI Group (UK) Ltd, Croydon, CR0 4YY

ISOQAR certified
Management System,
awarded to Emerald
for adherence to
Environmental
standard
ISO 14001:2004.

Certificate Number 1985
ISO 14001

INVESTOR IN PEOPLE

To my wife and my sons.

Acknowledgements

First and foremost, I would like to thank my family for their unwavering patience and support in the long years leading to the publication of this book. It was a sacrifice which cannot be repaid. I would also like to thank the Department of Sociology at the Faculty of Arts at Charles University for providing a fruitful academic environment, and for their continuing trust and support in my endeavours, as well as all of the students and colleagues who have provided vital feedback during discussions, conferences and in the classroom. I would also like to acknowledge the particularly invaluable and productive consultations with Dr. Jakub Macek from Masaryk University and with Dr. Suša from the Czech Academy of Sciences and express my gratitude to Professors Findahl, Petrusek and Sassen who instilled me with great inspiration and enthusiasm throughout the writing process. I would also like to thank Emerald's Commissioning Editor Jennifer McCall for her kindness, support and assistance. Last but not least, Lucy Halasek, who did a great job translating and editing the book.

I would also like to acknowledge the copyright holders who kindly granted me permission to adapt or reprint the required figures; namely Wiley (Fig. 4.5), the Center for the Digital Future at USC Annenberg (Fig. 4.6), Cambridge University Press (Fig. 4.12) and SAGE (Figs. 4.13 and 4.14).

This book was published with support from the European Regional Development Fund-Project 'Creativity and Adaptability as Conditions of the Success of Europe in an Interrelated World' (No. CZ.02.1.01/0.0/0.0/16_019/0000734), with support from the Charles University programme Progres Q15 'Life course, lifestyle and quality of life from the perspective of individual adaptation and the relationship of the actors and institutions', and with support from the Czech Science Foundation, Grant No. GA13-21024S, titled 'World Internet Project – The Czech Republic II: Analysis of the social and political aspects of unequal Internet use'.

Table of Contents

Acknowledgements   *vii*

List of Figures   *xi*

List of Tables   *xiii*

Chapter 1   **Introduction**   *1*

Chapter 2   **Searching for the Core of the Information
                 Society Theory: Developments, Versions, Arguments**   *7*

Chapter 3   **Manuel Castells: Towards the Digital Divide of
                 the Information Age**   *17*

Chapter 4   **Digital Divide Research**   *45*

Chapter 5   **Tenuous Assumptions in Digital Divide Research**   *133*

Chapter 6   **Understanding Indispensability: Contexts, Networks and
                 Discourses**   *159*

Chapter 7   **Conclusion: Towards a New Theory of
                 Information Society**   *175*

Bibliography   *181*

Index   *207*

List of Figures

Fig. 4.1. The Global Evolution of Internet Users between
1995 and 2017   46

Fig. 4.2. Evolution of Articles in the Web of Science Core
Collection Containing the Words 'Digital Divide' in the
Topic or Title   47

Fig. 4.3. Changes in the Percentage of Households with E-mail
in the United States between the Years 1994 and 1998 in
Selected Income Brackets   50

Fig. 4.4. Differences in the Growth Rate of Internet Users between
1998 and 2001 in Selected Income Brackets in American
Households   52

Fig. 4.5. Diffusion of Innovation Curves and Categorization of
Adopters According to E. M. Rogers   56

Fig. 4.6. Age Distribution of Internet Users in Selected
Countries in 2015   60

Fig. 4.7. Evolution of Internet Users by Age in EU-27 and
in Selected Countries, 2004–2016   62

Fig. 4.8. Evolution of Internet Users by Formal Educational
Attainment in EU-27, 2004–2016   69

Fig. 4.9. Evolution of Internet Users by Household Income
in EU-27, 2008–2014   70

Fig. 4.10. Evolution of Internet Users by Population
Density in EU-27, 2004–2016   72

Fig. 4.11. Evolution of Households with Internet Access
and Individuals Using the Internet in ITU Development
Regions, 2005–2017   77

Fig. 4.12. The Diffusion of Innovations Process across
Different Social Strata: The Normalization
Model and the Stratification Model   88

Fig. 4.13. Van Dijk's Causal Model of the Core Argument   96

Fig. 4.14. An Updated Version of van Dijk's Cumulative and Recursive
Model of Successive Types of Access to Digital Technology   98

Fig. 4.15. The Deepening Divide Thesis   114

Fig. 4.16. Thesis of the Growing Usage Gap   126

List of Tables

Table 2.1 Comparison of Webster and Duff's Typology
of the Information Society Theory 15

Table 4.1 Percentages of Households with Internet
Access by Household Composition in EU-27 from
2004 to 2016 64

Table 4.2 Percentages of Female and Male Internet
Users in EU-27 from 2004 to 2016 67

Table 4.3 Matrix of Digital Divide Dimensions at a
National Level 92

Chapter 1

Introduction

When confronted with the question 'How significantly has the proliferation of the Internet impacted society?', the answer that comes to mind is that the Internet has changed everything, including how we communicate, work, make decisions and even think. If, however, the Internet really has become such a key communication and information infrastructure governing our social lives, then Internet use suddenly becomes a precondition for participation in today's society, that is, a new dividing line between social success and exclusion. This is not a difficult sentiment to corroborate: How many of us would be unable to perform our jobs (well) without the Internet? How much would our social lives suffer and how much less informed would we be about politics, culture and our fields of work and interest? Gaining insight into unequal access to the Internet or any other information and communication technology (ICT) has thus become one of the key challenges of our times. Insight into this new form of inequality, which has been dubbed the digital divide, becomes increasingly valuable the more (proficient) Internet use proliferates into more and more domains of social life as a ubiquitous necessity. In this respect, it would seem counterintuitive to contest the above.

However, the critical overview of digital divide research presented throughout this book furnishes us with sufficient grounds to identify the misleading nature of these claims. The purported necessity of ICT use is called into question by such findings as the sizeable number of non-users who maintain that they do not need the Internet and the number of users with low digital skills claiming that their skill-set is sufficient as far as their job performance is concerned. Are such statements merely a testament to the poor judgement of these individuals or are they rationally justifiable? Digital divide research has, with only minor exceptions, favoured the first answer – and for good reason: if (the quality of) Internet use was irrelevant for a certain segment of the population on the basis of their social status, it would compromise the basic premise that non-users or weak users of the Internet are at a disadvantage. Conversely, in certain situations (proficient) Internet use has become an absolute necessity, with no other available alternative. How, then, can we reconcile these disparate experiences, that is, the indispensability of Internet use and the looming possibility of social disadvantage on the one hand and the irrelevance of ICT use or the adequacy of minimal, often 'non-productive' ICT use on the other?

Beyond the Digital Divide: Contextualizing the Information Society, 1–6
Copyright © Petr Lupač
All rights of reproduction in any form reserved
doi:10.1108/978-1-78756-547-020181004

In response to this dilemma, this book proposes a new approach which posits the Internet as one of many possible information and communication channels. The gravity of the digital divide is then assessed as situation-specific, defined by a contextually determined necessity to use the Internet as the only possible tool. The aim of this book is then not to refute the social gravity of the digital divide, but rather to demarcate the limits of its validity, as data reveal that the digital divide is not necessarily a permanent or pervasive condition of every aspect of daily life or society as a whole.

The added value of the following text is not, however, limited to providing a more adequate explication of the digital divide issue or proposing optimized information policies. The prevailing approach employed in digital divide research is problematized in this work in order to pave the way for a new theory of the information society and to investigate the role of the social sciences in the informatization process. How might shifting our approach to the digital divide open the doors to such large issues?

In order to answer this question, we must consider the fact that the correlation between a widespread societal transformation, catalysed by the proliferation of ICT (or the Internet), and the general need to be connected, is intrinsic to prominent scientific theories emphasizing the important role of ICT in contemporary society (the information society theory) as well as digital divide research and information policies designed to ameliorate this purportedly problematic state of affairs. The relatively obvious correlation between the exceptional role of ICT in contemporary society and the digital divide then applies in both ways; this means that limiting the validity of the digital divide to certain contexts would compromise the pervasive, socially ubiquitous nature of the information society construct.

The information society theory has long held a tenuous and thus uncertain position within the social sciences. It has been the subject of harsh criticism pointing to the theory's conceptual and argumentational shortcomings and the techno-deterministic, totalizing, and highly reductionist lines of reasoning observed among its proponents.[1] Nevertheless, the information society construct has been accepted (despite its problematic nature) by an overwhelming number of social scientists as a sufficient framework for explaining the specificity of current social phenomena. This can be explained using three supporting arguments: (i) the viewpoint of those advocating the validity of the information society concept has become an uncontested source of basic knowledge in the most popular sociology textbooks,[2] (ii) later versions of the information society theory are considered

---

[1]For example, Garnham (2000); Poster (1990); Roszak (1994); Webster (1995). More details in Chapters 3.5 and 7 of this book.

[2]See, for example, Macionis (2016), who in the 16th edition of one of the most widely used sociology textbooks worldwide claimed that 'Many rich nations, including the United States, have entered a post-industrial phase based on computers and new information technology' (p. 99). Another of the most frequently used textbooks, Giddens and Sutton's (2009) *Sociology*, strongly adheres to Castells' thesis. In the latest edition of *Introduction to sociology* by Thompson and Hickey (2012), ICT is presented as the most influential factor in changing social interactions (p. 137) and proliferates 'every aspect of society' (p. 12).

crucial for postulating a theoretical framework for studies empirically examining the social aspects of information technology[3] and (iii) at least two of the 10 living social scientists most cited during 2000–2010 were among the chief proponents of the thesis asserting a strong connection between the profound transformation of social organization from the 1970s onwards and the proliferation of information technologies (D. Bell and M. Castells).[4]

However, the 1990s saw something far more significant than the normalization of the concept in academic discourse – something that brings the vanishing debate on the validity of the information society construct full circle: the information society theory has, by way of mass media, investment strategies and information policies, become a part of the everyday life and future of societies around the world. Framed by themes of social progress, development and universal participation, the realization of an information society has made its way to the top of government agendas and long-term development strategies.

Unlike other widespread theoretical concepts, such as the knowledge society, post-industrial society and post-modern society, the concept of information society has served as a critical element in transformative practices in the fields of politics, economics, social sciences, and research and development. The information society thus functions both as a theory and a robust set of actions aimed at a specifically targeted transformation of society and thus the *reconstruction* of social institutions and social life *as a whole*. This process is generally understood as a natural phenomenon, extrinsic to human agency, with no rational alternative. However, this realization is not as striking as the absence of scientific analysis aimed at studying this process as an inherently human one, that is, one selected, created and managed by people.

The ultimate aim and purpose of this book is not limited to finding a solution to the insufficient or unequal expansion of one significant innovation. A better understanding of the mechanisms behind the societal proliferation of ICT can serve to provide clearer insight into deeper underlying issues, such as how human societies shape their material infrastructures and how these infrastructures are interconnected with such inherently sociological issues as social inequality, social change and social structures.

This book can thus also be read as part of a broader attempt at unmasking the process of the *social construction of the information society*. The successful completion of such an endeavour would require a comprehensive analysis of the participation and mutual interaction of the types of social actors, who, in the social structure of post-WWII society, occupy positions of power and who wield significant influence over the direction of future development: investors, mass media, politicians, high-ranking officials and scientists. What has already been relatively well mapped out is the constructive contribution of computer scientists from the

---

[3]This claim is posited based on the sources used in this book and a study by Raban, Gordon, and Geifman (2011) where the authors mapped out the consolidation of information society research.

[4]Castells (2012) from ISI Web of Science data.

1960s to the first half of the 1990s, whose power over the technological system of computer networks eventually collapsed.[5] There is one group of scientists, in particular, deserving of special attention – social scientists. What was and is their role in the process of informatization? Before we begin to address this question, we must first abandon the notion that information society research is merely a reflection of real-world processes, that is, that it represents a body of knowledge that simply mimics the constant social (re)construction of the social order. How then can the concept of the information society be grasped within its dichotomous role of scientific reflection and co-constructor of social reality?

This book offers a new approach to the information society as a set of socio-technological relationships that are emblematic of certain contexts with limited or very little validity in others. From this perspective, the information society is not a historical fact but rather an artefact constructed by social actors who, through their actions, have promoted the technologically embedded structuring of social and identity-based relationships. This book makes two observations in this regard. The first is the paradox of informatization policies which may inadvertently produce undesirable outcomes: by calling for the creation of an Internet-savvy society, the digital divide may grow wider for those who are either unable or unwilling to meet these expectations. In other words, the argumentation employed in this book suggests that current information policies may be catalysing rather than bridging the digital divide. Secondly, this book reveals that digital divide research and the information society theory have been treating informatization as a general fact, one to which we must conform if we are to maintain our positions in society. These scientific disciplines may have thus contributed to the legitimization of this artefact, that is, the information society, as an inevitable stage of socio-technological development.

The structure of the book investigates the aforementioned issues as follows.

Following the introduction, Chapter 2 presents the key arguments of the information society theory in order to illustrate technology's pivotal role in the theory and defend the book's focus on the theory's most recent and most respected exponent, Manuel Castells.

Chapter 3 introduces the roots and construction of Castells' latest social theory while emphasizing the close relationship between his theory of the information society and the digital divide thesis. This close correlation is not a new discovery in itself, as the digital divide issue has been interconnected with discourse on the burgeoning information society from the outset. The aim is to demonstrate that the dominant approach in digital divide research is interwoven with the argumentative structure of the information society theory and that to question this approach would also be to question certain parts of the information society theory. Readers who are well familiar with the information society theory and Castells' work can skip these two chapters.

Chapter 4 maps out existing digital divide research in order to understand the digital divide as a critical internal inconsistency in the information society theory. The chapter begins by introducing the early stages of digital divide research, its

---

[5]Abbate (2000); Castells (2001b); B.-K. Kim (2005).

treatment of the information society, and its relationship to government information policies, and also presents four basic arguments in opposition to the digital
divide thesis. The next section addresses the dynamics of physical access both
nationally and globally. A special section is dedicated to the diffusion of innovations theory as it bears great relevance to the digital divide. This section reveals
that this theory had engaged with the issue of unequal IT diffusion at least a
decade before digital divide research had and that it contains a wealth of inspiration that can be effectively applied to digital divide analyses. Nevertheless, this
discipline has remained untapped and ignored by digital divide research from
the very beginning. This section also presents discussions surrounding 'updated'
digital divides spurred by such technologies as broadband Internet and the
mobile phone. The fifth and longest section then gradually presents the arguments and current findings on the subjects of motivation, digital skills and online
activities. The concepts of the digital generation, knowledge gap, usage gap and
stratification model of Internet diffusion are also introduced and confronted with
empirical evidence and/or concerns about their logical consistency. This chapter reconstructs the current state of knowledge and in doing so also presents a
plethora of research questions which can be utilized by researchers, scholars and
advanced students in their future research endeavours.

The identified inadequacies of both the digital divide thesis and its empirical
footing are addressed in Chapter 5 with a critical examination of six assumptions
prevalent in digital divide research. To assess the validity of these assumptions,
the chapter also synthesizes empirical evidence of Internet-induced changes in
the domains of social and economic life. Despite the empirical (and in two cases
normative) inadequacies of the identified assumptions in digital divide research,
there is still a solid pool of data supporting the hypothesis that ICT use can pose
as an advantage (or disadvantage in the case of poor digital skills or non-use).
Unfortunately, at this point, it becomes clear that the prevailing approach cannot
house all of the presented findings without contradicting itself.

Given that any differences in Internet usage may be – and often are – interpreted
in connection with social differences, the digital divide issue thus overlaps with
the entire Internet studies research tradition, loosely linked by an interest in the
relationship between the Internet and society. This broad framework can be fruitfully enlisted as a means of analysing the tenuous assumptions in digital divide
research, as presented in Chapter 5.

Chapter 6 lays out a contextual approach to the digital divide. The first section
introduces the parameters that (in a given context) determine the social gravity
of the digital divide. Here, it becomes clear that employing a contextual approach
means having to analyse both the digital divide and the information society not as
static parameters of a certain epoch, but rather as a process of growing dependence on a single technological infrastructure. The second section then analyses
the rigidity and strong pro-ICT focus of current digital divide research. This is
followed by an introduction of findings that form a separate research tradition,
one which analyses the digital divide as a discourse and draws attention to the
symbiotic manner in which this issue operates alongside political and economic
interests.

The seventh, concluding, chapter focuses on the remaining unanswered question: What is the role of the information society theory in the process of informatization? Grounded in his synthesis of available digital divide discourse analyses, the author emphasizes the performative function of the information society theory and analyses the sources of the totalizing aspect of Castells' later theory of society. This allows the author to outline a possible approach for rethinking the information society theory in order to synthesize its dichotomous role of scientific reflection and co-constructor of social reality.

Chapter 2

Searching for the Core of the Information Society Theory: Developments, Versions, Arguments

> During Queen Victoria's reign, a new communications technology was developed that allowed people to communicate almost instantly across great distances, in effect shrinking the world faster and further than ever before. A world-wide communications network whose cables spanned continents and oceans, it revolutionised business practice, gave rise to new forms of crime, and inundated its users with a deluge of information. . . . The benefits of the network were relentlessly hyped by its advocates, and dismissed by the sceptics. Governments and regulators tried and failed to control the new medium. Attitudes to everything from newsgathering to diplomacy had to be completely rethought.[1]
>
> Tom Standage

The theory of the information society (TIS) is the composition of a wide set of diverse concepts,[2] all of which share certain fundamental arguments and beliefs, bordering on ideology, and a specifically structured imaginary. The aim of this chapter, however, is not to shed light on this demarcation (which will be explored more closely in Chapters 6 and 7), but rather to succinctly introduce the development, basic arguments and different versions of TIS in order to pave the way for our three main goals: First, this chapter shall reaffirm the notion of a 'proliferating system of ICTs' as an undeniable building block for the entire gamut of information society theories; the second aim of this chapter is to contextualize the relevance of this work by presenting the particulars and limits of recent efforts in order to exceed the scope of the existing TIS; lastly, this chapter shall justify the selection of a representative TIS, intended to serve as the pinnacle of recent efforts in the field.

Which arguments and authors should then be included in TIS? As we will later see, one can observe a set of arguments associated with the term 'information

---

[1]Standage, 1998 (pp. xiii–xiv).
[2]Karvalics (2008) makes a selection out of 50 different information society definitions.

Beyond the Digital Divide: Contextualizing the Information Society, 7–16
doi:10.1108/978-1-78756-547-020181005

society', though some are used to defend semantically close albeit non-identical terms such as the new economy, computer society, post-industrial society, the digital society, knowledge society, etc.[3] Every systematization and analysis of the information society theory then, to a large extent, depends on the criteria for selecting certain authors and arguments, that is, the appropriate scope of knowledge for developing and critiquing TIS. Given that one of our aims here is to find a new perspective from which to interpret the role of TIS in social change, we shall not delve into an overly detailed description of its development. Allow us to instead take a brief look at how TIS, as we know it today, has taken shape over time.

2.1. Milestones in the Development of the Information Society Theory

Although it is debatable whether it was the Japanese or the Americans who first coined the notion of the information society at the beginning of the 1960s,[4] it is Austrian-American economist Fritz Machlup's 1962 publication *The Production and Distribution of Knowledge in the United States* which is generally credited as the initial point of departure on the matter.[5] This work was the first to define and measure the 'knowledge industry', which Machlup divides into five principal categories: education, research and development, mass media, information machines (e.g., computers) and information services (e.g., finance and insurance). Based on an analysis of government data from 1958, he estimated that the information sector had generated 29% of the US gross national product that year, with 31% of the labour force employed in the sector; he also discovered that the sector's rate of growth was double the rate of the total US GNP growth from the years 1947 to 1958, meaning it would soon exceed the 50% threshold.[6] Although Machlup himself did not use the term 'information society', his concept was later adopted as 'the prototypical form'[7] of the information society thesis.

Machlup's classification of the 'knowledge industry', along with the calculated percentage of the labour force employed in the industry, inspired a large number of social scientists thinking about social change in terms of economically determined social stratification. An influential proponent of the management theory, Peter Drucker, applied Machlup's calculations and in the 1960s developed his own concept of the 'knowledge worker', who, much like the manual worker of the Industrial Age, represents the core of the new society's economic system. In 1969, he asserted that 'from an economy of goods, . . . we have changed into a knowledge economy'[8].

---

[3]See Beniger (1986) for a representative list.
[4]Duff, Craig, and McNeill (1996).
[5]See Beniger (1986); Cawkell (1986); Crawford (1983); May (2002); Salvaggio and Steinfield (1989); Webster (2006).
[6]Adapted from Beniger (1986, p. 22).
[7]Duff (2000, p. 24).
[8]Drucker (1968, p. 263).

In the mid-1970s, Machlup's categorization was elaborated on by Marc Porat, who was already using the term 'information economy'. The growth of the information sector was, according to Porat, directly spurred by the efficiency of 'non-information' production, where part of the produced surplus value was consumed via information goods and services. Porat's contribution lies in his distinction between the primary and secondary information sectors, where the primary information sector 'includes those firms which supply the bundle of information goods and services exchanged in a market context' (e.g., banks, research institutes, innovation centres, real estate offices, etc.), while the secondary information sector 'includes all the information services produced for internal consumption by government and non-information firms'[9] (e.g., research and marketing departments and government agencies producing nonmarketable information goods and services for internal use). While monitoring the development of these sectors in the US economy, Porat arrived at the conclusion that the United States was 'entering another phase in economic history' and was 'just on the edge of becoming an information economy'[10]. Porat posited the computer as the new 'central fact', which, together with the telecommunications network, serves as an essential component of the information infrastructure and is the driving force behind the shift towards an information economy. Machlup's notion of a knowledge-based economy, as elaborated by Porat, has become the point of departure for the entire research and theoretical tradition of the 'information economy' or 'new economy', serving as the economic basis for the transition towards an information society.[11]

At the beginning of the 1970s, Daniel Bell picked up where Machlup and Drucker left off with his ground-breaking study *The Coming of Post-industrial Society*. His work garnered great acclaim and overshadowed another, more critical theory of post-industrial society, penned by French sociologist Alain Touraine. Let us briefly summarize its basic features. Bell divides social life into three realms: the social (i.e., techno-economic) structure, polity and culture. He places great emphasis on the techno-economic structure, which, according to Bell, correlates with the social structure, that is, it corresponds very closely to the system of social stratification (it 'comprises the economy, technology, and the occupational system'[12]). Bell interprets societal relations along two axes – social (property) and technical. According to the dominant principle, society can be divided into feudalism, capitalism and socialism along the social axis, while the technical axis divides society into pre-industrial, industrial and post-industrial. The transition towards a post-industrial society is symptomatic of the rationalization of society, which is reflected in the streamlining of industrial production and which in turn results in an ever-increasing segment of the population crossing over to the service sector, the key component of which is expert knowledge. The respective features of post-industrial society are thus the centrality of

---

[9]Both quotations Porat (1977, p. 4).
[10]Porat (1977, p. 204).
[11]Duff (2000).
[12]D. Bell (1973, p. 12).

theoretical knowledge (with theoretical knowledge becoming the primary source of productivity and innovation), a focus on the creation of 'intellectual technologies' (i.e., the technology of modelling and rationalizing situations), a shift in the nature of labour (transition from the production of goods to services and towards an information economy), political meritocracy (the central institution of post-industrial society is longer the factory but rather the university) and an orientation towards the future (as opposed to a past-oriented pre-industrial society and present-oriented industrial society).

Although Bell's selection of the term 'post-industrial society' was a highly conscious one in an effort to emphasize the transitory nature of contemporary society, he rendered it virtually synonymous with the terms 'information society' and 'knowledge society'.[13] Towards the end of the 1970s, Bell freely equated post-industrial society with information society,[14] ushering in a slew of other theories emerging during the 1980s, where advocacy for the information society concept reached its peak. One of the most influential supporters of TIS at the time was American futurist Alvin Toffler, who, using a third-wave metaphor, presented informatization as the third revolution in human development following the Neolithic Agricultural Revolution and the Industrial Revolution.[15] The theory of the information society reached its apex in the second half of the 1990s in Castells' trilogy *The Information Age* (to be discussed in detail in Chapter 3).

2.2. Arguments and Versions

Two of the most notable attempts at a critical systematization of TIS are *Information Society Studies* by Alistair Duff and *Theories of the Information Society* by Frank Webster.[16] Both authors, having studied a wide range of relevant authors and arguments, agree that the concept of the information society has a solid foundation in that it reflects a significant societal change, allowing us to perceive today's economically and technologically developed societies in contrast to past systems. While Duff strives to create a framework for synthesizing different versions of TIS, Webster's aim is to reduce TIS to the empirically and argumentatively sound aspects which can be integrated into the general theory of society.

In this section, the basic arguments of TIS shall be presented, as extracted by the aforementioned authors, drawing attention to the shortcomings of this classification system and providing a rationale for the selection of Manuel Castells' theoretical system as the dominant variant of the information society theory.

---

[13]See D. Bell (1973, p. 212 and 467).
[14]D. Bell (1979).
[15]Toffler (1980).
[16]Duff (2000); Webster (1995, 2002, 2006); for older attempts at a systematization of TIS see, for example, Salvaggio and Steinfield (1989). As Webster's approach evolved while he was updating *Theories of the Information Society*, I always specify the edition in which the referenced information first appears when citing or referencing Webster's work.

This version shall then be the point of departure for outlining an improved approach to the information society in the conclusion of this work.

Webster postulates five basic definitions of the information society and criticizes the insufficient empirical footing and underdeveloped arguments of most TIS authors. The sources of social change, which the presented definitions are grounded in, can be categorized as follows (the authors whom Webster cites in the latest 2006 edition are indicated in parentheses):[17]

(1) *technological*: revolutionary innovation and the resulting changes in society's technological infrastructure (e.g., Connors, Evans, Gates, Martin, Negroponte and Toffler),

(2) *economic*: the prevalence of information activities in the total economic production (e.g., Porat),

(3) *occupational*: the majority of the labour force is engaged in activities related to the generation and distribution of information/knowledge (e.g., Bell, Drucker and Gouldner),

(4) *spatial*: unprecedented changes in social time-space, its acceleration and compression (e.g., Castells and Sassen),

(5) *cultural*: explosive growth of meanings circulating within society, associated with the defining role of the symbolic sphere, namely the media (e.g., Baudrillard and Poster).

Webster's typology of information society definitions also serve as (a) a list of basic arguments positing the information society as an emerging social reality and (b) a breakdown of the authors backing these definitions. The common denominator for these five definitions and the key criterion for categorizing an author or theory within the framework of TIS is, according to Webster, the increasing centrality of information in society. Barring a few exceptions, authors of TIS presuppose that the qualitative change is symptomatic of the quantitative increase of information in society, be it reflected in the employment structure, new technological systems or economic productivity. Given that the arguments supporting these definitions are 'either or both underdeveloped or imprecise'[18] Webster employs Roszak's critique of the reductive interpretation of the term 'information' in TIS[19] and adds a sixth definition, which he views as only marginally supported by TIS authors, though according to Webster, this definition is the most fitting.

The sixth definition emphasizes the role of theoretical knowledge as a distinctive feature of the current state of societal development; social life in the twentieth century was, according to Webster, increasingly dictated not by practical or situational knowledge as it had been in the past, but by a more theoretical knowledge, defined as 'abstract, generalizable and codified in media of one sort or another'[20].

---

[17]Extracted from Webster (2006, pp. 8–21).

[18]Webster (1995, p. 24).

[19]Roszak (1994) criticizes the omission of the qualitative component of information.

[20]Webster (2002, p. 26).

Not only does Webster consider the significance of people surrounding themselves with items constructed using theoretical knowledge and the use of this knowledge in increasingly specialized occupations, but that theoretical knowledge has become an integral component of their stock of knowledge at hand, a reference point for everyday interactions and interpretations of the world. Unlike authors who directly associate themselves with TIS or are considered typical representatives of TIS, Webster aligns himself with authors who, to a certain extent, operate outside or on the brink of this discourse, or at the very least do not implement the term information society as an umbrella concept for their theory (the sixth definition bears close resemblance to Beck and Giddens' theory of reflexive modernization[21]). This serves as a considerable step forward in terms of the overall tone of the book; while in the first edition, Webster subjects Bell's concept of theoretical knowledge to great criticism and scrutiny, from the second edition onwards, Webster recognizes the potential of this approach as a constructive reworking of TIS in the analysis of modernization and the development of capitalism.[22]

Webster's final typology, though a useful tool for navigating the maze that is TIS, poses three weaknesses for our purposes:

First, Webster himself draws attention to the fact that each definition should be read as an analytical category, though authors *always* apply them in certain combinations. One would be hard pressed to find, for example, an author who employs the economic definition without at the very least making reference to changes in the employment structure.[23] What is of greater importance here is that the validations and elaborations of definitions (b) to (e) always, to some extent, explicitly reference the impact of information technologies on current and future social change.[24] Webster's categorization of certain authors as adherents of TIS, although they do not emphasize information technologies as agents of change in contemporary society, can be accounted for due to their focus on the importance of information in contemporary society, though they make no use of the term 'information society' (e.g., Baudrillard). Webster's intention was likely not to reconstruct TIS based on critiques of the extracted arguments and referential significance, but rather to determine the *true* extent of discontinuity in contemporary social change with regard to the growing significance of information.

The second limitation is that the definitions of TIS do not carry equal weight: some (technological and economic) are emblematic of TIS, while others (i.e., spatial) are of a more inferred nature. The majority of authors who reduce the complexity of social change to one or a couple of factors can be somewhat laboriously categorized using this typology. However, this typology of definitions is scarcely applicable to the leading TIS authors, as all of the aforementioned definitions can technically be applied to them (see below), and Webster's failure to

---

[21]Beck (1997); Giddens (1990).

[22]Cf. Webster (1995, pp. 50–51, 2002, p. 58).

[23]For this reason, certain authors (Duff, 2000; Pintér, 2008) do not differentiate these two definitions.

[24]From the listed authors, for example, Drucker (1968), Porat (1977) and Poster (1990).

do so renders him inconsistent (e.g., he first attributes Castells to the spatial and occupational definitions before reproaching him for employing definitions that are too technological several chapters later).[25]

These two issues signal a certain internal incongruity in Webster's assessment of TIS: although he refutes the notion that we live in a new type of society defined by technologically induced relationships, he does acknowledge the centrality of information and information technologies in everyday contemporary life,[26] an 'unsurpassed'[27] analysis of which, according to Webster, can be found in the trilogy *The Information Age*, by Manuel Castells. The problem, however, is that Castells explicitly repudiates gradualism[28] and clearly functions as an emblematic author of the modern history of TIS, significantly bolstering the theory's position. Webster unfortunately does not satisfactorily elaborate on this discrepancy and instead directs his efforts at emphasizing the continuity of capitalism and the role of theoretical knowledge in everyday life.

Duff contends that TIS is, in fact, a set of three basic *versions* conceptualizing the transition towards an information society, all of which have developed in different geographic regions and scientific disciplines, employ different forms of argumentation and bring forth different evidence (the versions at hand are: information technology, information flows and information sector). According to Duff, these versions can be approached as different research traditions.

The first two versions correspond to the first three of Webster's definitions (Duff does not make a distinction between the economic and occupational definitions) and are, in Duff's estimation, characteristic of the Euro-American debate on the information society. Duff does not strive for an encyclopaedic categorization of authors representing these theories, but rather approaches each version with a detailed critique of the characteristic texts of canonical authors who empirically defend the transition towards an information society.[29]

Duff argues that the third version can be found in the Japanese discussion on *Joho Shakai* (translated as 'information society'). As this concept was developed within telecommunications and not information sciences, economics or sociology, it followed a different trajectory from that of the American version of the information sector and thus represents, according to Duff, an entirely different tradition of measuring the informatization of society. The difference between the two can be primarily viewed in the exploration of all communication media (not only electronic media) and in the emphasis on the population's consumption of an increasing volume of information rather than on the production and change in content. Duff considers the most beneficial aspect of the Japanese version

---

[25]Cf. Webster (2002, pp. 17 and 120).

[26]Webster (1995, p. 50), in other editions as well.

[27]Webster (2002, p. 123).

[28]Castells (2000b, p. 28).

[29]The reduction of the analysed works is so simplistic that it greatly reduces the value of the entire typology. The section of the book focusing on the information sector version provides a detailed critique of Machlup's 1962 work, the section on the information technologies version is almost entirely aimed at presenting and critiquing Ian Miles' texts.

of TIS to be the methodology modelled in the 1970s, which measures storage capacity dynamics and the transmission of all information in all communication media in the entire population of Japan. An illustrative example for our readers: the informatization of Japanese society can be evidenced, for example, by the finding that the volume of information transmitted via telephone calls rose from $2{,}557 \times 10^{10}$ minutes to $10{,}903 \times 10^{10}$ minutes between the years 1960 and 1972.[30] However, information flow statistics and the subsequently created diagrams in the Japanese version did not exhibit systematic critical reflections on the hypotheses, measurement methods and interpretation of results. Duff sees this as the result of institutionally grounded research, as the research was conducted almost exclusively within government institutions, with the results published predominantly as official government documents.[31] The Japanese TIS thus serves as an explicit legitimization of (technocratic) efforts to informatize Japanese society.

According to Duff, the ultimate aim and normative direction of expanding the theory and research on the information society should then be the formation of a 'synthetic methodology', which would combine the positive elements of all three versions while circumventing their inchoate hypotheses, operationalizations and interpretations. Duff considered Daniel Bell to be an exemplary proponent of the nascent synthetic TIS, claiming that if this synthetic methodology were further developed, it would have to overcome the shortcomings inherent in Bell's argumentation. From 2001 onwards, Bell's position in Duff's texts was gradually supplanted by Manuel Castells, whose trilogy, according to Duff, 'represents the latest important step in the direction of a synthetic theory of the "informational society"'.[32]

Although there are differing typology criteria at play here, the two typologies are not mutually exclusive. While Webster emphasizes the need for a complete list of basic definitions, devised to serve as an artificial construct to help readers navigate the deluge of authors and theories, Duff claims that his versions refer to factually existing traditions of empirically grounded TIS argumentation. This means that Duff penned the systematization of TIS from within, working with the assumption that the current TIS is merely an underdeveloped scientific response to the real process of significant historical change. Unsurprisingly, his goal is then to consolidate and empirically validate the three versions – all highlighting different aspects of one, real process. Webster refuses to work with the abstract postulation that informatization is a significant catalyst of social change, as he asserts that defining the role of information technologies should be the product of critical analysis. He is nevertheless still confronted with ascertaining the continuity or rather discontinuity in the transition between current and past structures, which he resolves by partially evading his own conceptualization of TIS. However, despite the aforementioned points of contention between the two, the authors come together on several notable points. Let us now summarize

---

[30]Duff (2000, p. 82).

[31]Duff (2000, pp. 96–99); cf. Masuda (1980).

[32]Duff (2001, p. 236).

Table 2.1:   Comparison of Webster and Duff's Typology of the Information Society Theory.

Webster (Definition)	Duff (Version/Research Tradition)
Technological	Information technology
Economic	Information sector, Occupational
Cultural	Information flows
Spatial	_[33]
Theoretical knowledge	Synthetic methodology

Source: Author according to Duff (2000) and Webster (2006).

which aspects serve as common ground for both authors and their differing approaches and consider how these parallels can be employed to bolster further interpretative efforts in this work.

First, as has already been suggested, the core TIS arguments for both authors are comparable. The Japanese version of TIS does not differ from the cultural definition of the Euro-American cultural sphere in terms of the nature of the proposed arguments, but rather in the argumentation method, which is grounded in impressive measurements and estimates of the total volume of stored and transmitted data. For the sake of clarity, the parallels between the information society theories of both authors are illustrated in Table 2.1.

Second, neither of the two authors provides satisfactory responses concerning the function of technology and specific technological development in TIS. The technological definition/version never ends with a nondescript declaration of the fundamental social changes spurred by informatization; similarly, each definition or version of TIS is always accompanied by some conceptualization of a specific (i.e., not arbitrary) technological development which hinges upon the development and proliferation of a certain technological infrastructure, the use of which brings about changes in the capacity, range and forms of communication. While Webster does draw attention to the opacity of TIS when confronted with the question of which technological artefacts in particular serve as the agents of the implied social changes, he avoids engaging with the role of the technological infrastructure in his definition of theoretical knowledge (in keeping with his position on the problematic significance of information).[34]

Third, both authors effectively agree that the TIS premise can neither be entirely refuted nor entirely accepted; the reason for this is not necessarily the

---

[33]Duff does not pay particular attention to the change in social space as symptomatic of the transition towards an information society.

[34]Webster (2006, p. 11).

obvious heterogeneity of approaches, argumentation methods and staggering volume of publications, but rather the contradictory assessments linking analyses of change in various domains of society with the assertion of the information society as a new form of social organization, as posited by two leading figures in particular: Daniel Bell and Manuel Castells. They hold unique positions in both of their attempts at a systematization of TIS, since, as has already been suggested, neither of these authors can be effectively aligned with single versions or definitions as their systems of thought encompass them all.

Fourth and last, both authors agree on the problematic lack of critical reflection regarding the reality of informatization in TIS – an issue which in itself calls for a reworking of TIS. Webster attempts to remedy this by shifting his focus to continuity, the role of theoretical knowledge in everyday life and more convincing empirical evidence when critically analysing the development of capitalism. For Duff, the formation of a unified TIS requires the academic consolidation of a new scientific discipline with its own adapted methodology.[35] However, a specific outline of a more sophisticated version of the current TIS is lacking in both authors.

The approaches of both authors pave the way for distinguishing two possible methods for reworking TIS. One leads via empirical grounding and a theoretical renovation of TIS as a reflection of real-life processes; the second method requires dismantling TIS and applying its valid features to the general theory of contemporary social dynamics. These approaches will be revisited once we are confronted with the task of not refuting TIS entirely, while attempting to find a way out of this crisis spurred by the compromised position of the digital divide thesis within TIS.

The aim of the following chapter shall be to present the symbiotic relationship between the prevailing concept of the digital divide and TIS (i.e., in that their current forms mutually validate one another). Although this chapter has furnished us with very solid groundwork, it is unlikely to be of much use in constructing a depersonalized, ideal form of TIS as an intersection of the presented definitions and versions; any subsequent criticism and reflection on the matter would have to be as equally abstract as this construct. The reworked version should ideally retain all of the core arguments of the entire TIS tradition and also be generally perceived as the unsurpassed apex of the whole theory's development while interlinking informatization with the nature of contemporary social transformation. If we were to select one author, one who applies all of the core arguments posited by Webster and Duff when postulating a new type of society, strives to conceptualize the role of ICT at the level of social change, and currently ranks among the most influential figures in the arenas of social science and communication studies,[36] it would be unseemly to choose anyone other than Manuel Castells.

Let us then revisit the sweeping lack of suspicion[37] towards the concept of the information society, to which he contributed significantly with his work.

---

[35]Webster (2002, pp. 263–273); Duff (2001, pp. 237–242).
[36]Castells (2017).
[37]Webster (1995, p. 4).

Chapter 3

Manuel Castells: Towards the Digital Divide of the Information Age

> No researcher engaging with the topic of information can afford
> to ignore the work of Manuel Castells. At the same time, our
> efforts cannot end with *The Information Age*.[1]
>
> Frank Webster

In this chapter, we shall observe the symbiotic manner in which Manuel Castells
fuses informatization and the digital divide in his work – a work whose information society thesis has been elevated to the status of esteemed social theory, with
even its greatest critics asserting that *The Information Age* trilogy is 'the most illuminating, imaginative and intellectually rigorous account of the major features
and dynamics of the world today'[2].

Since our main area of interest here is Castells' reflection on informatization,
we will not go into too much detail regarding his early research and books, which
primarily address the mechanisms and possibilities of the social articulation of
the urban space. We can symbolically frame this period around Castells' engagement with Touraine's research on Paris in the mid-1960s and with the publication of his 1989 book *The Informational City*, in which he postulates the first
comprehensive theoretical framework for investigating social change. However,
this period cannot be overlooked entirely, as we must establish Castells' primary
sources of inspiration as well as the texts which form the conceptual and epistemological basis of his later books and which must be taken into account when
reassessing Castells' theory in the concluding section of this work.

3.1. Earlier Castells: Epistemological Sources and Urban Sociology

In 1962, Castells left Francoist Spain and went into political exile in France,
where he studied sociology in Paris under the tutelage of renowned figures of

---

[1]Webster (2006, p. 123).
[2]Webster (2006, p. 98); similarly Garnham (2004, p. 165) and van Dijk (1999).

Beyond the Digital Divide: Contextualizing the Information Society, 17–44
Copyright © Petr Lupač
All rights of reproduction in any form reserved
doi:10.1108/978-1-78756-547-020181007

French post-war thinking such as Alain Touraine and Louise Althusser. Castells' approach to the analysis and critique of society was thus informed by the French intellectual milieu of the mid-1960s. With Marxism still dominating the scene, Castells found himself entering discussions centred on overcoming the existing social order (i.e., capitalism), allowing him to utilize the long-standing analytical framework as a platform for voicing his desire for radical social change – a sentiment he carried over from Spain.[3] The shape of Marxism was undergoing a transition during this period: in 1960, Lévi-Strauss, in his inaugural address at the Collége de France, announced a shift from phenomenology to structuralism, with structural anthropology taking on the role of a general theory of relations.[4] Althusser elaborated a distinctive version of structural Marxism, making a decisive epistemological break from Sartre's effort to merge Marxism with existentialism. In a structural reading of Marx's work, Althusser differentiated historical materialism as a science of history from dialectical materialism as the philosophy upon which this science was built; this allowed him to separate Marxism from the 'philosophy of history' as an ideology, but most importantly, by interconnecting structuralism with historical materialism, he was able to liberate Marxism from the thesis of an economy-driven understanding of ideology and politics. In Althusser's reading of Marx, there are no universally applicable, unilateral, causal relations between politics, ideology and economy, for which economy would serve as the ultimate determinant; certain social formations can reveal specific combinations of reciprocal determinations of varying degrees (e.g., the Middle Ages were dominated by Christian ideology, while economy is the last instance in capitalism). Though the field of reciprocal determinations is structured by economy as the dominant instance, society remains nonetheless a decentralized whole, where all instances retain a certain degree of autonomy in their internal development (the 'relative autonomy of superstructure' theory).[5] Althusser thus maintained that one cannot find a singular, ultimate explanation behind the shifts in social dynamics through history, just as social development does not arise out of the dialectics of a singular contradiction. Castells adopts the distinction of fundamental instances in the social structure, together with the relative autonomy of instances and the presupposed dominance of economy in the capitalist mode of production, and embeds them in different versions throughout his entire subsequent work.[6]

According to Castells, however, Althusser was not his main source of inspiration, nor does he explicitly cite him as often as he does Touraine, whom he considers his 'intellectual father', claiming that his 'entire intellectual life, career and life were shaped and protected by Touraine'[7]. What then was Touraine's

---

[3]Castells (2009, p. 2).
[4]Descombes (1980); cf. Lévi-Strauss (1963).
[5]Descombes (1980).
[6]Cf. the focus of three parts of *The Information Age* and also in Castells (1977, 1983, 1989). The role of Althusser's inspiration in Castells' 'redefinition' of urban sociology is further expanded upon by Saunders (2004).
[7]Castells and Ince (2003, p. 12).

role as Castells' 'intellectual father'? This can be summarized using three main points of influence: Touraine's effort to combine the objectivity of research with the social responsibility of the social scientist, an emphasis on the free actor and a focus on social movements as the crux of conceptualizing the possibilities of social change. Castells honours Touraine's rule that social scientists should shift the attention of social research towards social conflicts and problems (and away from themes of integrity, stability and growth).[8] Nonetheless, it should be the individual actors who actually tackle these issues in reality – sociological research should be 'just a tool' for those striving to build a better world, furnishing individuals with the results of sociological analyses which articulate the core of social problems and the formative power of the individual. Castells addresses the problematic relationship between observation and analysis in a combined emphasis on the comprehensive *description* of the examined subject (if injustice, pain, reasons for stagnation and the potential for change are part of the social order, they will emerge from analysis) and the use of theory as a *tool* for identifying research questions ('theoretical categories are just tools, working tools in my research. If I do not find a tool useful, or if it is too undefined to be utilized, regardless of its brilliance, I am not very interested in it'[9]). His approach can thus be best described as pragmatic positivism. Ultimately, Castells himself admitted that he adhered to the Marxist approach for as long as it proved useful in his research.

It is imperative that we examine Castells' categorical effort to maintain a non-ideological approach to his own scientific work – an effort which is (primarily from the 1980s onwards) manifested in the absence of an explicitly articulated normativity.[10] Allow us to have a look at Castells' own words as he ruminates on the topic:

> I do hope that this book, by raising some questions and providing empirical and theoretical elements to treat them, may contribute to informed social action in the pursuit of social change. In this sense, I am not, and I do not want to be, a neutral, detached observer of the human drama.
>
> However, I have seen so much misled sacrifice, so many dead ends induced by ideology, and such horrors provoked by artificial paradises of dogmatic politics that I want to convey a salutary reaction against trying to frame political practice in accordance with social theory, or, for that matter, with ideology. Theory and research, in general as well as in this book, should be considered as a means for understanding our world, and should be judged exclusively on their accuracy, rigor, and relevance. How these tools are used, and for what purpose, should be the exclusive prerogative of

---

[8]Cf. Touraine (1971).
[9]Roberts (1999, p. 34).
[10]We will revisit the topic of Castell's normativity in Chapter 7.

> social actors themselves, in specific social contexts, and on behalf
> of their values and interests. . . . The most fundamental political
> liberation is for people to free themselves from uncritical adher-
> ence to theoretical or ideological schemes.[11]

Castells thus believes in the individual's ability to overcome the human-imposed structural conditions of life. It is always the actor in his unique circumstances who, in opposition to the structures and systems at hand, negotiates and strives for a better social order. His claim that 'our societies are increasingly structured around a bipolar opposition between the Net and the self'[12] undoubtedly echoes Touraine's assertion that one of the chief social conflicts of the new society lies in 'the contradictions between the needs of these social systems (i.e. bureaucracy, technocracy and the market) and the needs of individuals'[13]. Both authors stress the position of social movements as the focal point of overcoming the instrumental rationality of technocratically oriented systems; Castells and Touraine also shared a mutual quest for the common denominator of various manifestations of resistance towards the dominant social order.[14]

Castells rose to the position of respected sociologist with his works on urban issues, the most widely known being *La Question Urbaine*[15] (1972), *City, Class and Power* (1978) and *The City and the Grassroots* (1983). In the 1980s, he seamlessly transitioned from studying structural influences on the formation of the urban space to studying the contemporary restructuring of society itself.

Influenced by the work of Henry Lefebvre and French structuralism at the turn of the 1960s and 1970s, Castells did not analyse the city as an autonomous entity, one that develops in accordance with its own laws, largely independent of the human factor (as advocated by the Chicago School), but rather as a social product, arising out of the intermingling of relationships situated within the social structure of the given social formation. Earlier Castells alleged that contemporary forms of urbanization (i.e., the formation of metropolitan areas) must be viewed in conjunction with the late-capitalist production process, which presents a framework of conflicts upon which the city grows.[16] During the 1970s, Castells expanded this frame of thought into three (relevant for our purposes) directions: an emphasis on collective consumption, the need to analyse the development of local (spatial and social) forms in the context of the globalization of capitalism and differentiating the mode of development from the mode of production.

---

[11]Castells (1998, p. 359).
[12]Castells (2000b, p. 3).
[13]Touraine (1971, p. 61).
[14]Cf. Castells (1983, 2004b, 2015) and Touraine (1971).
[15]In the United States published under the title *The Urban Question: A Marxist Approach*.
[16]Castells (1977).

As has already been suggested, earlier Castells was of the mind that:

> To analyse space as an expression of the social structure amounts, therefore, to studying its shaping by elements of the economic system, the political system and the ideological system, and by their combinations and the social practices that derive from them.[17]

The city can thus be understood as a material infrastructure (residential housing, factories, offices, roads, public transportation, playgrounds, parks, etc.) which mirrors the structure of social relations in its spatial order. At the level of the economic system, Castells does not seek opportunities for social change in the urban space in conflicts derived from relations in production, but instead creates a model which contains two interconnected components: production and consumption. Consumption is further categorized as individual and collective, with a greater emphasis placed on collective consumption, functioning as a structural complement to collective forms of production. By the second half of the 1970s, Castells considered consumption to be the central problem in understanding the dynamics of the urban space.[18] However, this means that disputes over the urban space cannot be reduced to a class struggle, calling for the need to create a theoretical framework for articulating the struggles between different groups, as defined by their positions within collective consumption. Such a newly defined field of social conflict requires identifying new actors of social change, who arise from the structural tension between 'a growing collectivized form of consumption on the one hand . . . and the capitalist logic of production and the distribution of consumption resources on the other'[19]. The stabilizing element here should be the state; however, given that its mode of functioning is closely intertwined with the distribution of power in the class structure of society, there is a clear overlap of interests between those of the state and the 'hegemonic factions of the dominant classes'[20] – in such a situation, systemic antagonisms become a pressing everyday concern, spurring a permanent political crisis. Resistance to the technocratic planning of a power aggregate by the exponents of the late-capitalist market and the state is formed from the bottom up by way of mobilized urban movements. Given that this form of protest is not, at its core, aimed at the interests of the local elite, but rather functions in defiance of the late-capitalist arrangement of social life, Castells employs this comparative analysis as a means of enriching our knowledge of the reproduction and changes of the urban space as well as society as a whole. The elaboration of this theme culminates in Castells' book *The City and the Grassroots*, where the author, following in the footsteps of Touraine, searches for the basic tenets and common aims of contemporary urban movements across different cultures and societies.[21]

---

[17]Castells (1977, p. 126).
[18]Castells (1978, Chapter 2).
[19]Castells (1983, p. 3).
[20]Castells (1983, p. 3).
[21]He revisits this theme in the context of contemporary movements in Castells (2015).

La Question Urbaine already exhibits Castells' dissatisfaction with the current model which studies the impact of changes in production relations on urban growth, despite the expansion of the model to include consumption. At the time, urbanization was considered the logical consequence of industrialization, resulting in its classification within the sociological conception of modernization as the transition from a traditional, agrarian, peasant community towards a modern society, functioning as its counterpart. Urbanization indicators were then equated with indicators of industrialization. Castells maintains however, that both indicators are informed by the capitalist mode of production. If nineteenth century cities did indeed look anomic, it was not spurred by technology or the spatial concentration of the population, as famously purported by Louis Wirth,[22] but was instead symptomatic of the poor social control of industrial activities, that is, a crisis in the mode of production. Castells refutes the notion of industrialization being the only catalyst for city growth by drawing attention to the global situation, characterized by an unprecedented growth of cities in 'underdeveloped' countries. It seems that the theories of Western urbanists were merely reinforcing the myth of modernization, overlooking the dependence of underdeveloped countries on the dominant capitalist system.[23]

Castells thus arrived at the concept of dependent urbanization, allowing him to better contextualize the relationship between the economic structure of the dominant social formation and the urbanization of the dependent country, as well as the correlation of urbanization and technological modernization within a single country. According to Castells, 'a society is dependent when the articulation of its social structure, at the economic, political and ideological level, expresses asymmetrical relations with another social formation that occupies, in relation to the first, a situation of power'[24].

The study of development, which reveals a new level of social exclusion in sprawled-out areas and entire subpopulations is, in these conditions, equal to 'studying the penetration of one social structure by another'. Migration (into cities) is then spurred by the destabilization of the periphery. This destabilization arises out of the interaction of old and new structures and is manifested in rapid population growth and the inability of rural areas to sustain themselves. Due to their position on the global periphery, cities in underdeveloped countries are not as equipped to tackle such large volumes as they lack the necessary tools for managing mass migration, that is, bureaucratic structure or developed urban networks. The associated (urban) social crisis of developing countries is then rather symptomatic of the implausible co-existence of two economic structures in a situation where the existing exchange system is subjugated by and restructured under the pressure of capitalism. In light of this book's theme, we cannot overlook Castells' explication (one we shall return to in the conclusion) that dualities such as agrarian/industrial, traditional/modern are but an 'ideological scheme'

---

[22]Wirth (1938).

[23]Castells arrived at this hypothesis two years prior to the publication of the first part of Wallerstein's trilogy on the world system.

[24]This and the following quotation are from Castells (1977, p. 44).

that should be done away with, and which reflect the 'reality of a single structure, in which the effects at one pole are produced by the particular and determined mode of its articulation with the other pole'[25].

The issue of dependent urbanization is elaborated in his book *The City and the Grassroots,* based on research conducted in Latin America.[26] In this work, Castells contests that socially marginalized individuals reside in the outskirts of cities, finding instead that a large number of immigrants gravitate to the city centre. Castells further asserts that the interpretation of marginality, as promoted by the state, confuses cause for effect – marginalized groups are not the cause of ill-conceived state policies but rather a consequence of them. Upon conducting an analysis on squatting in Lima, Mexico City, Monterrey and Santiago de Chile, Castells reached the conclusion that slums and squats and the informal economy tied to them are the characteristic traits of a dependent city. A large percentage of the population is relegated to illegal housing, leaving it at the mercy of governments which are, in turn, highly dependent on foreign capital flows which reflect the division of labour in the world system. For Castells then, urbanization is not an independent variable, as it too is subject to the global geography of capitalism.

It is now necessary to consider whether or not social change can be explained solely by studying the transformations and interactions between three fundamental, relatively autonomous substructures of society. Furthermore, are the capitalist mode of production and its global geography adequate explanations for understanding current social dynamics? At the turn of the 1970s and 1980s, Castells clearly leaned towards a negative answer to the above questions and attempted to lay down the foundations for a general model of contemporary social change which would explicitly include the factor of technological change. His point of departure here was the differentiation between two analytically independent axes which define the social landscape – the socio-economic axis of production relationships and the axis of the technical-organizational system of production.

3.2. Later Castells and His Theory of Society

An early version of a developed theory of society can already be found in *The City and the Grassroots*, with the most detailed elaboration of the theory appearing in his 1989 book *The Informational City* as well as his 2000 article 'Materials for an exploratory theory of the network society'.[27] After the year 2000, Castells no longer veered from his basic theoretical framework, although it is evident that he placed increasingly greater emphasis on the role of symbolic communication and the (re)production of meaning and power.[28] In the following text, we will work primarily with Castells' original formulations from his preliminary 1989 version and with the edits made in the first volume of *The Information Age: The Rise of the Network Society* (Castells merely tried to fine tune the model at this

---

[25]Castells (1977, p. 47).
[26]Castells (1983).
[27]Castells (1989, 2000a).
[28]Castells (2007, 2009); Castells, Fernández-Ardevol, Qui, and Sey (2007). Further on this below.

point, which is why only slight tweaks were made to his formulations after the turn of the 1980s and 1990s.) As the development of Castells' theory hinges upon empirical evidence, his theoretical research framework will be presented in terms of its empirical footing and the related arguments posed in the most significant and influential publication arising out of Castells' second productive phase: *The Information Age* trilogy. While working on the second edition of his work, Castells collected enough material for a separate book on the social impact of the Internet and published it under the title *The Internet Galaxy*. The guiding interpretive thread remains to be Castells' problematization of the geographically and socially asymmetrical development of information technologies, contextualized by the transition towards the Information Age.

The fundamental thesis that frames the second phase of Castells' work can be summarized thus:

From the 1970s to the 1980s, we bore witness to the creation of a new social structure, a network society, which is a historically and culturally specific incarnation of the informational mode of development in the context of the restructuring of capitalism.

Castells enlisted new analytical categories in order to approach the state of contemporary social change as one not limited to the urban space or a specific region. The respective terms are 'network society', 'mode of development' and 'restructuring of capitalism'. Let us take a closer look at the integration of these concepts in Castells' analysis of the logic of change in contemporary social life.

Castells posits that societies arise out of conflicting social interactions occurring within a specific social structure.[29] The social structure is made up of three basic sets of historically determined relationships: production, power and experience, which in turn interact to (re)produce the social structure.

> Production is the action of humankind on matter (nature), to appropriate it and transform it for its benefit by obtaining a product, consuming (unevenly) part of it, and accumulating the surplus for investment, according to socially decided goals.[30]

The mode of production is characterized by the structural principle of the appropriation, distribution and uses of the surplus, which generates a class-based division of society. The twentieth century saw two dominant modes of production: capitalism and etatism. Capitalism is, according to Castells, historically fluid and is constantly adapting by re-arranging (restructuring) its institutional and

---

[29]It nonetheless remains unclear which concept of structure Castells employs, as his theory fuses the two predominant traditions for defining the social structure: as an interpretive scheme, the rules for individual variations (a concept similar to de Saussure, Lévi-Strauss and Foucault) and as a set of historic forms of the dominant organizations of social life, something which functions as an oppressive external power over the individual (a concept similar to Durkheim and Touraine).

[30]Castells (2000a, p. 7).

organizational structure in order to preserve the essential building blocks of its functionality:

> the separation between producers and their means of produc-
> tion, the commodification of labour, and the private ownership of
> means of production based on the control of capital (commodi-
> fied surplus) . . . Capitalism is oriented toward profit-maximizing,
> that is, toward increasing the amount of surplus appropriated
> by capital via private control over the means of production and
> circulation.[31]

Let us note that there is no specific mention of a class of capitalists in the sense of an explicitly defined entity; the act of determining who (or what) capitalists are can only be furnished by context-sensitive research.

Castells does not engage with the theoretical construction of the develop-ment and restructuring of experience and power relationships as he does with production relationships. This can be accounted for due to the more expressly stated social implications of production among authors who informed Castells' line of reasoning and the resulting hypothesis of the role of economy as 'the last instance' in capitalist society. These two relationships, however important in Cas-tells' recent works, are of little consequence for our further endeavours and shall thus not be delved into in greater detail here.

All three instances are subjected to the historical and cultural realization of two inherently human characteristics – symbolic communication and the use of tools: 'Meaning is constantly produced and reproduced through symbolic inter-action between actors framed by this social structure [i.e. on all three levels – noted by PL], and, at the same time, acting to change it or to reproduce it'[32].

The perpetual (re)construction of the reasons and functions behind human behaviour is thus always structurally limited albeit never predetermined. The meaningfulness of this effort is constantly externalized onto struggles at all three levels of the relationships which form the social structure. The constant tension between freedom and necessity spurs the metaconflict of the epoch: it is always the expressed reaction of the experienced historical actor to the oppressive power of the dominant organizational principle of the age. For Castells, as we may have already observed, the central conflict at play today is that of Network versus Self.

Conceptualizing the role of technology in social development is, for Castells, rooted in an elaboration of the Marxist scheme of social change. The role of technology, however, has always been ambiguous in this scheme, and Marx's dia-lectics of technological and social forms leave open the question of the relation-ship between technological and social change.[33] Castells points out that – akin to symbolic communication – technology also permeates all three levels of the social

---

[31]Castells (2000b, p. 16).
[32]Castells (2000a, p. 7).
[33]For more details, see Feenberg (2002).

structure and its social impact cannot be limited to that of production; analytically speaking, it thus presents another autonomous layer: for example, hormonal contraceptives (a) alter the female experience by granting women greater control over their own biological processes, (b) impact economic relationships by enabling more efficient commodification of the female labour force, and lastly, (c) contribute significantly to the restructuring of power relations between men and women. Does this imply then that the capitalist mode of production does not necessarily have to be connected to a *specific* set of technological innovations organized in a *specific* system of the technological organization of production?

As early as the 1950s, Raymond Aron pointed out that although Soviet socialism and Western capitalism differ in their political regimes, when we examine the development of the mechanization, concentration and scientization of production (i.e., the concentration of workers in factories, the organization and division of labour, the bureaucratization of production, the development of the employment structure, the interconnection of science with production processes, etc.) and the related ideologies of growth and progress, both systems can be characterized as an industrial type of society.[34] This brings us closer to the reading of capitalism as a socio-economic formation, the development of which can be divided into stages based on shifts in the technological organization of production, inducing new organizational and institutional forms. This step was taken at the turn of the 1960s and 1970s by Touraine and Bell in their elaboration of post-industrial society as an emerging phase in the development of capitalism, a phase characterized by the growing significance of theoretical knowledge in the production and management of society. Castells draws on the work of these two authors and resolves the issue of technological and social production relations by employing a redefinition of Touraine's 'mode of development' concept,[35] which he distinguishes from 'mode of production' as an analytically independent category enabling a typology of societies along two separate axes.

While the mode of production dictates the rules of the appropriation, distribution and uses of the surplus, the volume and quality are categorically determined by 'the productivity of a particular process of production, that is, by the ratio of the value of each unit of output to the value of each unit of input'[36]. Labour acts upon matter in order to create a product in a specific technological configuration, that is, within a specific system of technological relationships and with a designated use of energy and knowledge. The mode of development is thus informed by 'the technological arrangements through which humans act upon matter (nature), upon themselves, and upon other humans'[37]. In Castells' estimation,

---

[34]Aron (1967).

[35]Castells very loosely draws on Touraine's concept of 'development formulas' (Touraine, 1981, Chapter 6), which is rooted in the nature of the ruling elite (defined in opposition to the masses) and differs from the mode of production which is defined by economic relations and divides society into classes.

[36]Castells (2000b, p. 16).

[37]Castells (2000a, p. 9).

we can historically distinguish three modes of development based on their main sources of productivity growth: agrarian, industrial and informational.

> In the agrarian mode of development, the source of increasing surplus results from quantitative increases of labor and natural resources (particularly land) in the production process, as well as from the natural endowment of these resources. In the industrial mode of development, the main source of productivity lies in the introduction of new energy sources, and in the ability to decentralize the use of energy throughout the production and circulation processes. In the new, informational mode of development the source of productivity lies in the technology of knowledge generation, information processing, and symbol communication.[38]

In order to emphasize the typological similarity with the term industrialism and to disengage with older information society theories, Castells employs the term 'informationalism' in order to articulate the appropriate stage of development. According to Castells, we cannot only speak of an 'information' society, as information plays a significant role in all human societies; what is more, Castells views the term 'information' as too closely interlinked with a set of techno-deterministic, progressivist theories using the term the information society, deeming it an innovated attempt at employing scientific discourse to legitimize a new version of universal modernization, which, in this case, is measured against the number of installed computers.[39] For these reasons, he adopts the adjective 'informational'[40] in order to signify a specific situation in which information-based operations become the main source of productivity. The informational mode of development does not only affect productivity however, as it significantly affects society as a whole. There are two primary reasons for this: first, as has already been discussed, technological change manifests itself at all levels of the social structure, thereby impacting not only production and consumption, but also power relationships, experience and symbolic communication; second, given that information and symbolic communication are inherently human activities, permeating the entire social structure, and because ICT is a technology facilitating the transmission and processing of information, the connection between production, experience and power is far more interlinked here than in any other socio-technical system. According to Castells, this shift in the mode of development infiltrates society as a whole (i.e., the entire social structure) and we

---

[38]Castells (2000b, p. 17).

[39]Castells (2000b, p. 20).

[40]The difference between informational and information, as implemented by Castells (2000b, p. 21) is no longer as relevant for us – if only for the reason that Castells, upon making this distinction, abandons it on the account of being more 'user friendly' and does not elaborate on this difference further (he merely reiterates it). It seems that this is the same rationale behind Castells' use of the term 'Information Age', which he renders synonymous with the term informational society, without further specifying its relation to capitalism.

can thus expect 'the emergence of historically new forms of social interaction, social control, and social change'[41].

Castells conceives of information technologies today as being akin to that of steam engines and electricity in the Industrial Age, that is, an innovation so ground-breaking that it defines the very essence of the entire subsequent era in the wave of derived innovations. He views the Information Technology Revolution as a historical product, stemming from the contingent development of specific economic and cultural formations in Western societies at the beginning of the 1970s and the interfering development of three key technological fields: telecommunications, computers and microelectronics. The historically unique nature of the combination of these three fields lies in digitalization (the shift to a binary numerical code), that is, in the ability to process and reversibly model any information, in this case, any set of codable data (communication, financial flows, maps, organizational structure, DNA, etc.). The productivity of informatization is not, in Castells' estimation, limited to the increasing ratio between inputs and outputs, but is primarily grounded in the processing of information and modification of processes.[42] Just as with the invention of electricity, we can observe a shift in the parameters of the innovation process; this new framework of rules and strategies, encompassing the technological shift and subsequent social change, is coined by Castells as the concept of 'the information technology paradigm'.[43]

In separating the mode of production from the mode of development, Castells does away with the premise that an agrarian society could not be a capitalist one, in the same way that it is plausible for informational etatism to exist.[44] Real societies are always the product of the historically and culturally specific combinations of the mode of production and mode of development (including specific technological and organizational forms). It is important to keep in mind that informationalism does not represent a specific historic society, but rather an analytical category for defining certain types of technologically structured relationships. Castells reads the transition from industrialism to informationalism as a process emerging in the background of interactions between the interconnected processes of information technology development, restructuring of capitalism and the gradual reorganization of production and distribution of goods. The historical realization of informatization and the social structure that forms in its wake is labelled by Castells as the 'network society'.

---

[41]Castells (2000b, p. 18).

[42]Castells (1989, pp. 10–14).

[43]Castells (1989, pp. 12–17).

[44]Provided that there is sufficient compatibility between the technological design, power structures and communication flow structures. See Castells' hypothesis on the collapse of the Soviet bloc as spurred by an inability to adapt to the conditions of an informational mode of development (Castells, 1998).

3.3. Network Society

Castells is cognizant of the fact that, akin to information, networks are one of the foundations of human life and thereby of all social formations. Castells defines a network very generally as a set of interconnected nodes, with each node being an intersection of curves/flows.[45] In the domain of social life, networks are created and 'programmed' by social actors as specific communication structures that, once established, become semi-autonomous entities operating in accordance with the designated aims and procedures.[46] Networks are, according to Castells, non-centralized; the significance of the node is contingent upon its position in the structure of flows in the given network and on its ability to processes throughputs. This also gives rise to his stipulation that networks are inherently horizontal and instead of centres have nodes with coordination and programming functions.[47] If a network arrangement is characteristic of *any* set of units that are bound by relationships (thereby including human collectives), why then should contemporary society be labelled a 'network society'? According to Castells, the emphasis of recent studies on networks as the universal pattern of social life fails to recognize the dominant position of hierarchical and vertically integrated forms of organization as seen in mythically and religiously defined societies (a reflection of the hierarchical order of the world), as well as in societies of industrial capitalism and etatism (reflected in the centralization and control of unilateral communication flows). Why then did social networks, as the defining forces of all social life, only appear towards the end of the twentieth century as a dominant form of organization in human activities? Castells chalks this up to the limited capacity of social networks to coordinate the activities of its members once they exceed 'a certain threshold of size, complexity, and volume of flows . . . *under the conditions of pre-electronic communication technology*'[48]. The traits of social networks, namely adaptability, flexibility and redundancy, become

---

[45]Castells (2000b, p. 501).

[46]Castells (2009, p. 20). Here we can see that Castells does not distinguish between the two layers of meaning in his conception of the term 'network', that is, a network as a general analytical category, a universal trait of human organization (where even hierarchical organization is a type of network formation), and a network as a socio-technical structure specific to informational capitalism. In order to defend his thesis of the network society as a historically new type of society, the usage of the term 'network' in his texts is most often associated with the second meaning, that is, as a non-human collective actor to which he freely applies the term automaton (see Lefort, 1999, p. 49). The significance of this glossed over difference in Castells' work is discussed in detail, for example, in van Dijk (1999) and is a matter that shall be revisited later in the book.

[47]Nonetheless, these claims are misleading and Castells clearly employs them in order to distinguish network society from that of its predecessors. Network science establishes centralization as an inherent feature of networks containing the preferential attachment of nodes (Barabási, 2002). The horizontal nature of social organization in network society is problematized by Castells himself in his analyses of contemporary organizational change (see Section 3.3.2) and in analyses of accelerating urbanization and the increasing significance of nodes in global trade (see Section 3.3.3).

[48]Castells (2009, p. 22), italics M. Castells. Similarly, also Castells (2001a, pp. 545–546).

the deciding factors of their dominance over vertically integrated formations once they acquire the required technological infrastructure, that is, the technology of computer-mediated communication which facilitates the transition towards information networks. Limited time, space and amount of nodes and flows no longer serve as an obstacle, as this tool exhibits an increased capacity for processing information and two-way communication in real time.[49] However, analyses on the integration of information technologies into financial and production organization in the 1970s and 1980s reveal that 'without organizational changes, technological advances are assimilated into the status quo'[50] and are used to reproduce existing relationships. An analysis of the historical realization of the network society must then also engage with an empirically rooted examination of the culturally, historically and organizationally conditioned adoption (together with the ongoing development) of information technologies.

Castells reads the historical realization of the network society as deriving from interactions between the global transformation of capitalism, the advancement of information technologies and the social organization of production and distribution of goods. His argumentation is grounded in two of the abovementioned premises: the structural position of production relationships in capitalist society and the structural impact of information technologies as tools for communication and information processing.

Castells thus finds himself engaged in a debate regarding the factuality of the 'new economy', where the argumentation employed in *The Informational City* (the issue of the aggregation of services and productivity based on knowledge) is coupled with an analysis of the impact of the proliferation of information technologies on national productivity (in the case of the United States). The purported existence of a new economy, grounded in new sources of productivity and the organization of economic activities, lies at the core of Castells' conviction of a new social order within the framework of restructured capitalism.

Castells specifies three fundamental traits of the new economy: informational (the main source of productivity growth is the generation and processing of information), global (key economic activities are organized globally) and networked (production and competition are formed 'in a global network of interaction between business networks'[51]). The new economy is the product of the longstanding process of the 'recapitalization of capitalism', overlapping with the stabilization period of the information mode of development. This process has its own distinct genesis, actors, and 'geometry'.

3.3.1. The Formation of a New Economy and Globalization

Castells cites the economic crisis, spurred by the oil price shock of the early 1970s, as the historical turning point in the evolution of capitalism. The vast majority of

---

[49]Castells (2001b, pp. 1–2).
[50]Zuboff (1988, p. 392), similarly Edwards (1995).
[51]Castells (2000b, p. 77).

companies responded by adopting new strategies: short-term measures included cost reductions, pressure to increase productivity, accelerated capital turnover and market expansion; long-term measures consisted primarily of decentralizing and investing in technological innovations. As a result, the 1980s saw a swift increase in international trade and an accelerated global integration of financial markets, followed by the gradual separation of capital flows from national economies. This process would have been unfathomable had it not been for the sizeable investments into the development and configuration of the necessary communication and information infrastructures. The highest rates of growth were experienced by high-tech companies and financial corporations, who were the first to effectively navigate the emerging arenas of multinational finance:

> The expanding global reach, integration of markets and maximization of comparative advantages of location, capital, capitalists and capitalist companies facilitated, namely during the 1990s, a significant increase in their profitability, thereby restoring the investment conditions upon which the capitalist economy depends on.[52]

Castells is justly ranked among the leading globalization theorists; in order to extend his research beyond the limits of the urban space to the broader issue of a transitioning Western society, he had to proceed contextually – in this case, that meant coming to terms with the impossibility of analysing informationalism outside of a global context. He belongs to the group of authors who interpret globalization primarily as a process of increasing economic interdependence – though he is by no means an economic determinist; he calls attention to the fact that markets alone did not shape the global economy, also crediting governments and financial institutions, and primarily the wealthiest nations (G7) and their affiliated international institutions, as they played the largest role in the formation of the global economy.[53] According to Castells, the foundations of globalization were brought to fruition by three policies: the deregulation of domestic economic activities, the liberalization of international trade and investment, and finally the privatization of publicly controlled corporations.

The process of the internationalization of production and distribution of goods and services continued to rapidly increase throughout the 1990s; this process encompassed three interdependent aspects: (a) an increased volume of direct foreign investment, (b) the formation of an international production network, in which (c) multinational corporations played a decisive role in the context of economic and organizational change in the 1990s, becoming an integral part of the highly dynamic transnational production networks formed via ad hoc strategic alliances. Castells conceptualizes the variability and 'fluidity' of this new form of production and distribution organization by employing the term 'network enterprise'.

---

[52]Castells (2000b, pp. 96–97).
[53]Similarly Sassen (2006).

3.3.2. Network Enterprise

According to Castells, the fabric that wove together production, distribution and management networks consisted of new, culturally differentiated organizational formations which emerged as an integral part of location-specific strategies designed to increase competitiveness. At the turn of the millennium, there were many perspectives regarding the sources and features of the organizational restructuring that had been underway since the 1970s. Castells tried to retrospectively reassess the validity of the primary concepts of organizational change which were dominant during the restructuring of capitalism. These included the transition from mass (Fordism) to flexible (post-Fordism) production, new management methods (e.g., Toyotism), inter-firm networking and the emergence of strategic ad hoc corporate alliances. These trends, to some extent mutually autonomous, were different dimensions of the same 'crisis of an old, powerful but excessively rigid model associated with the large, vertical corporation, and with oligopolistic control over markets'[54].

If we were to find a common denominator for these organizational transformations, it would undoubtedly be the horizontalization and decentralization of the organizational structure, coupled with the automatization of what were formerly considered lower levels of management. However, such a high level of decentralization also bore the risk of 'articulation errors' between individual conglomerate units – an issue which was reduced in corporations which reintegrated the coordination function of the vertical corporate system in decision-making centres, and which operated online with networked units in real time. In order to ensure high functionality and thus a competitive advantage, it is necessary to strike the perfect balance between flexibility and planning. The adaptive model requires the simultaneous flow of data from various sources and their immediate processing, adjusting the organization strategy and its components.

Castells deems it necessary to step away from the cultural specifics of contemporary forms of organization, which should instead be viewed as the manifestation of a certain general model. Castells labels this model the *network enterprise*. This model cannot be understood as a strictly horizontal corporation that approximates the notion of a 'dynamic and strategically planned network of self-programmed, self-directed units based on decentralization, participation, and coordination'[55]; the dynamic structure of resources in a network enterprise is contingent upon the general dynamic of targets, which are the product of subtargets of local units and the control and coordination efforts of the core (the central subnet) of the network enterprise. The network enterprise is thus the model of a partially decentralized organization that seeks to maximize the benefits of exploiting information technologies in order to dynamically adapt the enterprise's organizational structure and targets to the conditions of a highly dynamic social and economic environment.

---

[54]Castells (2000b, p. 179).
[55]Castells (2000b, p. 178).

3.3.3. The Global Geometry of the New Economy: Segmentation and Exclusion

The global network-based system can be viewed as a complex web of increasingly decentralized networks, organized in semi-autonomous units that converge in strategic ad hoc alliances with units in other networks. At the same time, each of these alliances is the node of an affiliated network of small- and medium-sized enterprises. These sets of production and distribution networks have a transnational topology that is perpetually being transformed by dynamically connecting and disconnecting from different companies depending on their ability to exploit local benefits. If we were to model a dynamic visualization of this entire process onto the Earth, the result would bear some semblance to *Solaris*: a mesmerizing vision of an incredibly complex and dynamic flow of people, goods, texts and images, percolating against a colossal mosaic of chrome, oil, weapons and glaring screens – a vision interrupted by momentary flashes of horror, ignited by the realization that the cold perfection of this system is meant to serve as a reflection of ourselves.

A key element of the entire system is the ad hoc connection, that is, a connection that dissolves once the comparative advantages offered by the affiliated unit or location begin to dissipate.

> Networks mean you can connect everything that carries value for this dominant system. . . . But this structure also means that anything for which it has little regard – individuals, regions, sectors and companies – don't get connected and are thereby condemned.[56]

The former modern constructs of an autonomous collective social existence (nation states, cities, etc.) are now divided – segmented – based on new selection practices, often laid down beyond their reach. This results in the dissolution of the contract between labour and capital – a connection that was labouriously enforced in the Industrial Age. Integral features of economic growth are thus the grey economy of dual cities, deindustrialization, mass migration, global unemployment and the dualization of the social structure.[57] The process of economic segmentation, characterized by high volatility and potentially leading to the deindustrialization of entire countries (i.e., the Mexican crisis, the Brazilian crisis, the Greek crisis, etc.), is accompanied by increasing geographic segmentation.

> However, while dominant segments of all national economies are linked to the global web, segments of countries, regions, economic sectors, and local societies are disconnected from the processes of accumulation and consumption that characterize the informational, global economy.[58]

---

[56]Lefort (1999, p. 46).
[57]Castells (1989, Chapter 4, 1998).
[58]Castells (2000b, p. 135).

Such a highly functioning system of global informational capitalism deepens old inequalities and creates a new 'fourth world' in the form of a black economy made up of geographically scattered areas plagued by unemployment, violence, drug addiction and poverty.[59]

After the formation of a networked production structure, enabled by the infrastructure of information technologies, the process of global integration was (from a network viewpoint) inevitable; once a network has been formed, any node that disconnects itself is simply replaced or bypassed and the resources continue to 'flow' throughout the network, relegating the disconnected segment to a site of failure, poverty and misery. 'The network society works on the basis of a binary logic of inclusion/exclusion', where the highly dynamic structure of the global network enterprise dominates, in all instances, 'over activities and people who are external to the networks'[60]. The shift here is a qualitative one, as while industrial capitalism saw peripheral regions and lower social classes as 'dependent exploitation', in the new economy they are considered 'structurally irrelevant'.[61] At the same time, Castells sees the disappearance of the capitalist as an autonomous, responsible (and culpable) actor in the production process, supplanted by a faceless, cold rationality of instrumental networks that is entirely divorced from human logic, and one which is not controlled by any particular actor. Castells dubs this type of network an *automaton,* exemplified by the global network of financial flows[62] and serving as the backbone of the new global economy. The geometry of the new economy is thus grounded in networks formed by the utilitarian interconnection of local segments and the ever-changing global web, the fibres of which consist of dynamically shifting flows of people, money, goods and information. There is simply no escaping a web of this magnitude that ensnares the entire globe.

Or is there?

3.4. In the Internet Galaxy

The implementation of the network society and its functionality are, according to Castells, seamlessly intertwined with the central technology of the Information Technology Revolution – the Internet. The Internet, however, is not merely a material infrastructure of a specific organizational form (network) – it is also a communication medium, giving rise to the assertion that 'since communication is the essence of everything that people do, all domains of social life are modified by the all-pervading use of the Internet'[63].

Historically speaking, a society's communication structure has always been intrinsically linked with its power structure. For the sake of analysis, we can differentiate two distinctly interconnected levels of communication in the communication structure of the Industrial Age: centralized mass media systems

---

[59]Castells (1998, Chapter 2).
[60]Both quotations Castells (2009, p. 26).
[61]Cf. Castells (1998).
[62]Castells (2009, p. 44); Lefort (1999, p. 49).
[63]Castells (2001b, p. 275).

of unidirectional communication flows tied to the economic and political system (i.e., print, centralized radio and television) and distributed interpersonal interactions conducted in social networks, primarily within local reach (e.g., interpersonal face-to-face communication, 'amateur radio', telephone and letters). Castells distinguishes between the two levels using the terms 'societal' and 'interpersonal'.[64] In order to integrate society and maintain a sense of hegemony, the industrial society places special significance on the regulation and control of societal communication, facilitated by the centralization of mass media on a nation-state level. The Internet is fundamentally changing the perceived functionality of the entire system, thereby changing the entire ecology of power associated with the traditional structure of communication flows. In the arena of social communication, we shall briefly look at the transformation of three areas which are tied to three important shifts in the system of social inclusion/exclusion: the transformation of the mass media system (mechanisms of societal formation and agenda setting), the transformation of sociability (integration of the individual into the social sphere) and the transformation of civic and social movements (strategies of civil–political conflicts).

3.4.1. The Transformation of Mass Communication

Roughly up until the 1970s, Castells read the entire media system as being structured around television. To become a member of the 'collective consciousness' of the entire society meant to enter this system, as social networks at this time were too limited in their range to fulfil a similar function. However, this rapidly changed with the reorganization of the media industry and the expansion of 'new media'.

The 1970s saw a drastic expansion in the range of tools which granted the individual control over the curation of music and television content: the Walkman, the video cassette recorder and other recording and playback devices. This shift was not so significant in itself as the culture industry maintained the power to influence the taste-making process by controlling system inputs, distribution networks and advertising. Since the 1990s, this power has been threatened by the emergence of expansive global networks of cultural content sharing (texts, images, music, and videos) and by a lowered material and competency bar in the creation of such content, thanks to the wide accessibility of tools for reprogramming or modifying this content. The Internet became a tool for the formation of horizontal social networks in which it became virtually impossible to differentiate interpersonal and societal levels of communication. The gates have swung open – the individual has become a direct participant in the creation of the symbolic environment of society as a whole. Though Castells categorizes this entire system as *mass self-communication*, it has 'the potential to make possible unlimited diversity and autonomous production of most of the communication flows that construct meaning in the public mind'[65]. According to Castells, the

---

[64]Castells (2009).
[65]Castells (2009, p. 71).

persisting economic, cultural and educational limits of ICT access will dictate the cultural impact of these technologies, as it will be 'primarily reflected in the bolstering of those social networks that dominate culture'[66], a phenomenon which Robert Putnam was quick to call 'cyberapartheid'[67].

It is not, however, governments that have the final say in the formation of a new multimedia system, but rather the economic sector. In this regard, Castells points out that 'whoever controls its first stages could decisively influence its future evolution, thus acquiring structural competitive advantage'[68]. In terms of investments into mass media, the preservation of the model of company-controlled one-way information flows from the emitter to the recipient still plays a crucial role; global mass media conglomerates have invested primarily into projects that serve as an extension of the traditional model of TV-centric mass media of the Industrial Age (e.g., video-on-demand, smart TVs, online streaming services, etc.) in an effort to maintain their privileged position, bolstered by mergers, organizational restructuring and changes in production and distribution strategies. In doing so, these conglomerates are also vying to preserve the established terms of participation in the entertainment-news complex, thereby contributing to the reproduction of the centralized mass culture model. The communication potential of computer-mediated interaction technologies, which extends far beyond processing and transmitting information in one-way communication, is being realized at a staggeringly slow pace.

In Castells' estimation, the turn of the millennium was a period fraught with the conflict between two fundamental and opposing cultural and technological tendencies. On the one hand, it is about mass media complexes, rooted in traditional models of organization and power, which are slowly evolving and striving to retain their position of power and whose visions are centred on multimedia market-oriented entertainment. On the other hand, there is a tendency towards exploiting and integrating accessible means of bilateral communication for the institutionalization of an 'interactive society', enabling the articulation of problems and addressing them 'from the bottom up' and potentially restoring the legitimacy of political authority. According to Castells, the result of this 'key cultural battle', manifesting itself in a certain structure of communication flows, dictates: 'who will interact and who will be interacted with in the new system, shaping, to a certain extent, the framework for a system of dominance and the process of liberation from the information society'[69].

3.4.2. The Transformation of Sociability

The technical parameters of the Internet and the social consequences of its expansion are closely tied to the climate and values of the universal milieu from

---

[66]Castells (2000b, p. 393).
[67]Putnam (2000, p. 175).
[68]Castells (2000b, p. 395).
[69]Castells (2000b, pp. 405–406).

which it arose: openness, sharing and academic freedom.[70] Internet use up until the beginning of the 1990s, was, on account of its geographic and technical parameters, predominantly in the hands of those with university and research backgrounds from around the world (with a clear US dominance). The common interests, beliefs and values of Internet users in the 1970s and 1980s came close to making social revolution a reality thanks to the geographically unrestricted, creative and computer-mediated human interaction between like-minded individuals. The reality of the Internet prior to the early 1990s genuinely consisted of virtual communities and relatively stabilized platforms for discussion governed by their own values and (n)etiquette.[71]

According to Castells, community-centric user activities collapsed during the acceleration of Internet diffusion in the 1990s due to the pressure of massive user growth, relegating these practices to marginal forms of use. In terms of Internet use as a means of interpersonal communication, user practices were informed by the prevailing value system, which is reflected at the level of social behaviour via individualization, that is, the restructuring of social relations around the individual. Castells draws on Wellman's studies and calls this type of sociability[72], facilitated by the expansion of computer-mediated technologies, *networked individualism*, as it presents a model of highly self-centred networking of individuals using ICT within the contemporary system of establishing and maintaining social relationships. Networked individualism is an 'operating system' of society, which 'confers social and economic advantages to those who behave effectively as networked individuals'[73]. Individuals who do not or choose not to behave accordingly then miss out on these advantages. However, it would be ill conceived to see this as spurring a mechanical increase in impersonal social connections, instrumentality upon social contact or complete disengagement from social relationships. Networked individualism can best be described as the concomitant creation and maintenance of two types of relationships: on the one hand, new communication technologies are used to create a wide network of weak ties which are used transiently for obtaining information, for communication, as a leisure time activity, entertainment and for civic engagement; on the other hand, they are also used to strengthen bonds with close friends and/or family members, who form the core social bonds that provide intimacy and bolster individual identity in the wake of the cultural and economic pressure of increased mobility and adaptability of the individual.[74]

---

[70]Abbate (2000); Castells (2001b); Hafner and Lyon (1996).

[71]See Hauben and Hauben (1997); McChesney (2013, pp. 102–109); Rheingold (2000).

[72]The term sociability in this book is not intended in a strictly psychological sense, reflecting an internal motivation to get to know other people and spend time with them, but rather in sociological terms, that is, as the by-product of this motivation in the form of a specifically structured set of social ties informed by specific historical, cultural and technological conditions. The transformation of sociability here then does not entirely indicate a change in the way individuals relate to others, but rather a change in the prevailing patterns of social behaviour in the form of available, specifically structured social networks.

[73]Rainie and Wellman (2012, p. 256).

[74]Castells (2001b, pp. 121–122, 130). Castells thus presents the same model for the development of sociability which Luhmann (2012) defines as the logical consequence of

This facilitates higher mobility, since social and spatial shifts no longer pose such a high risk of dwindling social bonds and the potential destabilization of the individual along with it. Rainie and Wellman, in their 2012 book *Networked,* go so far as to say that having constant access to a large social network creates a scenario in which social support no longer has to be a fixed group of people: 'The weakened comfort of group identity comes with the gain in manoeuvrability; the ease of organizing group-based activities has given way to more strenuous micro-coordination of networks'[75]. According to Castells, the societal implications of this triumphant reinforcement of the individual remain unclear unless we accept the idea that the entire process is a logical component in the formation of a new type of society: the network society.[76]

3.4.3. The Transformation of Resistance

One of the beacons of hope brought on by the expansion of the Internet was the proliferation of democratization. People could have access to a wealth of political information and could gain insight into the inner workings of their governments (and not vice versa); The deliberative democracy project could finally acquire the necessary material infrastructure for its realization. However, instead of a more democratic form of government, Castells observes the dominant political practice around the world to be that of a politics of scandal, stemming from the personalization of politics and the exclusive interdependence of politics and an increasingly tabloid-oriented media sector.[77] This only deepens the distrust of citizens, which, when coupled with the desire for change, deepens the crisis of democracy. The possibilities for resistance and the organized collective (articulation of) social change are within a network society, in Castells' estimation, inseparable from the Internet for the following three reasons: First, 'social movements in the Information Age are essentially mobilized around cultural values'[78]. What is more, 'the communication of values and mobilization around meaning' have become fundamental components in the fight for social change. 'Cultural movements (in the sense of movements aimed at defending or proposing specific ways of life and meaning) are built around communication systems – essentially the Internet and the media'[79] – as they are the main channels for reaching out to those who share in their values, opening up the gateway to shaping the consciousness of society as a whole. Second, the Internet facilitates the creation of spontaneous mass mobilizations, transitional associations and new social movements which fill the void created by the crisis of vertically integrated organization. A prototypical example of a social movement in

---

adapting an individual system to an increasingly complex environment of social bonds, conceptualized at the level of trust and intimacy by Giddens (1997).
[75]Rainie and Wellman (2012, p. 56).
[76]Castells (2001b, p. 133).
[77]Castells (2004b, 2007, 2009).
[78]Castells (2001b, p. 140).
[79]Castells (2001b, p. 140).

the network society is, according to Castells, the anti-globalization movement, which owes its existence to the Internet. Networking via the Internet has enabled this movement to be: a space for ongoing debate that is at once diverse and coordinated without running the risk of becoming paralysed, since 'each one of its nodes can reconfigure a network of its affinities and objectives, with partial overlappings and multiple connections'[80]. Finally, the third and primary reason behind the Internet's crucial role is the global reach of the demands and objectives of local movements, as the main issues of the Information Age are neither created nor can they be resolved locally. According to Castells, not only does employing the Internet as a communication and mobilization infrastructure transform social movements, it leads to a transformation within the Internet itself, allowing it to become a tool for social transformation. Nevertheless, Castells draws attention to the fact that the Internet's function as a tool for liberation is constantly being curbed and supressed by interest groups striving to use the Internet as a means of preserving and perfecting the old order: governments, political parties, interest groups, churches, criminal networks. It is precisely for this reason that Castells claims that:

> the most decisive social movements of our age are precisely those aimed at preserving a free Internet, in the face of both governments and corporations, carving a space of communication autonomy that constitutes the foundation of the new public space of the Information Age.[81]

***

Castells appears to furnish us with two directions for envisioning positive change under the current social conditions which we can tentatively call structural and adaptive. The structural approach towards change is based on the assumption that the revolutionary subject of historical change (more likely to be the mutation and combination of existing collective identities) will emerge and, upon redefining his own position in society, successfully attack by transforming the entire social structure rooted in the existing system of the network society's instrumental rationality (i.e., capitalist informationalism). Castells then goes on to claim that:

> In the Information Age, the prevailing logic of dominant, global networks is so pervasive and so penetrating that the only way out of their domination appears to be out of these networks, and to reconstruct meaning on the basis of an entirely distinct system of values and beliefs.[82]

---

[80]Castells (2001b, p. 142).
[81]Castells (2009, p. 413–414).
[82]Castells (1998, p. 351).

However, as we have discussed above and as Castells will once again explicitly confirm in the following section, such a (structural) solution is contingent upon the acceptance of the network logic of social organization *within* the given system of dominance and rules of symbolic production. The entire social structure could then neither be transformed, nor could these networks be abandoned for that matter, as the functional organization of a hypothetical revolutionary subject would require the preservation of the constitutive elements of the very system vying to be transformed. These elements include the information infrastructure, consisting of a relatively complex production, distribution, investment and regulation system that is symbiotically interwoven with the logic of the current social order. This discrepancy can mean two things: it either implies crucial shortcomings in the analyses found in Castells' later work,[83] that is, the analytical separation of informationalism and capitalism, the problematic content of his key concept of a "network" and possibly the overestimation of the societal significance of information technologies; or, Castells' system of thought is not inherently contradictory in this matter and the deliberate advocacy of an alternative to the dominant systemic logic is problematized in that the potential actors of change (social movements) are themselves adherents of this system. A structural solution in the second case would be a Trojan horse abiding by the implicit condition of retaining the technological system of information technologies.[84] The adaptive possibility of change requires examining the causes of exclusion from the system of the global production of wealth, as dictated by information capitalism. While Castells looks to social movements and the creation of new collective identities for a structural solution, an adaptive solution utilizes the potential of the Internet's technological infrastructure in addressing the digital divide issue.[85]

3.4.4. A Path to Change: Bridging the Digital Divide

It might now be clear to the reader as to why 'the Internet is the fabric of our lives'[86] are the very first words of Castells' *The Internet Galaxy*. In our dissection of Castells' analysis of contemporary social change, we saw the crucial role that

---

[83]These shortcomings are examined in closer detail in Chapter 3 footnote 46, in the following section and in Chapter 7.

[84]Similarly, Christian Fuchs (2008) reads capitalism and the Internet as contradictory in nature, as he considers negative competitiveness to be the essence of capitalism and positive cooperation to be the essence of the Internet (and man). The aim of positive social change is then, according to Fuchs, utilizing the Internet, deformed by capitalist competitiveness, to overthrow this 'inhumane' regime and to establish a cooperative, sustainable non-capitalist information society in its place. A brief look at the flaws in Fuchs' book and the rationale behind not using it can be found in Lupač (2011).

[85]This solution is given the label 'adaptive' for two reasons: First, no technology can incite social change in itself – technologies are inseparable from the social contexts of their creation and use; second, which will be the subject of further explication, this solution lies in the adaptation to the technological infrastructure of the network society and its utilization.

[86]Castells (2001b, p. 1).

this infrastructure plays in the new global economy (Castells thus often speaks of a techno-economic system), the (re)production of culture, the transformation of sociability as well as its impact on efforts to ameliorate current social conditions.

In a scenario where basic social processes and actors are reorganized around the Internet, the difference between being connected and being unconnected becomes the difference between social inclusion and exclusion, a new telling source of social inequality and signpost pointing to prosperity, prestige, liberty and autonomy in one direction and to redundancy, poverty, destitution and social isolation in the other. It is thus no coincidence that Castells concludes his work on the Internet with the issue of the digital divide.

First, Castells summarizes statistics on the dynamics of ethnicity, gender, age and geographic differences in Internet connectivity at the end of the 1990s and puts forth the argument that these differences have gradually been waning. The digital divide, in terms of Internet connection, would then become a matter concerning 'primarily the poorest and most discriminated segments of the population, thereby further reinforcing their marginality'[87]. He goes on to add that the digital divide will continue to reassert itself as more significant ICT innovations unfurl (i.e., broadband Internet). Furthermore, it will contribute to the issue of the intergenerational reproduction of social status, demand the transformation of the entire learning process and will also be highly selective in socio-demographic and geographic terms, thereby accelerating the marginalization of the fourth world.

The most dramatic manifestation of the digital divide is, according to Castells, the global process of uneven development. Castells puts forth eight arguments in order to demonstrate how unequal Internet access – an integral part of contemporary globalization – is linked to phenomena such as mass urbanization (incited by the eradication of local farming systems), high economic volatility which causes spontaneous declines in weaker and smaller economies, the jeopardized sovereignty and legitimacy of governments, the proliferation and global integration of criminal networks, etc.[88] The fragmentation of society brought on by connecting and disconnecting to the information infrastructure serves as a 'structural feature of the global network society'[89]. Non-technological alternatives for development have, according to Castells, been roadblocked as 'Internet-based information systems and the information economy . . . have confined the trajectories of further development to relatively narrow limits'[90]. The only path to development thus leads through the Internet:

> development without the Internet would be tantamount to industrialization without electricity in the Industrial Age . . ., without an Internet-based economy and management, any country would

---

[87]Castells (2001b, p. 254).
[88]Castells (2001b, pp. 265–268).
[89]Castells (2009, p. 25).
[90]Castells (2001b, p. 270).

be hard pressed to generate the resources necessary to cover the costs of development in an economically, socially and ecologically sustainable fashion.[91]

According to Castells, unequal informatization and the issues of global hunger, poverty, violence and exclusion are inextricably linked in today's world.

This correlation between unequal informatization and the fundamental issue of contemporary global development is revisited with newly found vigour by Castells in his examination of the information mode of development towards the end of the 1980s and which later led him to the concept of 'informational democracy'.[92] Although he has not systematically engaged with the issue of the digital divide since 2001, he has not strayed from the logic of the underlying argument either. A semantic shift in unequal informatization would trigger a necessary shift in the understanding of the central role of informatization in contemporary social change, which would greatly impede upon the entire framework of Castells' theory of the transition towards an Information Age.

3.5 Addendum: A Blunt Critique of Castells' Late Theory of Society

Critical reservations towards Castells' work can be divided into two types: the first being commentary on issues pertaining to the writing style and scholarly language while the second calls into question the competency, validity and theoretical adequacy of his fundamental arguments.[93]

What can already be found in early reviews[94] is the often Carnapian criticism of conceptual vagueness (primarily in such key terms as 'information' and 'network') and excessive poetic and metaphoric language at the expense of both clarity and use value for the scientific understanding of social reality (e.g., the sentence 'Timelessness sails in an ocean surrounded by time-bound shores, from where still can be heard the laments of time-chained creatures'[95]). This results in a lack of 'criteria of empirical adequacy',[96] which would allow one to assess the validity of what are often fundamental arguments. Bordering on the second type of commentary is the reproach of unoriginality, the triviality of a number of

---

[91]Castells (2001b, p. 269), can be similarly found in the earlier works of Castells (1989, p. 352, 1998, pp. 92–95).

[92]See Castells (1989, pp. 348–353, 2004b, pp. 414–418).

[93]The entire gamut of the critical debate over Castells' work (the collection of important reviews and review essays from Webster and Dimitriou alone spans approximately three volumes, i.e., 900 pages) do not need to be presented here in full detail, if not only due to the repetition of both negative and positive critiques; I shall thus only outline the basic aspects of these critiques for the purpose of assessing their relevance for further interpretation.

[94]For specific points of reference see Abell and Reyniers (2000); Calhoun (2000); Fischer (1999); Fishman (1986); Saunders (2004); Tilly (1985); van Dijk (1999); Webster (1995).

[95]Castells (2000b, p. 497).

[96]Saunders (2004, p. 105).

Castells' 'discoveries', eclecticism without appropriate synthesis and the presence of mutually contradictory arguments.

The common denominator at the forefront of most critiques aimed at assessing the empirical and theoretical adequacy of Castells' late theory of society is a 'strong techno-determinism', arising out of the erroneous thought process that casts aside 'technological relationships' as autonomous territory, independent of production relationships.[97] Such rationale bears grave implications for further analysis: (1) the separation of technology and capitalism (ICT as an independent variable spurring a specific transformation of capitalism, which thereby loses its traditional position as an explanatory and all-encompassing variable); (2) the associated depolitization of informatization, which then comes across as a process independent of human interests and decisions and (3) the ontological nature of the term 'network', reflected in the understanding of a network as an automatic, dehumanized structure that controls spaces and people yet is not controlled by anyone in particular (Castells speaks of 'the pre-eminence of social morphology over social action'[98]).[99] The second most recurring criticism is that of tautology, the afore-mentioned poor empirical verifiability, ('inherently self-confirming and immune from empirical evaluation'[100]) and conveniently selected data and approaches so as to not contradict the overall idea behind the work. The entire work then, according to some critics[101], produces an impression of uncontradictability and coherence by eliminating theories and approaches that are either controversial or incompatible with the theoretical framework of the book. In more extreme albeit rare cases, Castells' competence is scrutinized, primarily regarding economic matters and his analysis of organizational change. In these cases, Castells' theory is interpreted as being generally misleading or as the embodiment of 'the failure of social theory'.[102]

Castells was disappointed with the inadequacy of critical reactions to his work, which in his estimation were confined to criticisms of language, statements taken out of context and criticism regarding the absence of proposed solutions to the analysed situations.[103] While Castells' response to his critics does not seem entirely well thought-out, it is true that criticism of Castells' TIS lacks a middle ground which would enable a constructive utilization of Castells' long-standing work, thereby paving the way for a more adequate modification of the role of information technologies in contemporary social change. As it remains trapped between an entire refutation (primarily

---

[97]MacKenzie (1984) explains this as a source of strong technological determinism in 'scientific Marxism' (Castells builds on this logic via Bell).

[98]Castells (2000b, p. 500).

[99]Abell and Reyniers (2000); Callinicos (2004); Garnham (2004); Stehr (2000); van Dijk (1999); Webster (1995).

[100]Saunders (2004, p. 105).

[101]Fischer (1999); Abell and Reyniers (2000).

[102]Garnham (2000, 2004); Abell and Reyniers (2000).

[103]Fischer (1999); Castells (2001a).

stemming from the criticism of techno-determinism) and acceptance (only critiquing marginal shortcomings in the theoretical framework or empirical evidence) of the entire work, the latest criticism of Castells' TIS has provided only very limited possibilities for reconstructing and improving upon information society theory.[104] In the following chapters, a reconstruction of information society theory shall be proposed based on a reassessment of its correlation to the digital divide.

---

[104]The most striking efforts are those of Frank Webster, Nico Stehr and Jan van Dijk. While the first two authors divert the problematization away from a change in society's infrastructure towards the role of theoretically codified knowledge (cf. Webster, 2002, 2006), van Dijk remains, despite expanding his version of the network society, tied to digital divide research (see Chapter 4).

Chapter 4

Digital Divide Research

> ...saying there is a lack of research on the Digital Divide is like saying there is a lack of research on life.[1]
>
> IPTS report to the G8 Opportunities Task Force

In the United States, the 1990s were not only a time of great enthusiasm, following the collapse of the Eastern Bloc, but also a period of great expectations, given the rapid expansion of the Internet. The beginnings of this acceleration can be traced back to 1991, when a group of scientists in Switzerland's CERN launched the distributed hypertext database known as the World Wide Web (www), and to 1993, which marked the release of the first version of the www-based Internet browser, Mosaic. Mosaic enabled web surfing via a graphic user environment, thereby providing a more user-friendly interface and ultimately contributing to the 'Internet craze' in the United States. The year-on-year increase in network size for the year 1993, as estimated by the Internet Society, totalled a staggering 341,634%; that year, new networks were being connected at a rate of one every 10 minutes and the number of connected computers exceeded two million in the month of July.[2] By December 1995, the Internet had roughly 16 million individual users, according to the International Data Corporation – a mere 0.4% of the global population at the time. In 2017, the Internet is being used by half of the global population (see Fig. 4.1).

However, the 1990s never saw the fulfilment of Marshall McLuhan's prophesied unification of mankind into 'one family', brought together by the electric speed of information transmission.[3] On the contrary, the envisioned gateway to the Information Age was afforded primarily to the socially and economically privileged segments of the population. This was then seen as the dawn of a two-speed society, consisting of those connected to the infrastructure of the digital future and those lagging behind in the analogue, industrial past. In order to articulate the inequality between these two populations, the term 'digital divide' was established in the second half of the 1990s.

---

[1]Gourova et al. (2001, p. 15).
[2]J. Q. Anderson (2005, p. 9).
[3]McLuhan (1995, p. 253).

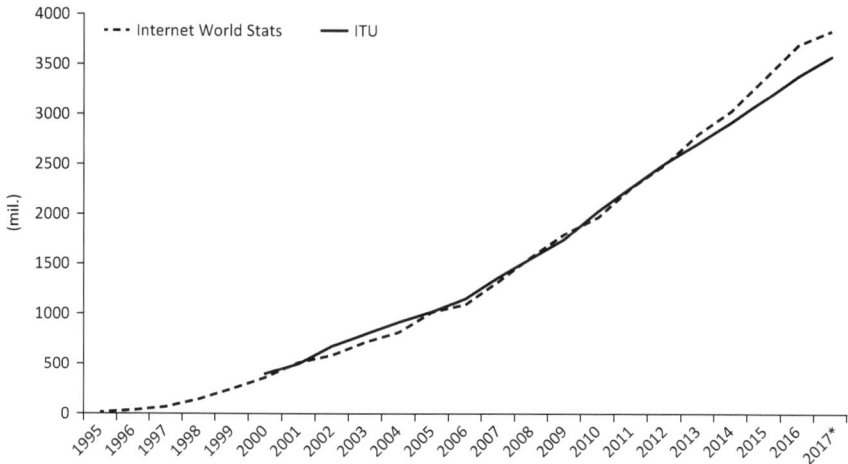

Fig. 4.1: The Global Evolution of Internet Users between 1995 and 2017.
Source: Author from the data of Internet World Stats and ITU, *estimation

The origin of the term is credited to the authors of a series of reports titled *Falling Through the Net* from the years 1998 and 1999, with the subheadings *New Data on the Digital Divide* and *Defining the Digital Divide*, conducted by the U.S. National Telecommunications and Information Administration (NTIA). While this trope likely made its first appearance in a 1995 issue of the LA Times, the above-mentioned NTIA reports were what most likely catapulted this term into popularity and solidified it as a means of expressing unequal Internet access.[4]

It did not take long before the concept of the 'digital divide' began to proliferate in the media, social science journals and political proclamations. As has already been stated in the introduction of this work, the role of political, economic and media actors in the informatization process will not be discussed in further detail here; allow us to instead look at the treatment of the digital divide in the social sciences. Readers familiar with the temporal context of the phenomenon might be tempted to conclude that the digital divide issue was borne out of the Internet craze of the mid-late 1990s and that the waning expectations associated with the arrival of the Information Age have relegated this issue to obscurity and insignificance in scientific circles. However, such an assumption would be a hasty one. Scientific interest in the digital divide did not fizzle out in the wake of the stock market crash of 2000, but instead continued to grow, becoming more differentiated, producing attempts at a theoretical synthesis of a wide array of empirical material.

One indication of the topic's relevance among the scientific public is the volume of professional articles published on the topic. In Fig. 4.2, we see an increase in the total amount of scientific articles obtained from the *Web of Science* database when searching for all scientific articles containing the term 'digital divide'

---

[4]Gunkel (2003, pp. 501–502); van Dijk (2005, p. 1).

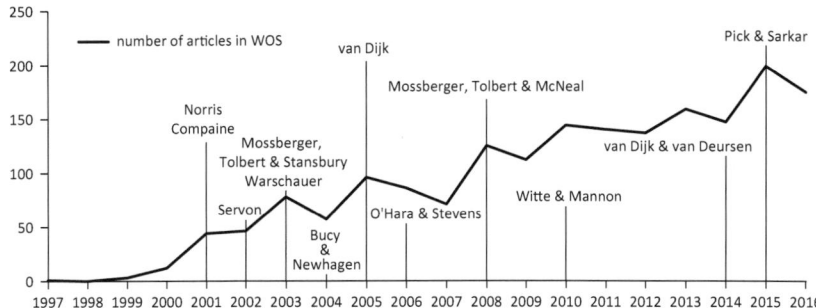

Fig. 4.2: Evolution of Articles in the Web of Science Core Collection
Containing the Words 'Digital Divide' in the Topic or Title.
Source: Author from Web of Science database

in the title or topic.[5] In order to ease the reader's navigation, authors of seminal digital divide texts have been added to the growth curve.

Fig. 4.2 should merely serve as an orientational tool, as synonymous terms for 'digital divide' were not searched for and *Web of Science* significantly decreases the real citation impact or volume of texts produced on a given topic, primarily in the social sciences (For the years 1995–2016, Google Scholar generates 69,000 search results for the use of the exact phrase 'digital divide' anywhere in the text).[6] For our purposes however, precise counts are not as significant as the dynamics of attention paid to the topic, for which our selected methodology is sufficient.

The growing number of scholarly articles attests to the claim that the digital divide is a real social problem. However, as the history of scientific practice has taught us, referring to the topic's relevance within the scientific community is not an adequate form of argumentation. The validity of the digital divide thesis, and the associated degree of social significance, should thus only be assessed after carefully analysing the hypotheses and arguments with which digital divide research has been operating. We shall only return to the issue of the concept's validity once we have mapped out its current developments.

This chapter shall present a wide array of scientific texts on the digital divide, summarizing their core arguments, key milestones in research development and up-to-date empirical evidence. The secondary aim of this chapter is to acquaint the reader with the main research issues and findings of digital divide research, as applied to current data. At this stage, the fundamental building blocks of the scientific, political and media sphere's reflection on this issue, referred to in this book as *the digital divide thesis*,[7] can be identified as follows: Unequal Internet

---

[5]Search criteria was limited to the exact phrase 'digital divide' in either the title or topic, limited to articles published in the years 1995–2016, the databases *SCI-EXPANDED, SSCI, A&HCI. Web of Science*, based on the applied algorithm, did not find any articles dating earlier than 1997. All data (including the following data from Google Scholar) were updated on 1 September 2017.

[6]For a comparison of both services, see, e.g., Harzing and van der Wal (2008).

[7]In the following text, I differentiate between the digital divide thesis (presented here),

access is a new source of social disadvantage which demands intervention. In other words, those with lacking or insufficient Internet access are at a social disadvantage in contrast to those who can (effectively) use it – a disadvantage which, without intervention,[8] will either persist or continue to grow and cement itself. This and the following chapter shall thus be aimed at presenting the arguments and findings which espouse the validity of this thesis.

4.1 Early Research: The Widening Divide

In the mid-1990s, countries with the highest number of devices connected to computer networks began conducting statistical research, studying e-mail and Internet use based on basic socio-demographic indicators. However, the majority of these surveys were problematic in their design and representation (primarily in the case of online surveys) in that they focused on a narrow segment of the population (urban populations, specific ethnic minorities, users of specific websites or services).[9] The largest response to emerging (initially predominantly American) digital divide research was to a 1995 NTIA report which focused on the potential social implications and consequences of unequal informatization. This report is, to this day, referenced as the 'starting' source of empirical data and its analyses.

The leading American think-tank RAND Corporation, in its 1995 report titled *Universal Access to E-mail: Feasibility and Societal Implications* (though it did not make explicit use of the term digital divide), addressed the implications of informatization thusly:

> as e-mail becomes more pervasive, as more commercial and government transactions in the United States take place on-line, those information haves may leave the have-nots further behind, unless we make concerted efforts today to provide all citizens with access to the technology.[10]

According to this report, there are no technological barriers standing in the way of this goal, as electronic mail can be made accessible once it is recognized as

---

discussions on the digital divide, meaning all texts and speeches addressing the topic (including in the spheres of politics, media, international relations, etc.) and digital divide research, meaning the (prevalently academic) discussions on the digital divide taking place in research institutions, publications and conferences.

[8]The recommendation of any form of intervention is a defining feature of digital divide research as Houston and Erdelez (2002) showed in their content analysis of 269 digital divide articles published between 2000 and 2001.

[9]See, e.g., Kohut and Bowman (1994); Pitkow and Recker (1995); Pitkow and Kehoe (1995); Clement and Shade (1996). Japanese surveys, mentioned in Chapter 2 have not been included, as they played only a marginal role in debates on the digital divide and the design of the surveys and research questions were formed under a different paradigm.

[10]R. H. Anderson, Bikson, Law, and Mitchell (1995, p. xiv).

a universal service.[11] The authors discuss four fundamental reasons as to why the social stratification spurred by computer use and network technologies is not commensurate with stratification arising out of the consumption of other goods, as far as the social implications are concerned:[12] (1) users of computer networks have greater amounts of accurate information at their disposal, (2) the societal nature of the media allows users to create and maintain new community formations (online groups, virtual communities, social networking sites), (3) interconnecting the nation would result in higher citizen participation and therefore democratization, which, due to technological globalization, could trickle down to the rest of the world, and (d) computer use is associated with the higher financial valuation of employees and with higher economic efficiency at a corporate and national level. Upon viewing data on access to PCs and network services through the lens of basic sociodemographic factors, the authors arrived at the conclusion that gender differences and differences between urban and rural areas diminished between 1989 and 1993, observing instead an increase in unequal access based on income and education.

In the same year, the NTIA published a research report titled *Falling Through the Net: A Survey of the 'Have Nots' in Rural and Urban America*, which scrutinizes the idea of limiting universal service to that of the standard telephone line at a time when 'the personal computer and modem are rapidly becoming the keys to the vault of the Information Age'[13]. The NTIA analysed data obtained from the Census Bureau's 1994 nation-wide survey, which included questions on the ownership of a telephone line, modem and personal computer, and found that those without access to a personal computer or modem were more likely than the national average to be residents of inner cities and rural areas (primarily states in the Northeast and South United States), and were made up primarily of poor households, ethnic minorities (with the exception of Asian and Pacific minorities) and elderly and less-educated Americans. Three years later, the NTIA followed up with another report confirming the previous findings and drawing attention to the widening digital divide – apparent in the noticeably quicker rate of Internet adoption among upper echelon individuals.[14] The same conclusion was reached in a research report published by the RAND Corporation the following year, lamentably concluding their analysis with the words 'we still have only half a revolution'[15].

---

[11]The innovative definition of universal service, including the guarante of equal access to telecommunications and information services, became part of the *Telecommunication Act* in the following year, that is, 1996.

[12]It is however important to note that the arguments presented in the report are based either on a small number of sub-studies, where generalizations prove problematic, or on studies which do not clearly indicate whether differences between users and non-users were sorted using other indicators in order to expose any spurious correlations, as well as findings from studies that are only valid in the context of user activities specific to the early 1990s. We shall return to a more updated state of knowledge in these areas in Chapter 5.

[13]NTIA (1995, p. 1).

[14]NTIA (1998).

[15]Bikson and Panis (1999, p. 30).

The data interpretation method on which these reports (and many future authors) build their digital divide arguments is illustrated in Fig. 4.3, which shows that while for the year 1994, e-mail was used by 1% of households with an annual income of US$5000–9900 and by 10% of households with an annual income exceeding US$75 000, in 1998, the numbers rose to 5% and 44% for the respective income brackets. The original single digit difference thus increased by almost 40%.

The 1999 NTIA report already sought to expand its research scope: in addition to the dynamics of socio-economic differences between connected and non-connected households, it also focused on the place of use, connection type, type of online activities and reasons for Internet non-use in households with computer access. With regard to reasons for non-connectivity, the NTIA touched on an issue which had been addressed two years earlier by Katz and Aspden,[16] that is, how exploring motivation, awareness, attitude and barriers can garner valuable insight for granting non-users a swifter transition towards Internet use. Though explaining the reasons for non-connectivity takes up only a small portion of the report's data analysis, it is precisely this issue which is called back into question in the conclusion, spearheaded with the question of how to extend Internet use to all tiers of American society the way it had (more or less) been accomplished with the telephone.[17] In the concluding chapter 'Challenges Ahead', the authors recommend the implementation of measures such as: price subsidies, promoting the Internet as a universal service, creating a network of community centres, and fostering awareness of the benefits of computers and the Internet even in the most remote areas, so that in the end 'no one should be left behind as our nation

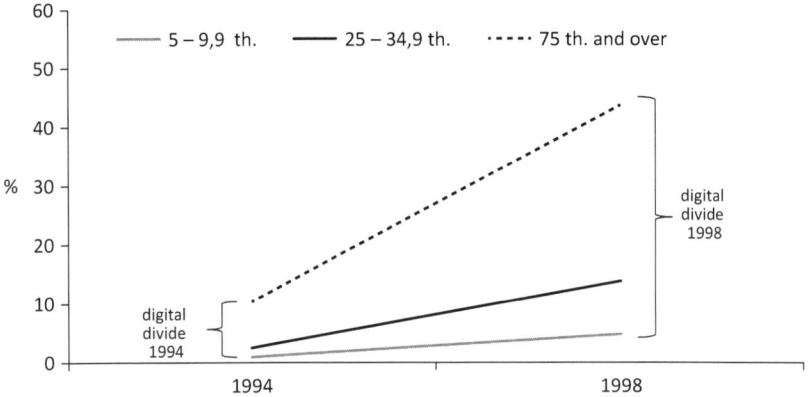

Fig. 4.3: Changes in the Percentage of Households with E-mail in the United
States between the Years 1994 and 1998 in Selected Income
Brackets (Household Income in Thousands of USD Per Year).
Source: Author, based on NTIA (1999, p. 100) data.

---

[16]Katz and Aspden (1997).
[17]Belinfante (2009) states that in 1998, 94.1% of American households had a fixed telephone line.

advances into the 21st century, where having access to computers and the Internet may be key to becoming a successful member of society'[18].

4.2 Turn of the Millennium: Closing the Digital Divide?

In response to claims of increasing stagnation in a large segment of the American population, Bill Clinton announced the *National Call to Action to Close the Digital Divide* initiative in 2000, signed by over 400 commercial and non-governmental IT organizations, who committed to contribute to the cause via financial donations, training sessions, donating computer equipment and raising public awareness in an effort to close the digital divide. During a period of pre-election promises, the government pledged to offer tax relief to companies that would contribute two billion dollars within a 10-year period, and vowed to allocate another US$380 million of the 2001 budget towards teacher training, school equipment, government grants and expanding the network of community technology centres in poor areas in order to coordinate the closure of the digital divide:

> For all families and communities to benefit from the New Economy, we must ensure that all Americans have access to technology and the skills needed to use it. We must work to meet the long-term goal of making home access to the Internet universal, bring technology to every neighborhood through community technology centers, empower all citizens with IT skills, and motivate more people to appreciate the value of 'getting connected'.[19]

However, the digital divide did not stay in the spotlight for long. The incoming administration emphasized an alternative interpretation of data on the proliferation of the Internet, arriving at the conclusion that the digital divide is in fact closing on its own, rendering governmental redistributive measures unnecessary. Between 2000 and 2002, the digital divide thus saw a significant drop on the government's list of priorities, resulting in abrupt cutbacks in financial support from the Technology Opportunities Program and the Community Technology Center Project – primary federal tools for combatting the digital divide in deprived inner city and rural areas in the United States.[20] These measures received relatively strong support from Republicans as well as those opposed to government funding for the expansion of certain technologies (not necessarily one and the same). We can analytically distinguish three main arguments here: the argument of different rates of Internet adoption across different population segments, the rejection of the Internet as a unique technology responsible for spurring a new type of social inequality, and the argument of the naturally quicker adoption of an innovation by certain social groups in the first stages of its diffusion. Although the digital divide had already been set as an official political priority

---

[18]NTIA (1999, p. 80).
[19]The White House, Office of the Press Secretary (2000, para. 4).
[20]Gordo (2003); Servon (2002).

in the European Union (EU) and other states around this time,[21] digital divide research was largely impacted by the US' backtracking on the matter.

4.2.1 The 'Different Rates of Internet Adoption' Argument

If we choose to interpret two concurrent time series, we can employ two basic methods. The first – from which the theory of the widening digital divide was derived in the first NTIA reports – is based on comparing variations in the magnitude of differences in absolute values over a certain period of time (see Fig. 4.3). The second method entails comparing the rate of growth, which, when applied to the evolution of the digital divide, can lead us to the contrary conclusion that the digital divide is in fact closing.

If, for example, Internet penetration in US households with an annual income of under US$15 000 increased from 14% to 25% between the years 1998 and 2001, and from 59% to 79% in households with an annual income higher than US$75 000, then the rate of Internet adoption for users in the lowest-income households was more than twice as high as for users in the highest-income households.[22] A graphic visualization of this data is presented in Fig. 4.4.

This (second) interpretation method was used in the NTIA report following the inauguration of the Bush administration as evidence of a narrowing digital divide. Just as the NTIA reports of the 1990s were symptomatic of Clinton era information policies, the 2002 report was an equally apt reflection of the Bush administration's policies. A report from 2000 is already depicted as ameliorating the grave tone of previous reports with the heading *Toward Digital Inclusion*;

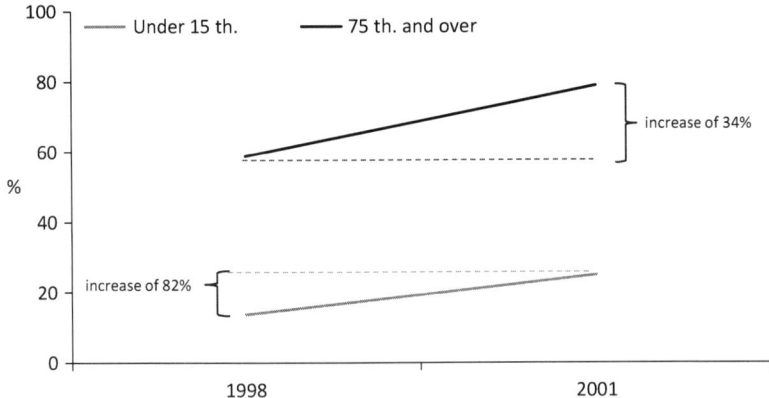

Fig. 4.4:   Differences in the Growth Rate of Internet Users between 1998 and 2001 in Selected Income Brackets in American Households (Household Income in Thousands of USD Per Year).
Source: Author from NTIA (2002, p. 28) data.

---

[21]'Information society for all' was one of the main pillars of the European Lisbon Strategy for the period 2000–2010 (European Council, 2000).
[22]From NTIA (2002, p. 80) data.

there is a semantic shift from the problem of the digital divide to the expansion of digital inclusion.[23] A focus on comparing growth rates in different population segments draws the authors of this fittingly named 2002 report, *A Nation Online: How Americans Are Expanding Their Use of the Internet*, to the discovery that 'Internet use is increasing for people regardless of income, education, age, races, ethnicity, or gender'[24]. This finding is supported by Gini coefficient calculations for computer and Internet use gaps across households based on income. The gradual decline of the Gini coefficient as early as the 1980s proves, according to the report's authors, that despite increasing income inequality in the United States, 'declining prices, increased availability in schools and libraries, and wider applications in many occupations have combined to reduce inequality in both computer and Internet use.'[25] This draws the authors to the conclusion that the Internet has become a widely accessible and adopted tool for Americans nationwide.[26]

4.2.2 The 'Non-Exceptionality of ICT' Argument

The rapidly cooling faith in the 'e-future', spurred by the drastic fall of IT company stocks, has prompted certain official sources, the media and the academic sphere to question the significance of the Internet as a technology which, when compared to other advances in modern science, should be so unique as to require government intervention. The new chairman of the *Federal Communications Commission*, Michael Powell, employed a famous analogy at his first press conference when asked what the commission's role should be in reducing gaps in access to new technologies:

> I think there is a Mercedes divide. I'd like to have one; I can't afford one. I'm not meaning to be completely flip about this. I think it's an important social issue. But it shouldn't be used to justify the notion of essentially the socialization of the deployment of the infrastructure.[27]

In a similar vein, Benjamin Compaine, Lead Associate Researcher at the MIT Program on Internet & Telecoms Convergence, made the assertion in 2001 that 'the issue is not one of information or knowledge gaps, any more than it is one of a protein gap or transportation gap'[28]. The group of authors who share this view are of the same mind in that, just as with other technologies, the entire Internet diffusion issue can be boiled down to the gradual reduction of computer costs (something which the sufficiently liberalized market will secure via competition), and efforts of commercial entities to expand their markets to the lower-income masses through dumping, product differentiation and simplifying their operational interfaces. These standard market mechanisms should

---

[23]NTIA (2000).
[24]NTIA (2002, p. 1).
[25]NTIA (2002, p. 88).
[26]NTIA (2002, p. 91).
[27]Labaton (2001).
[28]Compaine (2001, p. 116).

ensure the organic expansion of the Internet, just as they did for the many tech-nological advances that came before it.[29]

In the academic sphere, the issue of non-exceptionality has taken on a distinct form in terms of public policy and its priorities, primarily in the context of une-qual global development. A prominent figure in development informatics, Richard Heeks, pointed out the cost of sacrificed opportunities associated with ideologi-cally motivated investments into the expansion of ICT, enforced while overlook-ing the primary sources of social inequality which catalyse unequal ICT access.[30] Heeks saw this as a major flaw in global development programmes, purporting that "ICT fetishists' have so far been unable to demonstrate how ICT-based informa-tion represents a more important resource than water, food, land, shelter, produc-tion technology, money, skills or power in the development process'[31]. Heeks uses the term 'ICT-fetishists' to categorize a specific line of reasoning within develop-ment theory, dominated by the overestimation of the anticipated positive effects of ICT implementation along with the idea of technology's unidirectional causal influence on society (i.e., techno-determinism), articulated in equations such as 'technology=development' and 'technology=problem solution'.[32] Heeks and like-minded authors do not deny the utility and potential of ICT in the economic and social progress of developing countries, they merely criticize the prevalence of underdeveloped, uninformed, techno-deterministic solutions to the digital divide which monopolize resources from more important domains.[33]

Michel Menou identified with Heeks' perspective, perceiving a clear contradic-tion between public proclamations emphasizing the need for universal connectivity and observed political practices, rendering the digital divide more of an artfully veiled attempt at creating new markets in the context of ongoing neoliberal privati-zation.[34] Promoting the fastest possible solution to the digital divide on a global scale is, according to him, unethical and is a syndrome of a 'mental illness' which he dubs 'hICTeria'. Similarly to Heeks, he poses the question, 'Should not the people be first properly fed and cured before being given means to communicate?'[35]

At the turn of the century, the critique of techno-determinism and the sys-tematic reduction of the complex issue of the digital divide to the ownership of a personal computer or physical access became a common denominator in the development of socio-scientific reflections on the matter.[36] This critique is not pri-marily directed at the digital divide as such, but rather towards reductionist inter-pretations, meaning we shall not focus on it within the scope of an entire section.

---

[29]Murdock (2000); Samuelson (2002); Simons (2001); Thierer (2000); a list of other propo-nents of the non-exceptionality argument can be found in Gunkel (2003, p. 500).

[30]Similarly, Alden (2003).

[31]Heeks (1999, p. 16).

[32]Heeks (1999).

[33]Heeks (2010); Martínez-Santos, Cerván, Cano, and Díaz-Alcaide (2017).

[34]Menou (2001b). We shall return to this interpretation of the digital divide in Chapter 6.

[35]Menou (2001a, para. 8), similarly also Chowdhur (2000).

[36]See, e.g., Couldry (2003); DiMaggio and Hargittai (2001); Gordo (2003); Gourova, Hermann, Leijten, and Clements (2001); Gunkel (2003); Tuomi (2000); van Dijk and Hacker (2003); Warschauer (2002); Wyatt, Graham, and Terranova (2002).

It has, however, significantly impacted digital divide discourse and research, and so we shall return to it later in Chapter 5.

4.2.3 The 'Organically Closing Digital Divide' Argument

When rationalizing variations in Internet adoption rates across different segments of the population as a natural occurrence, both of the above-mentioned critiques draw on a general understanding of the diffusion of innovations theory (DOI), spearheaded by Everett Rogers. As we shall revisit this theory later in the book, allow us to briefly take a look at its basic features:

Diffusion is defined here as:

> the process by which (1) an *innovation* (2) is *communicated* through certain *channels* (3) *over time* (4) among the members of a *social system*. The four main elements are the innovation, communication channels, time, and the social system…These elements are identifiable in every diffusion research study and in every diffusion campaign or program.[37]

DOI is based on the assumption that an innovation does not spread through the entire social space at the same speed, but is gradually adopted by different segments of the population which exhibit varying degrees of innovativeness. Innovativeness is, for Rogers, an analytical category, defined as 'the degree, to which an individual or other unit of adoption is relatively earlier in adopting new ideas than the other members of a system'[38]. The distribution of this characteristic throughout the population is, in his estimation, approaching normal distribution, just as it has with other human characteristics. The cumulative share of innovation users (equalling its market share, in the case of commodified market spread innovations), takes the shape of a sigmoid curve over time, culminating at a level of absolute saturation (100% in an abstract model).

> At first, only a few individuals adopt the innovation in each time period (a year or a month, for example); these are the innovators. Soon the diffusion curve begins to climb, as more and more individuals adopt in each succeeding time period. Eventually, the trajectory of the rate of adoption begins to level off, as fewer and fewer individuals remain who have not yet adopted the innovation. Finally, the S-shaped curve reaches its asymptote, and the diffusion process is finished.[39]

Interleaved curves of the absolute and cumulative frequencies of innovation adopters over time are presented in Fig. 4.5.

---

[37]Rogers (2003, p. 11), italics by E. M. Rogers.
[38]Rogers (2003, p. 22).
[39]Rogers (2003, p. 23).

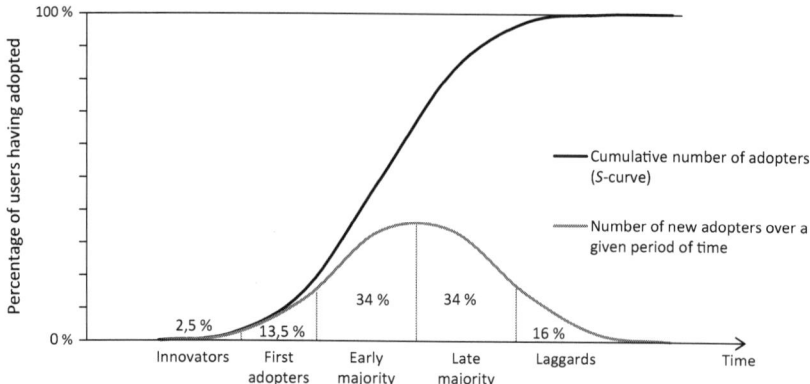

Fig. 4.5: Diffusion of Innovation Curves and Categorization of Adopters According to E. M. Rogers. *Source*: Adapted from Rogers (1958)

Based on studies mapping the dynamics of DOI (e.g., new corn seeds), Rogers, at the end of the 1950s, divided adopters into five categories and defined the size of acquired subpopulations using standard deviations from the average DOI rate, or the mean innovation value for a given population (i.e., from the first innovator's adoption of the innovation to the moment of adoption by the entire population). Subsequent innovation research yielded the following preliminary findings regarding the basic characteristics of ideal types of categories of adopters:[40]

(1) Innovators comprise 2.5% of the population. They have access to large social networks and have high media exposure. Individuals in this group are cosmopolitan, open to new ideas and risks and have apt financial resources. They are the gatekeepers between the world of new ideas and the social system.

(2) First Adopters represent 13.5% of the population. They form a group of strong, loyal opinion leaders, central in the rapid diffusion of innovations. First adopters are selective in their adoption of new innovations, stabilizing the ways in which they are used, thereby reducing the degree of uncertainty associated with the innovation for members of their social networks.

(3) The Early Majority represents 34% of the population. This group is made up of conformist individuals with access to large social networks in which they do not have a leading role. Their aim is to adopt the innovation earlier than the majority of society.

(4) The Later Majority is a sizeable segment of the population, though innovation adoption here is rather the result of external (economic and social) pressure. Individuals belonging to this group are careful and sceptical of new developments – at this stage, the innovation must be very stable, reliable and perceived as a social norm.

(5) Laggards make up the remaining 16% of the population. Laggards are highly locally rooted, have very limited resources and small social networks (or live

---

[40]Rogers (2003, pp. 22 and 281–292).

in social isolation), they are suspicious of and closed off from innovations. They tend to focus on the past; if they are forced to adopt a technology, it is often at the point when it is already being supplanted by another innovation.

According to DOI, the degree of innovativeness, an integral aspect of the above-stated categorization scheme, is inextricably linked to openness to new things, age, size of the social network, ability to exert influence over the opinions of others and social status. In other words, the gradual diffusion of an innovation in society reveals transformations in the psychological, demographic, economic and social traits of its adopters. This is where empirical findings on differences in Internet use overlap with the popular perception of the diffusion of innovations as a manifestation of historical repetition, leading to the logical conclusion that the Internet's unequal expansion is a naturally occurring consequence.[41] This is not even ameliorated by the paradoxical fact that at this time, Rogers was publishing texts falling under the digital divide mainstream, and which contained repeated arguments calling for the need to address unequal access to the Internet – a technology which he labels as historically unique.[42]

While both of the arguments found in scientific texts overlap and complement each other, the difference between the non-exceptionality of ICT argument and the argument of an organically closing digital divide lies in that while the former is directed at questioning the unique position of ICT in contrast to other innovations (in other words, unequal access does not constitute a new form of social inequality), the latter circumvents the issue of ICT's unique position by claiming that the observed inequality was and is merely a temporary phenomenon. Texts employing the argument of an organically closing digital divide thus differ in the perceived benefits of ICT use as well as the justification and form of government intervention,[43] thereby partially surpassing the scope of this section. As we shall see in Section 4.4, digital divide research has managed, in its basic knowledge of the *S*-curve, to justify the necessity of politically led interventions into ICT diffusion.

***

The presented arguments have furnished relatively solid support in defence of further exploring the digital divide, and have thus become (through various articulations and in varying degrees of detail and explicitness) integral components of introductory sections of scientific texts, defending the contribution of the given study and prompting the need for further scientific elaborations on the topic. It can be said that the entire gamut of socio-scientific research functions in large part as a response to the presented critiques, or rather as a response to the topic's key issues: Is the digital divide a political and widespread societal problem? Has the expansion of ICT produced a new form of social inequality? Does the digital

---

[41]For example, Bikson and Panis (1999, p. 34); Compaine and Weinraub (2001, p. 169); Sciadas (2002, p. 9); Warschauer (2003, p. 55).
[42]Rogers (2001, 2003, pp. 468–469).
[43]Cf., e.g., Compaine (2001); Norris (2001); Schement (2001).

divide necessitate government intervention? What is the basic 'formula' for ICT diffusion in society? Are ICT users more advantaged in society than non-users?

We shall not proceed in a strictly chronological fashion now, as digital divide research has a rather tenuous relationship with the accumulation of knowledge principle: a large number of authors use concepts and sources which have long been criticized by other authors as problematic, while, conversely, many cogent models and arguments have been left by the wayside. However, a systematic approach can still be adopted, provided that we employ a functional sorting mechanism. The functionality of such a mechanism can only arise out of a categorization of texts and arguments that strives to be exhaustive, avoids making any major overlaps, is capable of best capturing the diversity of debates on the issue and is derived from a single categorization principle.[44]

In the following Sections 4.3–4.5, the main branches of existing digital divide research are reconstructed, with responses to the presented critiques of early digital divide research serving as the guiding classification principle. We shall first take a closer look at counterarguments and supporting empirical evidence associated with the argument of a narrowing digital divide. Next, we shall focus on the criticism and utilization of the *S*-curve, which also extends to the issue of continuous innovations in the field of ICT. Section 4.5 will present the second branch of responses to the narrowing digital divide argument, based on defending the unique impact of ICT use on social participation and analyses of differences in motivation, skills and online activities. The defence of the Internet as a unique technology, the use or non-use of which poses a new dimension of social inequality, shall be revisited in greater detail in Chapter 5, where the assumptions of digital divide research shall be laid out and pitted against available empirical evidence.

Developments in the digital divide debate show that responses to the social impact of ICT have transitioned from the initial utopian optimism of the 1990s towards a phase of scepticism and rejection at the turn of the millennium, culminating in the current phase of increasingly sober assessments that 'Web-based human interaction really does have unique and politically significant properties'[45]. Let us then take a look at what this final sober phase of digital divide research has furnished us with.

4.3 ...And Yet it Widens!

The issue of persisting or even widening gaps in ICT access, in keeping with the first NTIA reports, still makes up a significant portion of digital divide research. There have, however, been two notable shifts. Due to the decreasing percentage of non-users in economically developed countries, this issue has increasingly been crossing over to texts on global differences and on the digital divide in developing countries, socially underprivileged populations, the oldest generation and in

---

[44]The list of categorization parameters was inspired by Rogers (2003, p. 280), and the condition of adequately capturing variability within the debate (so as not to produce categorization that is either too fragmented or too vague) was added.

[45]DiMaggio, Hargittai, Neuman, and Robinson (2001, p. 319).

health care. In addition to studying other phenomena, for example, gaps in digital skills or the impact of Internet use, it has remained a constant even in the mainstream. It did not take long before analyses of this issue began to take the shape of more advanced methods of data analysis via efforts to clean up the impact of studied variables on the odds of Internet use using multidimensional methods.

However, these two shifts do not indicate the eradication of the original problem of a widening digital divide. It is necessary to keep in mind that the findings referenced herein from various monographs, reports and professional articles are merely the tip of the iceberg of a deluge of texts and discourses (theses, conference papers, local and corporate studies, public announcements, reports from statistical offices and non-government organizations, etc.), which suggest that gaps in ICT access across (sub)populations x as defined by criteria y (income brackets, gender, ethnicity, country…) are not only an ongoing issue but an expanding one. In this section, we shall attempt to systematize this mass of texts by covering a substantial portion of the arguments and findings stemming from existing comparisons between connected and non-connected populations. We shall first examine the argument of a quicker rate of adoption in socially weaker subpopulations as well as the question of creating a comprehensive model of factors serving as predictors of Internet use. An analysis of the global digital divide will be presented hereafter.

4.3.1 National Level: Bridging the Divide is Far on the Horizon

It was only a matter of time before someone pointed out the misleading interpretation method employed in the 2002 NTIA report (introduced in Section 4.2.1). But what exactly makes this method of interpretation so misleading? The Internet use growth rate is calculated using the increment size ratio for a given period and the initial value, thereby favouring subpopulations with lower-initial values. This also means that if we were to invert the entire problem and instead of tracking the growth rate in selected segments of connected subpopulations tracked the rate of decline of selected segments of non-connected subpopulations, we would come to the opposite conclusion: the rate of decline in the number of non-connected individuals favours subpopulations with higher initial values. The rate of decline of non-users is, in this report, overshadowed by comparisons of the year-on-year growth rates of ICT users.[46] The following year, Steven Martin called attention to this misuse of statistics in his study *Is the digital divide really closing? A critique of inequality measurement in A Nation Online*, where he recalculated data from this report using odds ratios, combining the growth rate of users with the rate of decline of non-users to form an unskewed indicator. Following his reanalysis using odds ratios, Martin once again reached the conclusion that even though odds of Internet use increased across all groups, up until 2004, the odds of owning a computer in the United States increased the least for households in the

---

[46]See the quoted passages in Section 4.2.1, or directly NTIA (2002).

lowest income bracket (on a similar note, he criticizes the NTIA's erroneously calculated Gini coefficient, employed to bolster their argumentation).[47]

Does the general claim of a widening digital divide still hold true today? Let us address this issue by first examining the national statistics on Internet users and also look at which socio-demographic factors can serve as predictors of non-use.

When determining the extent of the digital divide, researchers continue to track the increase or decrease in user distribution gaps within selected subpopulations.[48] The most commonly used variables for defining subpopulations are the traditionally employed indicators: age, gender, education, ethnicity and race, income and location (rural vs urban areas). Let us now briefly summarize the preliminary findings gleaned from available data.

Age has been a significant differentiating factor in all countries, including those with the highest penetration rates such as Great Britain, Japan, Sweden, Switzerland and United States.[49] When comparing the age distribution of Internet users across different countries, we can hypothesize that generational differences are more pronounced the less pervasive Internet use is in a given society.[50] This is reflected in Fig. 4.6, which illustrates the age distribution of Internet users in selected countries in 2015. How then can we explain the variances in adoption rates across different age categories?

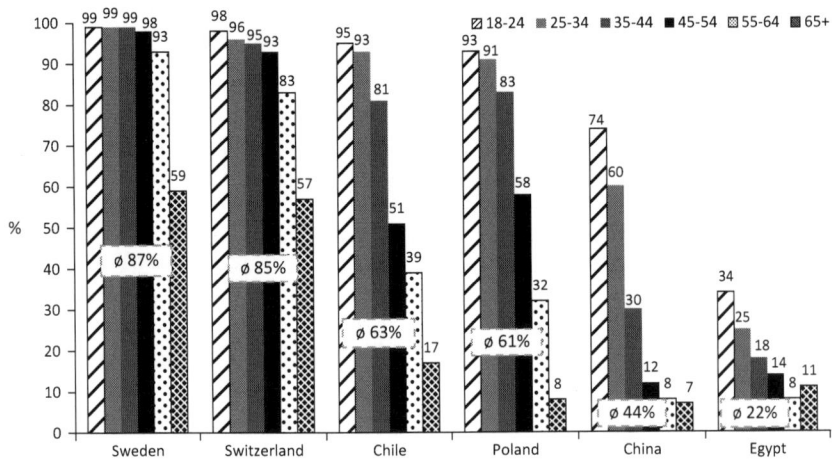

Fig. 4.6: Age Distribution of Internet Users in Selected Countries in 2015.
Source: The Center for the Digital Future at USC Annenberg (2016).
Graph designed by author.

---

[47]Martin (2003); Martin and Robinson (2004, 2007).

[48]For example, Hale, Cotten, Drentea, and Goldner (2010); Sciadas (2002); van Dijk (2005); Warschauer and Matuchniak (2010).

[49]Eurostat (2017); Findahl (2012); Perrin and Duggan (2015); Statistics Bureau, Ministry of Internal Affairs and Communications Japan (2017).

[50]See ITU (2016, p. 194).

Internet use rates in the youngest age categories (teenagers and early twenties) are nearing one hundred per cent; this can be historically explained by: (a) online businesses heavily targeting younger age categories; (b) higher innovativeness in this age category, that is, an openness to new things and willingness to experiment[51]; (c) the network effect[52] associated with increasing peer pressure; (d) the important role of personal electronic devices in contemporary youth subculture;[53] and (e) government programmes promoting the Internetization of schools and the incorporation of Computer and Information Technology-oriented classes in the compulsory curriculums of primary and secondary schools. The distribution of users continues to decrease with age up until the 50–70 age category, where there is an abrupt drop[54] followed by a rapid decline to very low values. This is part of the reason why the past few years have seen a rise in studies emphasizing sizeable internal differences within the senior population and which convincingly argue against the simplistic analysis of seniors as a singular, homogenous population, in which age plays a decisive explanatory role in Internet non-use.[55]

Based on comparisons of Internet diffusion patterns in economically developed countries, we can now roughly map out a general model of Internet diffusion according to age. At the beginning of the 1990s, the dominant age category comprised people aged approximately 25–45; by the end of the decade however, this group was surpassed by the youngest and fastest growing group (which was also the fastest growing group from 2000–2010). When the rate of growth of new users from the youngest age category began to decline, there was an increase in the rate of growth for those aged 30–50, followed by an increase in Internet use in older age categories several years later. This process is well in line with the previously mentioned diffusion of innovations model, where the first people to adopt such a new and complex technology are those in university settings and IT fields, followed by the vast majority in their social circles and younger age groups. The continuously increasing rate of adoption in the middle-age category is attributed to the external pressure to adopt (from employers, media, friends, children), which then ends up as an 'acknowledged necessity' for the remaining segment of the population.

---

[51]Although the relationship between age and innovativeness is not clearly demonstrated in Rogers' DOI model (Rogers, 2003, p. 288), the correlation is substantiated in ICT adoption when the analysis is not limited to the population of innovators and early adopters alone.

[52]The term 'network effect' (also referred to as 'network externality' and 'demand-side economies of scale') is used primarily in the field of IT economics and is based on the observation that the value of certain products (e.g., in the sharing economy) is determined in part by the number of people who own/use the product. The most widely used formulation of the network effect in ICT is Metcalfe's law, which shall be discussed in greater detail in Chapter 6.

[53]Campbell and Park (2008); Castells et al. (2007).

[54]Findahl (2008); Friemel (2016); van Deursen and Helsper (2015); van Dijk (2005).

[55]Friemel (2016); van Deursen and Helsper (2015).

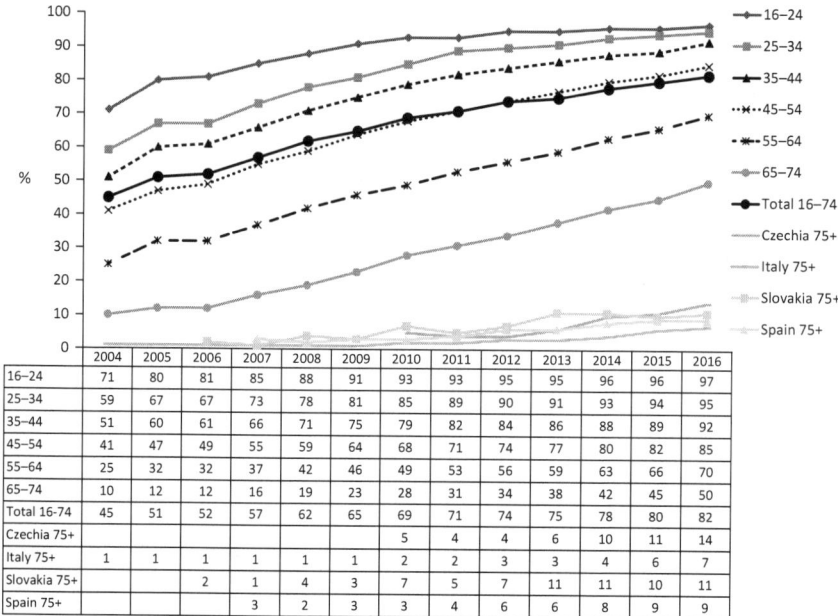

	2004	2005	2006	2007	2008	2009	2010	2011	2012	2013	2014	2015	2016
16–24	71	80	81	85	88	91	93	93	95	95	96	96	97
25–34	59	67	67	73	78	81	85	89	90	91	93	94	95
35–44	51	60	61	66	71	75	79	82	84	86	88	89	92
45–54	41	47	49	55	59	64	68	71	74	77	80	82	85
55–64	25	32	32	37	42	46	49	53	56	59	63	66	70
65–74	10	12	12	16	19	23	28	31	34	38	42	45	50
Total 16-74	45	51	52	57	62	65	69	71	74	75	78	80	82
Czechia 75+							5	4	4	6	10	11	14
Italy 75+	1	1	1	1	1	1	2	2	3	3	4	6	7
Slovakia 75+			2	1	4	3	7	5	7	11	11	10	11
Spain 75+				3	2	3	3	4	6	6	8	9	9

Fig. 4.7: Evolution of Internet Users by Age in EU-27 and in Selected
Countries, 2004–2016. *Source*: Eurostat (2017) database.
(Graph designed by author.)

Fig. 4.7 depicts the rise in Internet use across different age categories in the
EU between 2004 and 2016.[56] Here we can clearly observe an increase in all of
the monitored groups, even though the oldest group (75+) saw only an insignifi-
cant increase when compared to other age categories (almost consistently falling
below the margin of error in annual comparisons). The stagnation of growth in
two of the youngest monitored age groups, approximately since 2010, is associated with a nearly attained saturation point, where the number of connected
individuals will no longer rise due to income, cultural, physiological and psychological population differentiation (physically and/or mentally disabled, inhabitants of ghettos, people with less technology-oriented lifestyles, prisoners, people
with the lowest income, the homeless, etc.). This naturally imposed cap leaves us
with reasonable doubt regarding countries that declare a 100% user rate for their
youngest population segments, for example, South Korea and Iceland. American
teenagers (aged 12–17) have been hovering at a comparably stable rate of 95% as
of late 2006.[57]

---

[56]The Eurostat methodology works with the general population aged 16–74 only on
exception. Data from EU-28 was not used, as it was only made available in 2007 and is
identical to the previous data set. Long-term, reliable time series for the 75+ population are
only available for the listed countries.
[57]Madden, Lenhart, Duggan, Cortesi, and Gasser (2013).

The EU data clearly provide interpretive leeway when comparing changes in user distribution across subpopulations: the question of whether the digital divide is narrowing or widening depends, to a great extent, on which groups and years are included in the comparative analysis. If we compare differences between the youngest and oldest age segments, then the digital divide undoubtedly widened between the years 2004 and 2016. However, when we compare the youngest age group with all age groups under 74, the gap appears to be closing. Based on the current growth rate of the 25–74 population, we can thus expect at least a partial closure of the digital divide in the upcoming years; the validity of this assertion as it pertains to the oldest age segments depends on to what extent the increases observed over the past few years signify a consistent (perhaps even accelerating) trend, or whether it is merely the case of a temporary, modest increase, as can be observed in US time series data.[58]

The Eurostat data clearly elucidate that the overall rate of growth of new users in the EU has been on the decline for several years, thereby substantiating the hypothesis of a more equal distribution of new adopters over time. This claim is further bolstered by more long-term time series from Sweden and the United States, where the break in new user growth came roughly at a time when the number of users in the population reached 50–60% (i.e., around the year 2000).[59] The main catalyst of future growth from here on in will be the older generations who now form the majority of the non-connected population. Even if the average annual growth rates from 2006–2016 were maintained, the 55–64 age category (within the EU) would not match the 16–24 age group until 2028, and the 75 and over age category in its respective countries would only reach this level in the latter half of the twenty-first century.[60] Whether or not the Internet diffusion ceiling is the same across all age groups remains an open question for future research (see also Section 4.4.4), along with the question of if and what percentage of today's aging population will stop using the Internet and if and how rapidly Internet diffusion will accelerate among this population.

The composition of the household has often been a neglected factor due to the long-ingrained focus of social research on the respondent as an isolated analytical unit. Nevertheless, it is a salient predictor of Internet use, primarily in the case of school-attending children in the household.[61] According to a Chilean study conducted by Teresa Correa, the influence of children on their parents' adoption of ICT is more pronounced primarily in older parents (over 35), in women and poorer households.[62] EU data (see Table 4.1) confirm the persisting and considerable role played by the presence of dependent children in the household – provided that one or two adults are in the picture; we can also observe comparable differences based

---

[58]Cf. Perrin and Duggan (2015).

[59]Findahl (2008); Zickuhr (2013).

[60]This information presupposes a uniform Internet use ceiling of 97% across all segments of the population, a stable year-on-year increase averaging at the annual increase rates for the years 2006–2016.

[61]Brown, Venkatesh, and Bala (2006); Eynon and Helsper (2015); Reisdorf (2011); van Dijk (2005, p. 56).

[62]Correa (2014, 2016); Correa, Straubhaar, Chen, and Spence (2015).

Table 4.1:   Percentages of Households with Internet Access by Household Composition in EU-27 from 2004 to 2016.

Type of Household / Year	2004	2006	2008	2010	2012	2014	2016
Single person	29	34	44	55	61	68	74
Single person with dependent children	42	47	68	79	85	91	94
Two adults	36	45	55	64	71	77	82
Two adults with dependent children	55	65	76	86	91	95	97
3+ Adults	51	60	72	81	86	91	94
3+ Adults with dependent children	50	57	70	82	89	92	95
Total EU-27 without dependent children	37	44	55	64	71	76	82
Total EU-27 with dependent children	54	61	74	84	90	94	96
Total EU-27	41	49	60	70	76	81	85

Source: Eurostat (2017). Table designed by author.

on the number of adults. Larger households indicate higher odds of Internet use – most likely in young adults or employees – and a higher number of earners (which increases the total household income). The fourth, often neglected, factor,[63] is that the larger the household, the larger the aggregated social network, thereby increasing the probability of a higher number of users in this network, which in turn increases the odds of adoption in the household. When considering the role of household size however, the term 'household' here becomes too restrictive when reflecting upon the impact of an individual's social environment – when assessing an individual's odds of Internet use, it is not of great consequence whether the social relationship is of a parental nature or whether the social interactions responsible for influencing Internet adoption stem from the extended family, peer groups, workplace or any other environment. It would thus be of greater value to incorporate the impact of the size and composition of the household into a broader framework when examining the role of various parameters in an individual's social network.

The first qualitative studies on the impact of social networks on computer and Internet adoption were conducted as early as the second half of the 1990s. The picture these studies painted is a familiar one: close friends or children of

---

[63]For example, van Dijk (2005, p. 56) includes the presence of dependents, more potential users and more potential earners in his assessment of household composition.

interviewed respondents are often depicted as 'warm experts', who help increase the respondent's awareness of the usefulness of ICT, encourage the respondent to either acquire or start using ICT (be it in the form of a gift, practical demonstration, or simply motivating the respondent), and help overcome initial user issues and frustration.[64] This finding resonates with DOI experts, as it echoes one of the most fundamental mechanisms of the diffusion of innovations: '*An individual is more likely to adopt an innovation if more of the other individuals in his or her personal network have adopted previously*'[65]. In the mid-1980s, Rogers confirmed the crucial impact of interpersonal relations on the odds of PC adoption in the United States, despite the massive ad campaigns run by IBM, Apple and other manufacturers (prior to purchasing a PC, every new adopter had on average five PC owners in their social network and every owner recommended buying a PC to roughly eight other people).[66] Similarly, a 2001 study from the San Diego Regional Technology Alliance revealed that for those who own/use computers/ the Internet, social relations prove to be a more revealing factor than the respondent's individual traits, such as ethnicity, education and income.[67] This discovery was bolstered by later studies which strove to shed light on Internet diffusion in university environments, to explain lower levels of Internet diffusion in rural areas and to examine the impact of low sociability in the remaining non-users on decreasing Internet diffusion rates.[68] Despite the number of indicators emphasizing the relevance of the number of users in a respondent's social network and attempts to incorporate the 'social support' factor into theoretical models of ICT adoption,[69] it is puzzling that digital divide research has not spent much time engaging with this factor.[70] While there are a select few studies focusing on 'peer effects' based on the number of users in the studied area,[71] this method is, nonetheless, insufficient for verifying and refining the key parameters of this factor – that is, how strong of an influence does the interconnectedness of the examined population have on the Internet diffusion process, and, on a microlevel, how do various social network parameters (e.g., size, composition and number of users) and the immediate social environment impact adoption during the Internet diffusion process, when pitted against the adopter's other attributes.

---

[64]Bakardjieva (2005, pp. 98–103); Haddon (2004, pp. 72–76); Rojas, Straubhaar, Roychowdhury, and Okur (2004, pp. 120–122). The term 'warm expert' comes from Maria Bakardjieva.

[65]Rogers (2003, p. 359), italics E. M. Rogers.

[66]Rogers (1986, pp. 123–126).

[67]Dowling (2001, p. 12).

[68]Albert, Dávid, and Molnár (2008); Boase (2010); Goldfarb (2006); Helsper and Reisdorf (2017); Verdegem and Verhoest (2009).

[69]DiMaggio and Hargittai (2001); Valadez and Duran (2007); Warschauer (2003). The issue later appears in research on social support for users (see p. 115).

[70]As noted also by van Deursen and Helsper (2015).

[71]Agarwal, Animesh, and Prasad (2009); Schleife (2010). Similarly, Pick and Sarkar (2015, p. 90) argue for the number of scientists and engineers as a significant predictor of ICT use in a given population.

Gender differences in Internet access are closely linked to the culturally conditioned significance and weight of certain socio-demographic factors. If, for example, we were to observe Internet diffusion in a culture that prioritizes the adoption and use of a new technology by the oldest member of the family, the age distribution of Internet users would not necessarily follow the general model outlined above. However, even in countries belonging to the same cultural sphere, we can find significant differences associated with intergenerational interconnectedness and the specific values and lifestyles of different generations. Similarly, differences in the number of male and female users should only be considered within the context of local gender dynamics, which are reflected in the social barriers and opportunities for the use of new ICT innovations and which are internalized, experienced or realized via (non-)user practices.[72] For example, in the EU, the most significant gender differences in Internet use can be observed among individuals with lower educational attainment and to some degree among the older population, that is, in segments of the population whose lifestyles reflect a more conservative approach to male and female roles; conversely, younger and more educated individuals do not present such gender differences in Internet access (see Table 4.2). This is further illustrated in results stemming from the application of multidimensional models on international data, leading to the conclusion that gender differences in Internet access can be entirely accounted for by other variables, primarily income and education.[73]

The countries for which comparable data are available can be divided into three basic categories based on size and the persisting differences between men and women. The first category includes countries with significant gender parity, where such differences are currently either nearing the margin of error or are not at all discernible (namely Denmark, Ireland, France, Sweden, United States, Canada and the Baltic states). Gender differences in Internet access evened out gradually in these countries: in, for example, the United States, Ireland and Canada, the gender gap began to subside as early as the late 1990s.[74] The second category includes countries in which both genders exhibit the same rate of adoption, with persisting or only incrementally waning differences of 5–10% (e.g., Chile, Italy, South Korea, Germany, Portugal, Greece). The vast majority of countries in the second category do not exhibit almost any gender differences in the youngest population segments – this gender gap is localized in older age cohorts. The third category includes countries with deep-rooted male and female stereotypes, which are noticeably mirrored onto the education system, household relationships and labour market. The differences in the distribution of male and female Internet users in these countries have been in excess of 10% over a span of several years (e.g., Egypt, Jordan, Turkey, Iran, India, Mexico, Azerbaijan).[75]

---

[72]Castells et al. (2007, pp. 41–55); Cooper and Weaver (2003); van Dijk (2005).

[73]Bimber (2000); Eynon (2009); Friemel (2016); Goldfarb and Prince (2008); Hindman (2000); Mossberger, Tolbert, and McNeal (2008); Wilson, Wallin, and Reiser (2003).

[74]Eurostat (2017); Fallows (2005); NTIA (2002); Sciadas (2002).

[75]ITU (2010, 2016); The Center for the Digital Future at USC Annenberg (2010, 2012, 2016); Eurostat (2017).

Table 4.2:   Percentages of Female and Male Internet Users in EU-27 from 2004 to 2016.

Group \ Year	2004	2006	2008	2010	2012	2014	2016
Females, 16–74 years	41	48	59	66	71	76	80
Males, 16–74 years	48	56	64	71	76	80	84
Females, 16–24 years	73	81	88	93	95	96	97
Males, 16–24 years	75	81	88	92	95	96	97
Females, 55–74 years	15	18	28	34	43	49	57
Males, 55–74 years	25	29	38	46	51	59	65
Females, low education	21	27	33	40	46	51	58
Males, low education	28	35	42	49	55	60	66
Females, high education	72	80	88	91	94	96	97
Males, high education	79	85	90	93	94	96	97

Source: Eurostat (2017). Table designed by author.

Race or *ethnicity* was, similar to gender, a rather closely studied variable primarily during the first wave of digital divide research in the United States. This is well in line with the emphatic focus on race and gender issues in the US social science tradition, which generated the majority of the first scientific texts on the matter (unfortunately, data on this variable from other countries is scarce). In the United States, the percentage of computer owners and Internet users of Asian or Pacific American descent was comparable to that of white Americans, while Native Americans, Latin Americans and African Americans were lagging behind considerably in Internet adoption. The digital divide between these two ethnic groups continued to widen until the year 2000.[76] Authors engaging with this issue found these differences problematic primarily with regard to the paucity and poor quality of ICT equipment in the households and schools of less-connected ethnic minorities – something which could further deepen ethnic or racial inequality due to the risk of low prospects in the school system and the increasingly informatized job market.[77] Whether or not the digital divide between different ethnic groups in the United States is narrowing is still a matter of debate.[78] What is clear, however, is that the more rapid Internet diffusion among Black and Hispanic Americans is symptomatic of the proliferation of smartphones, which are, however, presumed to offer only limited options for use and thus lower potential benefits to be reaped from Internet use.[79]

[76]Fairlie (2007); Hoffman, Novak, and Schlosser (2001); NTIA (2002).
[77]Fairlie (2005); Hess and Leal (2001); 'The racial digital divide just won't go away' (2004).
[78]See, e.g., Campos-Castillo (2015); S. Kim (2011).
[79]van Dijk and van Deursen (2014, pp. 99–101); Washington (2011).

The earliest reports on racial gaps in computer ownership and Internet access made it clear that these inequalities are context-sensitive and are not bound to any particular race or ethnicity. Findings furnished by sociology and social and cultural anthropology have made it abundantly clear that members of the same race or ethnicity can attain diametrically different social status, cognitive abilities, personality traits, value preferences, etc., by being socialized in different social environments. The distribution of Samoan and Indian users in New Zealand, even after controlling for age and gender, varies depending on whether the individual was born in or relocated to New Zealand.[80] Similar differences can be found in the United States between native- and foreign-born ethnic minorities.[81] The explanatory power of the standalone factors 'Asian', 'Latino' or 'Samoan' is thus almost non-existent when not examined in the appropriate context. The generalization of the specifically American experience onto the dynamics of Internet access across specific racial or ethnic groups would perhaps only be possible at a level sufficiently abstracted from the particularities of the social context, by removing all of the social odds and obstacles pertaining to immigrants and members of a certain generation.

When attempting to generalize partial findings, we cannot do so without addressing one of the key facets of the racial dimension of the digital divide: the possibility that racial gaps in Internet access are only an indicator of other forms of inequality, such as unequal education and access to the labour market. Studies on this issue (including those outside of the United States) reveal that even though income, education and employment explain a significant amount of racial/ethnic inequality, the impact of this variable does not disappear entirely as it does with gender.[82] This can be justified either in the different 'cultural resources'[83] at play, or the language barrier associated with the fact that most online content in a given country is available either in English or the language of the core ethnicity.[84] However, language skills or certain cultural patterns are not static markers of a particular race or ethnicity; the impact of these categories is more of a testament to the failure of including the explanatory variables of attitudes, values and language skills in analyses rather than a purely racially or ethnically predetermined relationship to ICT use. Race/ethnicity as an explanatory variable is then used as more of a crutch, which, in the context of the digital divide, raises the question of whether this is not merely another manifestation of academic racism, unintentionally contributing to the preservation of racial and ethnic demarcations and the inequalities spurred as a result.[85]

Educational attainment, along with age and income, is one of the strongest predictors of Internet use. Very high figures for the secondary school and university educated population are associated with a combination of five features: (a) faster and more intensive computerization in higher levels of the school system, the graduates of which are always Internet users, (b) the substantially more rapid

---

[80]Greenbrook-Held and Morrison (2011).

[81]Livingston, Parker, and Fox (2009).

[82]Campos-Castillo (2015); Fairlie (2004); Korupp and Szydlik (2005); Wei and Hindman (2011); Wilson et al. (2003).

[83]van Dijk (2005, p. 60).

[84]Fairlie (2004, 2007); Poushter, Bell, and Oates (2015).

[85]As noted also in Tuomi (2000, p. 7).

informatization of labour market segments which demand secondary school and university level education, (c) higher income and the associated consumption patterns promoting luxury consumption, (d) higher probability of social ties to influential individuals already using the Internet and (e) an inverse proportion between age and education. Lower education, on the other hand, is often associated with manual labour which does not involve computer use, and lifestyle, where ICT ownership or use is mainly associated with the degree of ICT use in member and reference groups, pressure imposed by institutions (schools, authorities, cultural institutions, the mass media…) and with the subjective perception of the benefits of Internet use in terms of day-to-day tasks and activities. The development of the situation in the EU is an adequate reflection of the varied dynamics of Internet diffusion in different education categories as seen in Fig. 4.8.

The graph clearly illustrates that the adoption curve for the university educated population is already approaching its ceiling, with the secondary school educated levelling off; the primary contributors to the overall rise in Internet users in the United States are now those with low formal education. The evolution of the digital divide among different education groups in the EU is not atypical, though educational differences in European countries are among the smallest in the world – in poorer countries, we can observe immense differences between the high and low end of the education spectrum, relegating efforts of bridging this gap as a thing of the distant future.[86]

The 'classic' approach to examining the educational dimension of the digital divide, as presented here, has now become marginalized within the larger scope of texts on the matter. This is akin to the once popular issue of unequal computer and Internet access in the school system, an issue that has become obsolete in countries producing the highest number of digital divide-related texts as a result of government programmes promoting the computerization and Internetization of the school system – in the United States, 98% of public schools were connected to the Internet in 1998, the EU reached 96% by 2006, with none of the member states falling below 90%.[87]

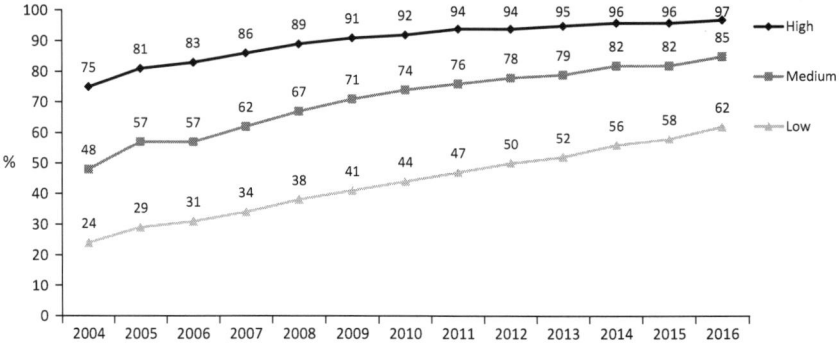

Fig. 4.8: Evolution of Internet Users by Formal Educational Attainment in EU-27, 2004–2016. *Source*: Author from Eurostat (2017) database

---

[86]See ITU (2016, p. 192).
[87]Cattagni and Farris (2001); Korte and Hüsing (2006).

Proponents of the digital divide thesis were then drawn to other research issues: differences between schools in terms of the quality and quantity of ICT,[88] exploring the relationship between education and user skills and adjusting the impact of independent variables and determining the significance and weight of their impact.

Since *income,* traditionally the focal point of social inequality studies, is correlated with all of the sociodemographic attributes detailed here (education, gender, age...), it is evident that the picture of the digital divide will not differ greatly when comparing different income categories. Current EU data reveal only a slow narrowing of the digital divide, illustrated via differences in household income (see Fig. 4.9). These differences are more pronounced in countries with lower income levels and higher income inequality – certain OECD countries, for example, Hungary, Slovenia, Lithuania and Portugal, exhibited an approximately 50% difference in the distribution of at-home users from the first and fourth quarter in 2015.[89] As is the case with education, these differences are much more pronounced in developing countries.

The effort to adjust the impact of income in the context of other related variables has led to the current hypothesis that for countries within the Euro-American cultural sphere, income, together with age, are the strongest predictors of ICT ownership, followed by education – the significance of which is proportional to the relationship between connection costs and the average income in the given country. The impact of education is thus noticeably higher in more economically developed countries, while income remains the deciding variable in developing countries.[90]

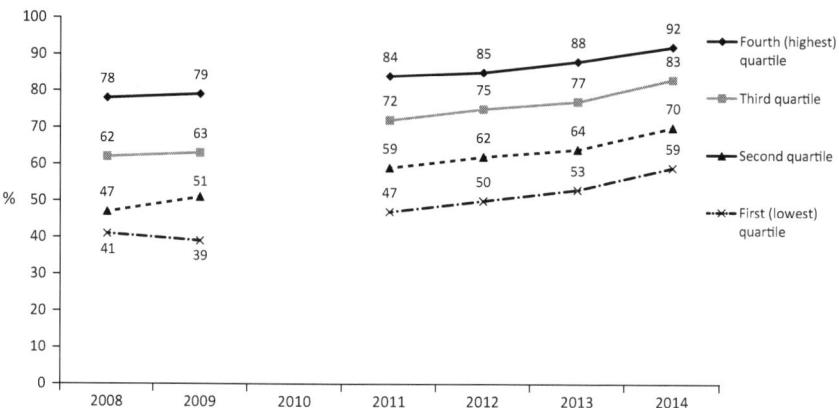

Fig. 4.9: Evolution of Internet Users by Household Income in EU-27, 2008–2014 (No Data for 2010). *Source*: Author from Eurostat (2017) database

[88]For example, Hess and Leal (2001); Valadez and Duran (2007); Valentine, Holloway, and Bingham (2002); Warschauer and Matuchniak (2010).

[89]ITU (2016, p. 189).

[90]J. E. Katz and Rice (2002, pp. 54–55); NTIA (2002, p. 19); van Dijk (2006a, p. 226); van Dijk and Hacker (2003, p. 319).

If, instead of ownership, we shifted our focus to use, then the categories of age, income and education would also have to be considered alongside *employment position,* which has a significant impact on the possibility (or necessity) of using the Internet at work. Internet use in the workplace then leads to a higher probability of Internet use at home – a relationship which is unlikely to be explained by income.[91]

The last 'major' dimension of social inequality, which we should not fail to include here, is the impact of *location in a socially structured space* on the probability of Internet use. The emphasis on the spatial dimension of social theories and practices (i.e., including certain systems of institutionalized social inequality) poses an underdeveloped and undervalued contribution from the fields of urban studies, social geography and sociology.[92] According to Tickamyer, this oversight is reflected in the omission of three important issues: (a) analyses using an implicit, unreflected and often inappropriately selected scale, neglecting the multiplicity of scales for social phenomena and processes, resulting in 'the tendency to confuse, conflate, or ignore spatial processes at different scales'[93], (b) analyses of a selected spatial segment as an isolated entity, neglecting its relational nature in the context of other spaces and relevant social processes at other scales, and (c) neglecting the socially constructed – and thereby fluid – nature of the examined space and the configuration of elements by which it is constituted. These three issues shall serve as the foundation of the following questions in order to better our understanding of the spatial dimension of the digital divide. They are as follows: (A) What are the basic scales with which texts operate, and what are the basic signs of Internet use gaps at these levels? (B) To what extent are the most frequently studied scales interconnected and if and how can they affect the interpretation of results? (C) What spatial elements and scales of analysis are currently lacking in digital divide research and how will expanding analysis using these scales and abandoning the dominant scales of analysis aid in our understanding of the digital divide? The first two questions can be answered immediately, while the third requires a shift in perspective, which is why we shall return to it only once we have presented the basic structure of digital divide argumentation and its drawbacks (i.e., in Chapter 6).

Spatial inequality on a national level has been a part of digital divide discourse from the very outset, and has involved studying differences in Internet adoption rates across the primary types of subnational spaces – as defined in administrative or traditionally statistical terms – such as rural and urban areas, states, prefectures (Japan), microregions (EU) and metropolitan areas or counties (US). These spaces are most often used in analysis as stable, internally homogenous and undifferentiated units.

Let us not forget that one of the central texts which helped usher in the digital divide debate was subtitled, *A Survey of the 'Have Nots' in Rural and Urban America,*[94] and that lower household penetration in rural areas in the 1990s

---

[91]NTIA (2002); Peng (2010).
[92]See the still relevant and applicable Tickamyer (2000).
[93]Tickamyer (2000, p. 810).
[94]NTIA (1995).

became a frequently cited argument in debates on the need to bridge the digital divide and to expand universal services to include new communication technologies.[95] Current US records indicate a persisting or only slight decline in differences between the distribution of rural and urban Internet users, around 10%, similar to Canada and the EU (for this development in the EU see Fig. 4.10).[96] In countries with more pronounced spatial inequality, for example, China, India and Indonesia, the differences are far more striking.[97]

How can these geographic differences be explained? The first step in addressing this question requires establishing whether or not location (in this case) is an independent variable that cannot be explained by other items. Generally speaking, rural areas exhibit a higher average age and lower educational attainment and income, which can be explained by the structure of the labour market in sparsely populated areas that have a generally lower added value, the corresponding cost/earnings ratio, higher unemployment and the migration of young and educated segments of the population to cities. Given that age, education and income are important factors of innovativeness, people from rural, sparsely populated areas generally adopt new technologies later than inhabitants of cities, densely populated or metropolitan areas. A significant number of studies, however, have found that when controlling for age, education, income and other individual traits, differences across geographic locations are explained 'only' to a large extent, albeit not entirely,[98] indicating that location can have its own distinct impact on the odds of Internet use. In this case, we would have to refocus our question: Which specific features of rural, sparsely populated *areas* (or inner cities, socio-economically deprived neighbourhoods, regions, etc.) contribute to the lower

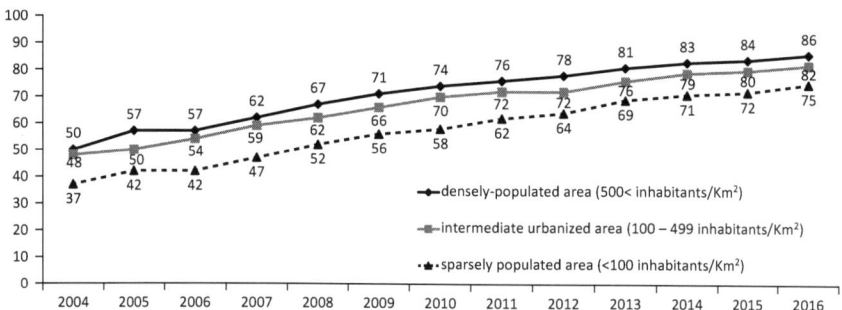

Fig. 4.10: Evolution of Internet Users by Population Density in EU-27, 2004–2016. *Source*: Author from Eurostat (2017) database

---

[95] See H. Anderson et al. (1995); Hindman (2000); NTIA (1998, 1999).
[96] Haight, Quan-Haase, and Corbett (2014); Perrin and Duggan (2015).
[97] Pick and Sarkar (2015); Sujarwoto and Tampubolon (2016).
[98] Haight et al. (2014); Hale et al. (2010); Hindman (2000); Noce and McKeown (2008); Whitacre (2010). The impact of location disappeared after controlling for other variables in P. Bell, Reddy, and Rainie (2004) and Vehovar, Sicherl, Hüsing, and Dolnicar (2006).

odds of Internet use among their inhabitants? We are now seeking structural (i.e., non-individual, infrastructural) determinants as opposed to features of a locality obtained via aggregating isolated traits of individuals within the said locality. It is useful to implement the market metaphor here when distinguishing these causes: an assessment of the spatially specific differences in the supply on the one hand, and the spatially conditioned differences in the demand on the other.

The geography of the Internet can be examined at three levels: the spatial distribution of users, the geography of the technical infrastructure and the economic geography of ICT business.[99] In order to continue, we need to justify why the spatial distribution of users should follow and mirror the technical and economic geographies. If the geography of users were independent of space, just as it has been declared by many critics and 'prophets' postulating the abolition of (centralized) space,[100] it would be fruitless to seek out its relation to the economic and technical infrastructure, and the specifics of location should thus be sought elsewhere. However, the thesis purporting the devaluation of space as a result of ICT diffusion was more a display of ideological short-sightedness than an argument reacting to real processes: as early as the 1980s, it was evident that Internet geography is a highly concentrated contributor, correlate and consequence of the specific geography of power in the global economy, with central nodes located in places where the highest flows of people, information and goods converge. The resulting flow network, to a large extent, disregards traditional spatial boundaries (cities, country borders) and enables locations with strategic value, in terms of global finances, production and distribution networks, to loosen their attachment to their geographic surroundings. These key locations are usually strategic cores of cities with highly sophisticated service sectors for players operating at a global level. A by-product of this is the heightened inequality between centres and their peripheries and their waning interdependence, something traditionally associated with geographic proximity.[101]

Due to these changes in the geographical makeup of the social space, the act of tracing the development of gaps at a nation or state level can be misleading – the new economic geography is being formed on increasingly varied levels of subnational and global divisions of space. When analysing gaps in Internet use, we can use this knowledge to confront claims of a narrowing digital divide in economically advanced countries through the lens of the geographic space – once we apply a more detailed scale of analysis, the divide opens up before us with an intensity not otherwise found when employing traditional national divisions.[102]

---

[99]Classification adapted from Castells (2001b).

[100]For example, Cairncross (1997); Mitchell (1996); Negroponte (1995); see J. Q. Anderson (2005) for more examples.

[101]Castells (1989); Sassen (1991, 1998a, 1998b, 2002a); Warf (2001); Zook (2005). Similarly also Section 3.4.4.

[102]Holloway (2005); Perkins and Neumayer (2011); Pick and Sarkar (2015); Vicente and López (2011).

However, the confrontation of findings from different scales is still quite rare in digital divide research.[103]

Let us now return to the interconnection of the user, technical and economic geographies of ICT. Highly interconnected centres exercise a centrifugal force on resources, talents and other capacities from their territories, exploiting them in a bid to maintain and increase their competitive edge in a globalizing economy. The biggest Internet service providers, the latest network technologies, high-quality services – these are all developed and localized in urban areas. High communication density and the presence of large social networks with a higher incidence of innovators and early adopters create the ideal environment for a more rapid diffusion of innovations.[104] The provision of Internet service is most lucrative in such densely populated areas with high market potential due to the well-developed infrastructure and mass consumption of luxury goods – the lower the population density and the further away from the centre, the higher the costs of building up an infrastructure for a less profitable target group, resulting in a lower number of providers (less competition), higher costs and lower speeds.[105] In terms of demand, there is a specific labour market, an overall lower density of social connections, specific local values and lower representation of accompanying services – parameters which are associated with lower motivation and need to connect.[106] The interplay of these factors appears to be at the root of certain unexplained differences between the examined subnational spaces. Akin to other dimensions of the digital divide, we can see that without any external interference, the geographical divide will likely remain an unmoveable constant for years to come.

The conclusion of this section confronts us with two related questions: first, what is the resulting shape of evidence of either a widening or narrowing digital divide at a nation-state level? and second, to what extent are the applied methods and approaches conducive to answering this question? The current state and analyses of Internet use gaps have been presented in this book alongside the most frequently used methodological and interpretive approaches: the discussion arose out of (a) an emphasis on the persisting assessment of changes in the distribution of users in selected subpopulations to the more balanced (b) indicators of changes in odds ratios to (c) advanced analyses measuring the net influence of individual variables on the probability of Internet use.

As we have seen in the application of the first two approaches on recent developments, the development of gaps across different subpopulations seems to indicate a gradual narrowing of the digital divide, though the rate of change is in some cases so subtle that the possibility of bridging the digital divide has become a task for several generations down the line.

---

[103] As noted also by Pick and Sarkar (2015, pp. 6, 313).

[104] Cf. Rogers (2003).

[105] García (2002); Greenstein and Prince (2009); Hale et al. (2010); Schneir and Xiong (2016).

[106] Boase (2010); Holloway (2005).

The third approach, as a specific set of attempts at creating a general model for factors of Internet use, is undoubtedly of analytical interest. However, the theoretical applicability of this model is problematic and its potential for future development is limited in terms of broadening our understanding of the digital divide or creating a solid argument in favour of government intervention. The creation of a singular, universally applicable model for factors of Internet use on a national level is seemingly problematic for four reasons: First, the significance and weight of the presented, most commonly used variables, which would allow for an international comparison and validation of such a model, is culturally conditioned; this is why these variables have different predictive cogency in different contexts. However, the cultural conditionality affecting the weight and significance of the observed variables is not the only obstacle hindering the construction of such a model – the other is the changing significance and predictive power of variables as the studied population undergoes informatization.[107] Models applied to the same country over several years thus often yield contradictory findings regarding the significance and weight of the observed variables. Thirdly, the vast majority of the constructed models are based on a select few economically developed countries in the Euro-American cultural sphere with high Internet penetration rates, which largely produces skewed generalizations. The latest analyses on the function of location and context seem to negate the possibility of creating a singular, generally applicable model.[108] Lastly, such a model could hardly take into account the structural meso- and macro-social factors, such as national information policies, local ICT infrastructure solutions, the country's position within the global infrastructure or economy, the quality of the education system, etc.

Most of the primary and indisputable findings gleaned from applications of these complex models have been long-established within DOI, and could thus aid in the verification and expansion of this theory; however, the added value of validating the social gravity of the digital divide is relatively low due to the above-stated reasons, and is limited to adjusting the impact of basic socio-demographic factors. The resulting findings are, however, either so trivial (the most impactful factors being education and income) or tenuous (the role of gender or ethnicity depending on the context), that their contribution, beyond exploring their mutual relationships in concrete data sets, is debatable. The time and space-sensitive findings of such models could then perhaps be valuable tools for local policymakers – though they are often not faced with the issue of tackling the digital divide, but rather with addressing the issue of social inequality as such.

4.3.2 The Global Digital Divide

We have already touched on the issue of the global digital divide in sections of this book overlapping with the subject of global inequality. The United States' first research efforts on the digital divide, along with those in other industrialized countries, were accompanied by burgeoning research on global differences in ICT use.

---

[107]Greenstein and Prince (2009); Noce and McKeown (2008); Peng (2010).
[108]See Hampton (2010); Pick and Sarkar (2015).

Global institutions such as the UN, OECD, ITU and World Bank incorporated the issue of unequal Internet diffusion into their reports in the second half of the 1990s, presupposing the significant impact of ICT on social progress.[109] These reports, along with analyses of the technical and economic geography of ICT and the first estimates of the global number of ICT users, made it clear that the differences observed within industrialized countries were incomparable to the state of the digital divide within developing countries and similarly between developing and developed countries. For example, the 1999 *Human Development Report* conducted by the United Nations Development Programme states that 'In mid-1998...North America alone—with less than 5% of all people—had more than 50% of Internet users. By contrast, South Asia is home to over 20% of all people but had less than 1% of the world's Internet users'[110]. The year 2000 was a turning point for political awareness of the global digital divide, with the vast majority of leading actors on the global scene lending their voices to the issue (United States, Britain, Japan, IMF, World Bank, UN, Microsoft...).[111] The World Summit on the Information Society, held by the UN in 2003 and 2005, became the formal affirmation of bridging the digital divide as a key principal in the global transition towards an information society.[112]

Post-2000, we can still find arguments insisting on a narrowing global digital divide and rebuttals to the necessity of political intervention – arguments similarly found in proclamations denying the political gravity of the digital divide in the United States: a declining Gini coefficient in unequal ICT access, higher rate of growth of ICT users in developing countries, graphs indicating a narrowing divide using a logarithmic scale on a vertical axis and the decreasing ratio of connected users across developed and developing countries.[113] However, when monitoring the development of the percentage of connected households up to 2017, it is apparent that the gap between the number of users in developed and developing countries is not on the decline (see Fig. 4.11). While data on individual use paints a different picture, the differences between the graphs most probably arise out of the rapid diffusion of mobile Internet in developing countries (see below), where fixed subscriptions mimic the dynamics of households. Composite analyses of the global digital divide however arrive at the conclusion that the global digital divide is widening, both in terms of use and connection speed.[114]

A dissection of the global digital divide issue extending beyond a simplistic comparison of the number of Internet users across individual countries (or continents, regions) is characterized by several typical traits in comparison to studies conducted on a national level.

---

[109]A summary and brief presentation of reports conducted by these institutions can be found in Norris (2001, pp. 5–6) and Hwang (2006, pp. 18–25).

[110]UNDP (1999, p. 62).

[111]See Hwang (2006, p. 14).

[112]WSIS (2005).

[113]For a summary of counter-argumentation see James (2008a).

[114]Hilbert (2016); Park, Choi, and Hong (2015); Rath (2016).

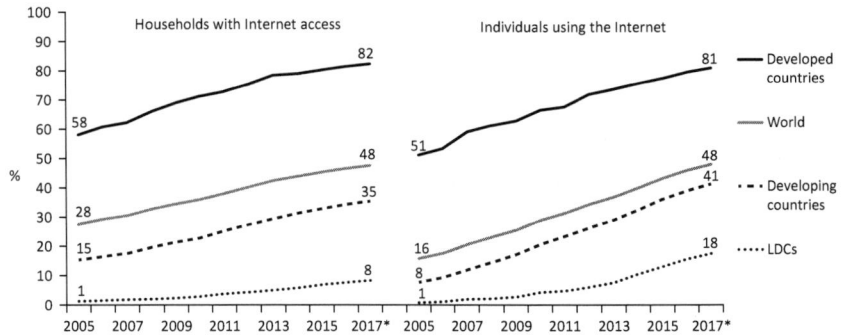

Fig. 4.11: Evolution of Households with Internet Access and Individuals
using the Internet in ITU Development Regions, 2005–2017.
Source: Author from ITU (2017) global and regional ICT data, *-estimate

When analysing global differences in ICT adoption rates, the basic unit of
analysis is the nation state.[115] The availability of data sources is heavily limited
when applying this scale, leaving authors to rely on data sources from a select
few supranational institutions (OECD, ITU, World Bank, UN, Eurostat). Usable
data have thus long been defined by the possibilities, optics and methodologies of
these institutions, thereby significantly limiting the variability and results of conducted analyses (and thus subsequent critical debates). The undeniable absence
of alternative data sources, primarily in the case of poor countries, is evidently
one of the main factors behind the limited efforts to interlink different scales. The
result is a relatively narrow focus on both complex models and the creation of
highly accurate indexes.

The design, use and enforcement of indexes are primarily the concern of
the above-mentioned supranational institutions, which employ these indexes as
indicators of social development.[116] The added value but also greatest weakness
of the constructed indexes, in comparison to digital divide analyses conducted
on a national level, lies primarily in the merging of a large number of indicators into a single piece of information, thereby allowing countries to be unequivocally ranked according to their obtained scores and using the rankings of
these countries to monitor the development of the digital divide. From a socio-
scientific point of view, it may seem unfortunate that the focus of academic
studies should culminate in such efforts, relegating their ultimate goal to the
creation of 'a robust compound digital divide measure, which would identify
all key segments and incorporate all relevant ICTs and thus reflect the "true"

---

[115]An exception being (comparative) analyses of subnational administrative divisions,
where the selection of the nation state as the basic unit of analysis becomes problematized
(as we have seen above). There is a difference between global digital divide research and this
tradition that focuses on the spatial divide at a national level and its generalization through
comparisons (see Pick and Sarkar, 2015).

[116]For an overview of indexes see Vehovar et al. (2006) or Bruno, Esposito, Genovese, and
Gwebu (2010).

digital divide'[117]. In addition to the usual criticism of substantial information loss, these indexes are also problematic in their design: they are compiled using indicators from international databases with varying degrees of conclusiveness and relevance to the studied phenomenon (e.g., the ICT skills component, serving as one-fifth of the IDI index, consists of 'mean years of schooling' and 'secondary and tertiary gross enrolment ratio'). What is more, the definitions are broadened to such an extent that their connection to digital divide research on a national level and to the theory of the information society is compromised (e.g., another component of the IDI index, ICT access, also includes the number of fixed-telephone subscriptions and mobile-cellular telephone subscriptions).[118]

If we were to take a closer look at which national parameters could be used to explain the degree of a country's informatization in comparison to that of other countries, the level of wealth (GNI per capita) presents itself as the obvious option. While this item does serve as the strongest predictor of a society's informatization,[119] it is by no means an exhaustive one. Other factors which play a prominent role in explaining differences across countries include the telecommunications infrastructure (number of landlines and/or registered SIM cards), electricity (consumption), telecommunications policies (degree of privatization, deregulation and competition support), institutional quality (the quality of institutional regulation, rule of law and political culture), international trade, human capital (i.e., educational attainment of the population), and the degree of urbanization.[120] Marginally verified factors with an observed influence on the degree of informatization include the unique strength of certain geographic locations (Scandinavia and the United States being at the forefront), degree of income inequality, R&D expenditure and the country's position in the world-system (core – semi-periphery – periphery). The impact of telecommunications service pricing (i.e., including connection charges) is most likely negligible, and the effect of a country's level of democracy proves questionable.[121]

Does the attempt at creating a general model of global digital divide factors face the same challenges as those found on a national level? The argument for designing a model primarily based on the databases of developed countries

---

[117]Vehovar et al. (2006, p. 285). For examples, see Bruno et al. (2010); Hanafizadeh, Saghaei, and Hanafizadeh (2009).

[118]See, e.g., ITU (2016). For an overview of UNDP, OECD, UNCTAD and ITU index compositions, see Hwang (2006, pp. 20–21).

[119]Chinn and Fairlie (2007, 2010); Fuchs (2009); Norris (2001); Skaletsky, Galliers, Haughton, and Soremekun (2016).

[120]Billon, Lera-Lopez, and Marco (2010); Chinn and Fairlie (2006, 2010); Fuchs (2009); Guillén and Suárez (2005); Norris (2001); Perkins and Neumayer (2011); Pick and Sarkar (2015); Skaletsky et al. (2016); Vicente and López (2011); Yu (2006); F. Zhao, Collier, and Deng (2014). Findings from this and the following two paragraphs have been adapted from these sources.

[121]Guillén and Suárez (2005) and Fuchs (2009) espouse the significant role of democracy, Norris (2001) found that the effect of this variable disappeared when controlling for other variables.

and the problem of neglecting meso- and macro-structural factors would most certainly not be applicable here. Unfortunately, the significance and strength of many factors obtained from global digital divide analyses are unusable at a national scale, as they reflect the qualities of the entire examined population or territory as a whole. Furthermore, local dynamics and cultural traits problematize the informative value of globally defined and standardized data – for example, the number of mobile-cellular subscriptions per 100 inhabitants or the number of fixed-telephone subscriptions carries different weight in countries with individual versus collective user practices.[122] Furthermore, major discrepancies have been detected on a global scale in terms of the significance and strength of different factors based on region, level of development and degree of informatization.

The last feature common to nearly all[123] texts on the global digital divide is the explicit insistence on interventions aimed at promoting the closure of the global digital divide, whether by way of privatizing or liberalizing the telecommunications market, increasing investments into the infrastructure (ITU, OECD, World Bank) or implementing ICT training and support centres like those in India and the United States.

However, in the face of persistent global disproportionalities in electricity or television diffusion, sceptical voices have been emerging regarding the novelty of the global digital divide issue. In 2001, Pippa Norris, upon comparing TV, radio and Internet diffusion curves, came to the conclusion that the Internet is not a particularly unique technology.[124] Jeffrey James falls back on Singer's 1970s concept of international technological dualism in his claim that 'the digital divide should be viewed instead as part of the same general mechanism that gives rise to other technology gaps between these two groups of countries'[125]. These claims have been bolstered by the more solid empirical argument posited by geographers Erica Perkins and Richard Neumayer in their study *Is the Internet really new after all? The determinants of telecommunications diffusion in historical perspective*. In their analysis of the basic factors of diffusion for the mail, telegram, telephone and Internet over a period of one and a half centuries, these authors reached the conclusion that there is a 'striking level of continuity in the territorially grounded socioeconomic attributes shaping the uptake of different communication technologies'[126]. However, in contrast to the mail or television, the Internet is a very complex technology, and its expansion into developing countries and subsequent effective use is hindered by several other factors that have not yet

---

[122]We will return to this in Section 5.

[123]The need for social intervention in the expansion of ICT on a global scale can be found in nearly all texts on the global digital divide issue used in this work.

[124]Norris (2001, pp. 64–66).

[125]James (2007, p. 285). Singer explains the lasting power of technological dualism in the focus of research and development, which is, on a global scale, concentrated in economically advanced countries, thus limiting their efforts to these very same countries. James estimates that at the time of the article's composition, over 90% of global research and development was being conducted in wealthy nations.

[126]Perkins and Neumayer (2011, p. 66).

been mentioned: (a) cultures with a low number of software developers and localized online content struggle to find content in their own language, thus putting the most economically and educationally deprived populations at a disadvantage; (b) Internet use is subjected to service fees, which are much more expensive in developing countries than in developed countries – in the poorest countries, these fees exceed or are even several times higher than the average monthly income; (c) a lack of motivation and digital skills in developing countries results in the underuse of available computers in community IT centres and similar access points, where computers and IT are freely available to the public; (d) due to the technical geography of the Internet, connection quality is very low and ICT equipment in developing countries is often outdated and of lower quality than equipment being used in developed countries.[127]

4.4. Applying the Diffusion of Innovations Theory: A Tenuous Relationship

The confrontation between the digital divide theory and the argument that the divide is closing of its own accord due to the natural diffusion of innovations process (see Section 4.2.3) has not abounded in academic debates on the applicability of DOI to Internet diffusion, as perhaps implied in our succinct overview of the basic elements of DOI; the issue has gained more traction in criticism and controversy surrounding the widespread ideas that stem from DOI, some aspects of which are even misleading in nature, for example, purporting the liberalized market to be the exclusive channel for the diffusion of innovations. This has had significant implications for the argumentation employed in digital divide research.

In this section, we shall try to shed light on the position of DOI in digital divide research as something which was, and to some extent still is, only tangentially considered and plagued with internal inconsistencies: on the one hand, academic thought on the digital divide has not drawn on DOI directly and certain prominent digital divide researchers have wrongly interpreted the lay version of DOI; on the other hand, modified versions of the *S*-curve have been used to validate the social gravity of the digital divide and the subsequent need for intervention.

4.4.1 The Disconnect between Diffusion of Innovations Research and Digital Divide Research

The last half-century of diffusion of innovations research has produced quite a complex theory, offering a plethora of findings and hypotheses that could benefit research on the relationship between Internet diffusion and social inequality.

Everett Rogers, one of the central figures of DOI, systematically explored the relationship between the expansion of new communication technologies and

---

[127]For (a) see UNDP (1999); Norris (2001); OECD, ISOC, and UNESCO (2013); Pearce and Rice (2014); for (b) and (d) see UN (2006); ITU (2016); Hilbert (2016) and for (c) see James (2008b).

social inequality as early as the mid-1980s,[128] thus engaging with the issue a decade before the discussion surrounding the digital divide even came to light. In 1987, together with Dutton and Jun, he published a meta-analysis of 11 studies on home computer diffusion, concluding the review with a set of useful recommendations for future research in the field. All of the referenced studies address problems and questions that are of pivotal importance for digital divide discourse. For example, in the section titled 'Social Impacts of Home Computers', the authors infer that 'equity issues in the future will depend on the rate of diffusion of home computers among American households'[129]. Among recommendations for future research in the field, we can find the request to use multivariate approaches that 'are required to rule out alternative explanations for the relationships found between independent variables and home computer adoption, use, and social impacts'[130]. They also call attention to the need to study individual motivation for adopting complicated IT and to the fact that 'the uses and social impacts of home computing vary across light versus heavy users'[131], resulting in their insistence on a more complex differentiation of different types of computer users. Their findings and research topics had to wait for more than a decade to be – without direct succession – laboriously rediscovered by digital divide research.

Similarly, at the same time when the term digital divide came to fruition, Prescott and Conger published a comprehensive review of 70 studies dated 1984–1995, in which DOI was applied to the diffusion of various information technologies. The study contains the following recommendations for future research in the field: a more thorough examination of contextual factors of diffusion, the integration of DOI and communication research, a greater focus on communication channels in the diffusion process and an elaboration of the decision-making process behind innovation adoption at various levels of social practice (e.g., managerial or individual level).[132] And, once again, digital divide research has re-discovered these research questions without directly drawing on these studies.

The digital divide discussion is thus not a direct successor of DOI, a theory which digital divide authors have been using very scarcely as one of the main sources of their research questions.[133] In addition, most applications primarily involve the fundamental theoretical model and do not elaborate on findings from older DOI studies (e.g., those aimed at analysing IT diffusion). In this regard, a lot of (primarily earlier) digital divide research comes across as somewhat curious, as the 'surprising' differences in adoption rates that they present are *consistent* with basic, well-proven DOI findings and thus do not effectively yield any surprising results (at least not

---

[128]Rogers (1986).

[129]Dutton, Rogers, and Jun (1987, p. 242).

[130]Dutton, Rogers, and Jun (1987, p. 245).

[131]Dutton, Rogers, and Jun (1987, p. 245).

[132]Prescott and Conger (1995).

[133]See, e.g., Correa, Straubhaar, Chen, and Spence (2013); S. Kim (2011); Mason and Hacker (2003); Nguyen and Western (2007); Norris (2001); G. Peng (2010); T.-Q. Peng, Zhu, Tong, and Jiang (2012); Pick and Sarkar (2015); Steyaert (2002); Verdegem and Verhoest (2009).

where researchers studying the systematic diffusion of innovations are concerned). A side-effect of this has been the perceptible negligence and re-emergence of significant factors of Internet diffusion – even today, digital divide research produces but a negligible number of studies focusing on, for example, the significance and interaction of providers, social networks and communication media within the dynamics of diffusion, research on change agents, research on the impact of the cultural compatibility of an innovation, the decision-making process in potential ICT users, etc. Research on the mechanisms of the diffusion of home computers did not end with the emergence of the digital divide debate; these studies, along with applications of DOI on Internet diffusion, however, have been neglected by digital divide research and its theoretical syntheses.[134]

Unequal Internet diffusion however *is* a diffusion of innovations issue by nature, meaning that even if digital divide research is not a direct successor of DOI, *a certain concept* of diffusion must be at play here – after all, digital divide research presupposes the existence of general Internet diffusion patterns hidden behind data on Internet penetration rates. Instead of applying existing knowledge in this field, digital divide theory has developed and legitimized itself by criticizing and refuting DOI, reducing it to the layman's idea of a basic *S*-curve model. Discussions around the popular, simplified version have borne crucial implications for the quality of this critique, its validity and the employed application of the *S*-curve.

4.4.2 Critique of the Diffusion of Innovations Theory: A False Target

Although the *S*-curve has been a part of sociological thought on the diffusion of innovations since Gabriel Tarde's time, the first empirical studies did not appear until the Second World War as the product of American rural sociology. The diffusion of innovations process has been modelled based on two basic variants and one mixed variant in DOI: the external-influence variant (assuming zero interaction between individuals, adoption on the basis of external influence, e.g., mass media), the internal-influence variant which corresponds to the *S*-curve (assuming zero influence of external factors, the diffusion of innovations solely via interpersonal social interactions) and mixed-influence (i.e., a combination of mass media and social interactions as influential factors). Since the 1950s, the stock of knowledge has been intertwined with findings on the diffusion of innovations from other socio-scientific fields (primarily pedagogy and social and cultural anthropology), mathematized and embedded in the burgeoning synthetic theory of diffusion of innovations.[135] Since then, efforts have also been made to integrate more factors into the fundamental diffusion model, leading to, for example, the dynamic diffusion model, space and time diffusion models, repeat-purchase

---

[134]The absence of studies published by Susan Brown and Venkatesh (e.g., Brown and Venkatesh, 2003; Brown et al., 2006; Venkatesh and Brown, 2001) in the most important books on the digital divide can serve as an example here.

[135]See Rogers (2003, pp. 39–75) for more details.

model, multistage innovation diffusion process model, etc. However, digital divide texts almost exclusively present a highly simplified, layman's idea of technological diffusion, comparable to the rudimentary, almost half a century-old model.

Today, the fundamental model of diffusion is a theoretically grounded mathematical construction, derived from a set of several necessary assumptions. The assumptions (and limits) of the fundamental model can be summarized in seven points:[136]

(1) *The adoption of an innovation is seen as a binary, discreet value* and the fundamental model thus does not factor in individual stages of adoption: awareness, decision-making, the acquisition of user skills, etc. (i.e., the innovation was either adopted or not adopted).

(2) *The assumption of a fixed ceiling of potential adopters,* the number of which remains static throughout the course of the diffusion of the innovation (this includes the assumption that the size of the social system in which the innovation is being diffused also remains fixed).

(3) *The assumption of one-time adoption,* that is, the model neither includes the repeated adoption or acquisition of the innovation, nor does it include the decision to stop using the innovation.

(4) The internal and mixed-influence model works with the assumption of the *interconnection of all members of the social system* with paired interpersonal ties (i.e., there is always a connection between those who have adopted the innovation and those who have not), the external-influence model works with the assumption of the constant influence of external factors throughout the entire diffusion phase.

(5) *The assumption of the innovation's stasis* throughout the diffusion process (i.e., the parameters of the innovation do not change during the diffusion process).

(6) *The assumption that diffusion occurs within a social system with fixed geographic boundaries* (the model does not include the factor of resistance towards a specifically structured space).

(7) The viability of prediction is based on the *presupposed knowledge of all significant variables* and their stability throughout the diffusion process.

In reality, the actual diffusion of innovations rarely corresponds with this fundamental model (the internal variant of which is seen in Fig. 4.5): most innovations are unsuccessful and are thus never diffused, some innovations quickly die out after initial success, while others may be diffused at a rate completely out of line with the *S*-curve. No scientist systematically engaging with DOI research would thus apply the fundamental model to any innovation without considering the distinct parameters of the innovation as proliferating a distinct social system, that is, parameters that are only evident in retrospect.[137] Such caution towards

---

[136]Summarized from Mahajan and Peterson (1985).

[137]Rogers (2003); Mahajan and Peterson (1985).

definitive a priori assessments on the diffusion of innovations process in complex social environments does, on the one hand, weaken the predictive potential of DOI; on the other hand, it bolsters DOI by clearly demarcating the limits of its validity and practical applicability. This might also explain why some authors associated with the digital divide do not gear their DOI criticism towards Rogers, Bass or other prominent representatives of DOI, but rather to the 'mainstream diffusion theory and interpretations of the *S*-curve in public opinion and by policy makers' that are plagued with 'simplicity and determinism'[138]. DOI is criticized for the assumptions presented in the fundamental model – assumptions which have been kept alive for decades with attempts to incorporate them in more complex models.

The relative disconnect between DOI and its criticism in digital divide research can be substantiated in how little digital divide research draws on the DOI tradition as well as in the claim that the fundamental diffusion model is more of an unreflected premise in digital divide analyses rather than a model which would be abstracted from these analyses. The creation of a research tradition separate from and only marginally tied to DOI has, on the one hand, led to the rediscovery of what had already been discovered, and on the other, has been accused of glossing over fundamental problems for which DOI has long been criticized – problems which may also extend to digital divide research, as both disciplines address the same issue: the diffusion of an innovation in society. The problems common to both traditions could indicate that their critiques could be of use when identifying the assumptions of the digital divide thesis and assessing its very validity. However, as our illustration of digital divide research is far from complete and because such critiques are truly pertinent to the digital divide thesis, we shall revisit the matter in Chapter 5 in our final assessment of the validity of the digital divide thesis. In the following two sections, we shall examine two methods of application for the *S*-curve that are conducive to the digital divide thesis, drawing attention to the ongoing innovations in ICT and to the possibility of different ICT diffusion ceilings across different subpopulations.

4.4.3 The Perpetual Resurgence of the Digital Divide

Plotting a uniform *S*-curve, given the technical specifications of ICT innovations, is problematic for two reasons.

First, the labels 'Internet', 'Internet access', 'computer' and 'mobile phone' employed in diffusion statistics and graphs suggest an idea of static, homogenous artefacts. In reality however, every curve represents rapidly evolving technological clusters with changing properties. The price variability of components (hardware, software), a reflection of their novelty, rarity, speed, etc., are then manifested in the preferential adoption of more high-performance and, for participation in (an information) society, more efficient combinations of technology clusters by the socio-economically privileged. Certain technology clusters can be less user

---

[138]Both quotations van Dijk (2005, p. 62).

friendly than others, which may be associated with a more gradual adoption (or lack thereof) in less innovative or less-skilled population segments. If we were to trace the quality of the examined ICT across various social strata, the digital divide would then take on a new dimension, thereby significantly problematizing arguments of a closing divide.[139]

Compared to older communication technologies, ICTs are evolving so rapidly that the diffusion process of a new ICT innovation begins at a point when the diffusion process of the former is still far from complete. Since segments of the population with a higher degree of innovativeness are the first to adopt an innovation (in the case of ICT, primarily those in higher social strata), they constantly surpass population segments with lower degrees of innovativeness by adopting newer, better and more efficient ICT.[140] The entire situation can be depicted as a series of several superimposed *S*-curves, where late adopters are adopting a technology while innovators and first adopters are already adopting the new generation of the said technology. The digital divide between users of different generations or types of ICT can thus remain stable or expand, despite general statistics insinuating a closure of the divide.[141]

In the digital divide debate, broadband Internet and the mobile phone have been viewed as fundamentally distinct technologies spurring new (types of) digital divides. The rationale as to why these particular technologies have become significant informatization indicators lies behind their added value vis-à-vis the use or ownership of the vaguely defined 'Internet', which has long been associated with fixed and wired PCs.

At a time when the digital divide was purported to be closing, and the entire discussion began to subside in the public sphere, the term *broadband divide*[142] emerged – identifying the gap between those who were connected to high-speed Internet and those who were lagging behind with slow dial-up. The data illustrate that the adoption of broadband Internet followed a socio-demographic distribution in line with that of Internet adoption – the gradual, relatively rapid convergence peaked at several per cent below the number of users in countries without aggressive digital inclusion policies (in the United States, the number of dial-up subscribers has been at approximately 5% of all users since 2011, and since 2013 approximately 3% of connected households in the EU have been without broadband)[143], with the majority of these users belonging to groups with the lowest overall Internet adoption rates.[144] What is more, greater differences (than those of Internet adoption in general) were recorded across rural and urban areas and across minorities. The problem of

---

[139]van Dijk (2005, pp. 62–63). See, e.g., Hilbert (2016).

[140]Rogers (1986, pp. 169–172).

[141]van Dijk (2005).

[142]Furthermore, this term did not gain much traction in the academic sphere, and similarly as in the case of 'mobile divide', its use was predominantly relegated to the sphere of political declarations, documents and reports.

[143]Horrigan and Duggan (2015); Eurostat (2017).

[144]Fox (2005); Horrigan and Rainie (2002); Mossberger et al. (2008); Smith (2010a).

the unequal or insufficient diffusion of broadband very quickly became the priority of national and transnational information policies, positing the general expansion of broadband as the gateway to economic prosperity and improved quality of life.[145] On what grounds are these promises justified? After adjusting for the impact of socio-demographic variables, it was revealed that broadband users hone different skills and use Internet in a different manner than dial-up users: they spend more time on the Internet, post more content online, exhibit a significantly greater scope and frequency of online activities and they also use more advanced functions and services to a much greater extent.[146] However, the direct effect of connection speed on quality of life has not been sufficiently scientifically tested.

Mobile phones have long remained on the fringe of digital divide discourse, and have only experienced a slight upswing in recent years due to the proliferation of smartphones and the correlated increase in mobile Internet speeds, allowing for the use of more demanding online applications and services.[147]

However, mobile phones first garnered great attention in connection to critiques of computerization as a form of aid for developing countries. Authors writing on this issue draw attention to the irrationality of such programmes in areas with often non-existing or poor power systems, education systems, telecommunications markets or even basic hydro and medical infrastructures.[148] For the poorest countries, the mobile phone is an undeniably more suitable technology due to the significantly lower infrastructure requirements (in the absence of power grids, batteries can be charged using cars or aggregates and the implementation of mobile networks in remote areas and otherwise unfavourable terrain is significantly more economical than for fixed-line networks) and in terms of user-friendliness (basic mobile phone functions do not require literacy, mobile phones are significantly cheaper than computers, phone credit can be topped up based on the individual's current financial situation, etc.). The advent of the mobile phone has also ushered in the cost-effective use of applications which enable online calling and texting. As a result, there has been an overwhelmingly rapid diffusion of mobiles in developing countries over the past few years. For example in Morocco, Ghana, Armenia and Columbia, the number of mobile subscriptions per capita has reached the same level as in the Netherlands; in Kenya, Cameroon, Tanzania and Nigeria, around four-fifths of the population aged 15 and over owned a mobile phone in 2015.[149] Mobile Internet has also impacted the

---

[145]See the overview of broadband initiatives in The Broadband Commission for Digital Development (2013).

[146]Fox (2005); Horrigan (2006, 2010); Horrigan and Rainie (2002, 2006); Mossberger et al. (2008); van Dijk (2005).

[147]Until then, the mobile phone had almost exclusively appeared in general overviews of different adoption rates of digital technologies (e.g., Cooper and Kimmelman, 2001) or within population categorizations based on the extent of digital technology use (e.g., Horrigan, 2007).

[148]See Section 4.2.2.

[149]ITU (2016).

dynamics of Internet diffusion in the economically developed world: for example in the United States, the wider availability of mobile Internet connections has led to increased Internet adoption in low-income households and in the Hispanic and Afro-American population, who use mobile Internet more often than White Americans.[150]

While the mobile phone is purported by multinational organizations and even some scientists to be catalysing the closure of the digital divide, the actual ameliorating impact of this technology's expansion on global and local inequality has not yet been established. Day-to-day tasks in Third World countries have certainly benefited from the innovative and locally tailored use of mobile phones as a source of information (e.g., looking up product prices or weather forecasts for local farmers), social and economic coordination, increased interconnectedness of the population, and as a payment card substitute;[151] however, the link between the mobile phone and economic and social growth in the most socially and economically deprived countries is a question that is yet to be answered. Despite the relatively rapid mobile phone diffusion in recent years, the geographic and socio-demographic distribution in the poorest countries remains significantly skewed in favour of urban areas and higher social classes.[152]

The long-standing negligence of the mobile phone in digital divide research is alarming due to the fact that the number of mobile-cellular subscriptions worldwide surpassed that of Internet subscriptions as early as the second half of the 1990s. According to ITU estimates, the number of mobile-cellular subscriptions worldwide matched that of the global population in 2016, thereby exceeding the number of Internet subscriptions more than twofold; in the same year, the number of prepaid SIM cards was on average higher than the number of inhabitants and 90% of the population of developing countries had a mobile phone subscription, according to the GSMA Intelligence survey.[153] However, the mobile phone did not only surpass the Internet in terms of diffusion but as early as 2007, it acquired the status of the number one most indispensable communication technology in the United States.[154] The consequences of such momentous and large-scale diffusion of the mobile phone have yet to be reflected in the digital divide thesis (we shall thus return to this issue in Chapter 5).

Broadband Internet and mobile phone connections have been receiving a great deal of attention in official political documents and proclamations espousing informatization efforts. Considering how easily these technologies have become new sources of the digital divide, it would be naïve to think that the entire digital divide debate ends here.

---

[150]Brown, Campbell, and Ling (2011); Smith (2010b).

[151]For examples and discussions see, e.g., Castells et al. (2007); Donner (2008); Fafchamps and Minten (2012); Jagun, Heeks, and Whalley (2008); James (2007); Overå (2008).

[152]James (2007, p. 288); ITU (2016).

[153]ITU (2016, Section 5).

[154]Horrigan (2008).

4.4.4 Adaptation of the S-Curve: Stratification and Normalization Model

While this book has cast verifiable doubt over the foreseeable closure of the digital divide in Section 4.3, it has not expanded upon the subject of its future development, as the argument of the social gravity of the digital divide has remained quelled by projections of the divide closing of its own accord. This argument, however, could be weakened if we were to plot *S*-curves for every studied subpopulation.

American political scientist Pippa Norris took inspiration from Rogers' theory and from the established practice of presenting a widening digital divide by plotting separate adoption curves for different social strata, based on which she presented two basic models in 2001 in order to assess the future evolution of the digital divide. According to Norris, the future course of ICT adoption will either favour the optimists who presuppose a uniform ceiling in the diffusion of these technologies, with variances only in the adoption rates of different subpopulations, or the pessimists, who project that adoption across socially and economically deprived groups will come to a halt before it even nears the saturation level attained by higher social strata.[155] Norris presents two basic models for the evolution of the digital divide on the basis of these two hypotheses: the normalization model and the stratification model (see Fig. 4.12).

These two scenarios resonated significantly within digital divide discourse, as any empirical evidence in validation of the stratification model would bolster argumentation calling for rapid social intervention; the looming threat of the irreversible stabilization of a two-speed society comprising ICT users and non-users would then be an imminent one. However, despite applications of this distinction,[156] up until the mid-2000s, no efforts had been made to model the dynamics of the diffusion process across different subpopulations in order to ascertain the validity of either model. One of the main reasons behind the cautiously formulated conclusions following similarly targeted attempts was the

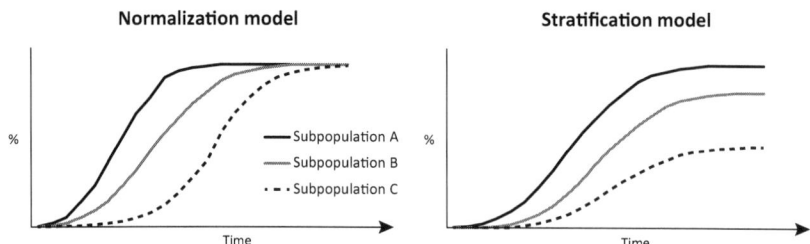

Fig. 4.12:   The Diffusion of Innovations Process Across Different Social Strata: The Normalization Model and the Stratification Model
Source: Adapted from Norris (2001).

---

[155]Norris (2001).

[156]From the texts referenced in this work see, e.g., Gonzales, Ems, and Suri (2016); Martin (2003); Martin and Robinson (2007); Sujarwoto and Tampubolon (2016); van Dijk (2005, 2006a); Willis and Tranter (2006).

paucity of long-term time series from different countries.[157] Approximately from 2010 onwards, and predominantly in global digital divide research, there have been several studies testing empirical data based on these models, arriving at the unanimous conclusion of divergence, or rather 'a lack of long term convergence in Internet diffusion between low- and high-income countries'[158].

Despite the fact that the distinction between the normalization and stratification model was well received in digital divide research, and despite the empirical testing that followed, this entire concept will not hold up when pitted against the fundamental DOI model and its assumptions as outlined above. This entire distinction can be refuted simply by adjusting the vertical axis of both graphs so that the saturation level of subpopulation A corresponds with the diffusion ceiling equalling 100% of population. If the ceiling ended up being above the saturation level of subpopulation A, it would indicate that the normalization model does not represent the population segment falling between the ceiling and saturation level – and adding this population segment to the model would effectively render the two models identical.[159] The normalization model thus assumes that the technology will gradually be adopted by the *entire* population, unlike the stratification model, which assumes only partial adoption by the population. However, this is at odds with the claims of authors who use the distinction of these two models in their work. In the early 2000s, Pippa Norris and Jan van Dijk hypothesized that the saturation level in the United States and other post-industrial countries would be around 70–85%, with a much lower level in the case of more complex ICT innovations and Third World countries – provided that the hypothetical global informatization policies aimed at stabilizing opportunities in the global information economy would remain unrealized.[160] Furthermore, we have already established (Section 4.2.3) that innovations are, almost without exception, first adopted by those with higher educational attainment and socio-economic status: plotting adoption curves for various subpopulations for innovations with a saturation level falling below 100% will then *always* produce a picture corresponding to the stratification model. The stratification model thus depicts the diffusion of any innovation that does not impact 100% of the population. In such a case, however, the distinction between the two models poses no added value. The discovery that the stratification model in all likelihood depicts the reality of the future evolution

---

[157]For example, van Dijk (2005); Martin and Robinson (2007).

[158]Andrés, Cuberes, Diouf, and Serebrisky (2010, p. 327). Similarly, Park et al. (2015), Rath (2016) and S. Kim (2011) for the United States.

[159]It should be noted, however, that a similar error can be found in the work of Rogers, who in 1986 presented the diffusion of television as an example of the normalization model in effect, for which the claim that 'in the end the innovation was adopted by everyone' contradicts the graphical representation, where even in the last studied period, we can observe a difference – albeit a small one – between the monitored income groups in the United States (Rogers 1986, pp. 170–171).

[160]Norris (2001); van Dijk (2005). In the United States the number of users has been around 85% as of 2012, and around 94% in Sweden as of 2011.

of ICT is a critical one for the digital divide thesis: the digital divide would, in this case, be an intrinsic aspect of the informatized social order.[161]

In Section 4.3, we have seen that the target group of digital divide research and the resulting statistics on the dynamics of Internet use always centre on the entire population of a given political, administrative or statistical unit: most frequently the entire nation, state, global population or region. These data, and the manner in which it is presented in digital divide research, thus *equate the entire population with the population of potential users*. This is underscored by efforts to identify a hierarchy of reasons explaining the unconnected segment of the population in order to enable more effective policies to integrate this 'vulnerable' population segment into the information society. The fact that digital divide research, as a frame of reference for data interpretation, employs the normalization model and dismisses the stratification model as undesirable, indicates that despite all explicit declarations of a saturation level below 100%, the demand to bridge the digital divide may be nothing more than a demand for the *absolute* informatization of society.

4.5 The Deepening Divide: The Final Argument

If the entire issue of the digital divide rested solely upon the ownership of a certain device or being granted physical access to the said device, then the prognosis laid out by the stratification model would no longer give such cause for alarm; a problem of this magnitude would seemingly be easily remedied by 'carpet-bombing those geographic and demographic regions' with 'Internet-ready computers'[162]. As naïve as this may seem to the reader, it is not far removed from the deluge of informatization programmes and initiatives touted by governments, authorities and international institutions over the past two decades, devised to catapult entire schools, districts, cities and regions into the information future. Whether it was the efforts of the Irish government to create 'An Information Age Town' prototype, the 'Hole-in-the-Wall' experiment carried out by the government of New Delhi to bring computers to Indian slums or the global project titled 'One Laptop per Child' spearheaded by Nicolas Negroponte, all of these initiatives fell short as effective solutions[163] for the following reason: they failed to consider the entire gamut of preconditions for successful ICT adoption, beginning with the individual's first encounter with the innovation to developing interest and finally culminating in efficient use of the innovation.

Critiques of the binary, techno-deterministic leanings of digital divide research and related efforts to extend the model beyond physical access are as old as academic discourse on the digital divide itself. As early as the mid-1990s, several studies cropped up focusing on gaps in computer and Internet skills in

---

[161]We shall return to this option in Chapter 6.
[162]Bucy and Newhagen (2004, p. xi).
[163]See, e.g., Leslie Steeves and Kwami (2017); Meza-Cordero (2017); Warschauer (2002, 2003).

the Netherlands, also drawing attention to other significant factors that hinder effective use: uneasiness towards computer use, insufficiently user-friendly computers and Internet, lack of opportunities for use, and significant gaps in required skills across users.[164] Around the same time, warnings of a 'second digital divide' resounded from North America, pointing to an unevenly distributed awareness of the existence, availability and added value of ICT.[165] In 2001, DiMaggio and Hargittai, in light of the constantly growing number of users, recommended shifting the focus of digital divide research from gaps between users and non-users to differences across various types of access and users. Identifying the different dimensions of digital inequality and subsequent empirical analysis should, in the authors' estimation, facilitate the development of a 'testable model of the relationship between individual characteristics, dimensions of inequality, and positive outcomes of technology use'[166]. While the distinction between the digital divide and digital inequality have not gained much traction in digital divide research, the above-stated efforts to differentiate the various dimensions of the digital divide (or types of digital divides)[167] and possibly even create a theoretically and empirically grounded general model have by no means remained entirely marginal.

Presenting each existing classification one by one in order to better our understanding of these efforts would be a tedious and unnecessary endeavour due to the amount of overlap. Also, there is no single model that would be exhaustive enough to house all of the findings, perspectives and dimensions that have been postulated to date. It then seems most appropriate to select a theoretical model which is most in line with the other classifications. Van Dijk's pursuit of a theoretically grounded model is one which fulfils the aforementioned criteria. Allow us to examine it in closer detail below.

If we were to take a closer look at the texts in the resultant matrix of dimensions (see Table 4.3), the most striking feature would not be the relatively strong overlap, but rather the sheer amount of overlap despite repeated refutations of 'a homogeneous perspective, which describes uneven ICT access as a simplified binary divide, which can lead to immature academic conclusions'[168]. This can either indicate that such efforts of expanding the scope of research are merely isolated, progressive islands in a sea of scholars with a reductionist binary understanding of the digital divide, or that such a refutation is at odds with the real state of academic discourse on the digital divide. In the first case, we would have to ask ourselves why the vast majority have latched on to this highly reductionist perspective; in the second case, we would have to ascertain the function and catalyst of such a 'discursive operation'. Many of the scientific texts used in this

---

[164]van Dijk (2000).

[165]Katz and Aspden (1997); Reddick, Boucher, and Groseilliers (2000).

[166]DiMaggio and Hargittai (2001, p. 1).

[167]Certain authors interpret dimensions as divides, though this is a more metaphorical use of the word. To avoid any confusion, I employ the term 'dimension of the digital divide' throughout.

[168]Lei, Gibbs, Chang, and Lee (2008, p. 541).

Table 4.3:   Matrix of Digital Divide Dimensions at a National Level. [169]

Appears in van Dijk (2005)	Dimension A (Motivational)	Dimension B (Material)	Dimension C (Skills)	Dimension D (Usage)	Dimension E (–)
Katz & Aspden (1997)	First divide (awareness)	Second divide (usage)			
Reddick, Boucher, and Groseilliers (2000)	Second divide (interest)	First divide (users and non-users)			
Attewell (2001)		First divide (access)		Second divide (computer use)	
Castells (2001b)		Digital divide, new technological divide	Knowledge gap (skills)		
DiMaggio and Hargittai (2001)		Digital divide, equipment	Skills	Autonomy of use / Purposes of use	Social support
M.-C. Kim & Kim (2001)		Opportunity divide → Utilization D. → Reception D.			

[169]This matrix is not necessarily an exhaustive one, though I consider it sufficiently representative and functional given its purpose in this book. Due to the variances between definitions and perspectives employed by the different authors, their categorization using van Dijk's dimensions is intended to serve as an approximation only.

Author				
Katz and Rice (2002)	Awareness, Internet dropouts	Access divide, cohort digital divide		
Steyaert (2002)		Physical	Informacy, info skills	Usage
Warschauer (2002, 2003)		Devices, conduits	Literacy	
Mossberger, Tolbert, and Stansbury (2003)		Access	Skills	Democratic divide, economic opportunity divide
Bucy and Newhagen (2004)		Physical, system	Cognitive		Social
Dewan and Riggins (2005)		First-order digital divide	Second-order digital divide	
Vehovar (2006)	Dual divide	First divide	Second divide	
Valadez and Durán (2007)		Physical		Use	Social support, social consequences
Helsper (2012)	Social impact mediators: attitudes access skills			Digital fields of resources	Digital impact mediators
van Deursen and Helsper (2015b)		First-level digital divide (physical access)	Second-level digital divide (skills and usage)		Third-level digital divide (outcomes)

Source: Author.

work[170] adopt this stance though the majority of researchers appear cognizant of these one-dimensional reductions and try to distance themselves from them. It thus appears that academic digital divide research has long made a habit of opposing the reduction of the digital divide to that of physical access. The value and function of such a discursive creation of opponents in the academic defence of the digital divide's social relevance remains, without an appropriate interpretive framework, unclear at this moment, and is why we shall reserve this finding for Chapter 6 of this book.

The second distinct feature of efforts to formulate a theoretical model of the digital divide is the almost exclusive aim of creating a 'container theory of society' rooted in methodological individualism, that is, a theory implicitly constructed as a model of relations in the homogenous space of the abstract nation state, the inner-workings of which are extrapolated from the characteristics of the discrete individuals studied and not, for example, from certain configurations of relationships between them.[171]

At a global level, we would be hard pressed to find a multidimensional model extending beyond the analysis of factors contributing to a certain one-dimensional degree of informatization (as observed in Section 4.3.2), despite the fact that the issue of social inequality in relation to the ICT infrastructure has already been a topic of debate in globalization sociology and development sociology.[172]

4.5.1 Van Dijk's Digital Divide Model

The growing number of empirical studies spanning beyond the binary principle of physical access has furnished us with a robust set of findings, indicating that the purported narrowing of the digital divide is but a dangerous chimera intended to divert attention from a serious social problem. Such an argument, however, could only be presented credibly via a theoretical framework which would facilitate the logical arrangement of results from empirical studies, thereby validating the digital divide theory. Efforts to formulate an adequately robust theoretical model have been confronted with two key issues: (1) creating a robust and logically compiled classification of digital divide dimensions and establishing its relevance to the (2) argument of unequal access to ICT as a new, standalone source of social inequality.

The most sophisticated synthesis of the digital divide theory and research to date, which addresses these issues by employing two testable models ('A Causal Model of the Core Argument' and the four-stage model 'A Cumulative and

---

[170]For examples, see Chapter 4 footnote 36.

[171]The concept of the container theory of society was developed by Ulrich Beck (2000), for a more detailed description of the difference between the individualistic and structural approach see, e.g., Wellman (1988). A shift towards context or to the relational approach has only been observed in recent years (e.g., Helsper, 2017b), prior to that, the relational perspective had been explicitly championed by, e.g., van Dijk (see Section 4.5.2), though digital divide research did not heed this call. We shall revisit this grave oversight in Chapter 6.

[172]See, e.g., Sklair (1994); Sassen (2006); Castells (2000b, 2001a).

Recursive Model of Successive Kinds of Access to Digital Technologies')[173] can be found in van Dijk's book *The deepening divide: Inequality in the information society* and in later, updated versions of these models.[174] These models shall serve as a solid foundation for structuring the remaining portion of Section 4.5, allowing us to present empirical evidence in support of the argument of a deepening digital divide. The aspects of van Dijk's model which are given the most weight in this book are its sophisticated and systematic character, impact as well as the 'typicality' of elements used in the argumentative framework in defence of the digital divide thesis.

When forming his key argument, van Dijk adopts Tilly's concept of categorical inequality, that is, inequality between binary categories (man–woman, white–black, citizen–foreigner, etc.), present in the system of socially sustained mechanisms of resource distribution (material, social, cognitive, etc.). Inspired by the resulting understanding of social inequality as both a relational and individual phenomenon, van Dijk makes a distinction between individual (age, gender, ethnicity, personality, intelligence, etc.) and positional (inequality between positions in the workforce, education, household and social geography) inequality in order to systematize empirical evidence of categorical inequality. The potential added value of using Tilly's approach lies in its emphasis on the relational nature of the digital divide, that is, the call to shift our attention from identifying and analysing the socio-demographic profile of the population, defined in terms such as 'non-use' or 'inefficient use', towards a more constructivist-based analysis of the (re)production of interactions, relationships and institutions which actively limit and underestimate ICT use. Van Dijk is nonetheless limited by the (individualistic) model he uses and by the individualistically grounded methodology of studies on ICT use and non-use which he employs (an issue which we shall cover in greater detail in Chapter 5).

A socially sustained system of categorical inequality produces the unequal distribution of resources relevant for ICT access (understood primarily as Internet access). Given that characteristics of ICT, such as user friendliness and technological complexity, significantly inform the extent and quality of a new technology's use in a given population, van Dijk posits this factor, together with the distribution of resources, as two explanans of unequal access. The next step in the construction of this model is a critical one for the digital divide thesis: 'unequal access to digital technologies brings about unequal participation in society'[175]. The resulting increase in the participation gap subsequently impacts the system of resource distribution which in turn bolsters categorical inequality. The key argument thus leads us to one primary aim: to demonstrate that in the absence of effective intervention, unequal access to ICT will become a new structural factor of social inequality, producing second- and third-class citizens, and in some cases entirely ostracizing

---

[173]Van Dijk and van Deursen (2014) label the first model 'A Casual Model of Resources and Appropriation Theory' and the second 'Four Stages of Access to Digital Technologies'.
[174]van Deursen and Helsper (2015b); van Dijk (2005); van Dijk and van Deursen (2014).
[175]van Dijk (2005, p. 15).

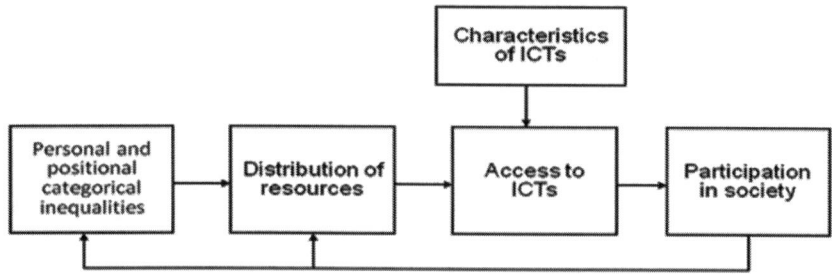

Fig. 4.13:   Van Dijk's Causal Model of the Core Argument. *Source*: van Dijk (2005, p. 15).

certain segments of the population from public life.[176] Van Dijk's goal is to gain an understanding of this process, to refine our knowledge of the causes and consequences of unequal ICT access and to propose a set of interventions as a means of neutralizing or subverting the role of ICT access in growing social inequality.[177] A graphic representation of the key argument can be seen in Fig. 4.13:

The key argument here seems to lend fairly salient support to the digital divide thesis – the biggest advantages being its footing in the broader framework of sociological theory and its empirical testability. However, there are two tenuous points which are crucial for maintaining the validity of van Dijk's core argument.

First, it can be argued that ICT access in itself can be understood as an unequally distributed resource. Why then is it plotted separately next to the unequal distribution of resources and unequal participation in society? The separation of ICT access from resources is not made sufficiently apparent in van Dijk's model; while he does explain this analytically out of the necessity of explaining ICT access apropos of the current system of social inequality,[178] he fails to give credence to the potential bias that such a privileged classification is imbued with. Van Dijk's interpretation of access to ICTs as including computer ownership and Internet access results in an explicit rift from the world of other material resources directly linked to categorical inequality and removed from any direct impact on participation in society. The ramifications of this oversight are reflected in the absence of other means of communication and information-processing tools – testing the model in their absence could lead to heavily skewed conclusions, potentially overestimating the real impact of ICT on participation. The separation of access to ICTs and resources and the absence of other media could thus significantly destabilize the entire model and diminish the key role of ICT access as a mediator between unequal starting conditions and participation.[179]

---

[176]van Dijk (2005, 2006b).

[177]'The ultimate purpose of this elaboration is to find ways to intervene in the process to solve the problem of the digital divide as it is currently defined.' (van Dijk, 2005, p. 14).

[178]van Dijk (2005, p. 20).

[179]I use this objection along with its consequences for maintaining the digital divide thesis in Chapter 5.

This leads us to the second, more crucial objection – one which needs to be addressed if we are to maintain the validity of the entire digital divide thesis: what exactly characterizes ICT access as an exceptional new source of inequality (i.e., unequal participation) when compared to other scarce resources? Van Dijk was aware of this issue and of the fact that existing digital divide research had yet to provide a satisfactory answer.[180] He thus elaborated an affirmative response by grounding the entire issue within information and network society theories in the Bell-Castells tradition. Given that this theoretical context guarantees the Internet a pivotal position as a material infrastructure within an ongoing structural transformation into a new type of society, it was of no great difficulty to posit Internet access as a necessary precondition for social 'survival', maintaining participation in increasingly digitized social networks and finding employment in the computerized job market.[181] More recent responses to this issue draw attention to ongoing informatization as a reality which often renders Internet use a necessity, and to findings from segments of the population which attest to the positive impact of the Internet.[182]

Van Dijk laid out the foundations of the cumulative and recursive model of the successive types of access to digital technologies as early as the late 1990s, in his critique of the techno-deterministic character of nascent digital divide research and policies aimed at bridging this divide.[183] His model is rooted in the understanding of 'access to ICTs' as a set of four successive levels of access of a certain quality: motivational, material, skills and usage. The successive nature of the model lies in the fact that each additionally attained level of access is conditioned upon access at lower levels – the individual can only become a user once he has successfully 'passed' all four levels (e.g., the use of skills presupposes motivation and physical access to the technology). The model is considered a cumulative one in that the quality of use and its impact on participation in society are the result of inequalities that accumulate throughout all four levels of access. The dynamic, recursive nature of the model is rooted in the momentum of the technological innovation, indicating that the hypothetical user will need to go through all four levels again, albeit under different conditions (e.g., using a smartphone requires different motivation – familiarization with new applications, software, etc.). If we were to replace 'access to ICTs' with a recursive sequence using a four-level approach, the result would be the previously mentioned synthetic causal and sequential model of individual access to digital technology.

As we have discussed the level of physical/material access in sufficient detail, the following sections will address the remaining three levels of access, presenting up-to-date data and its implications for the digital divide thesis. This should, as explained above, allow us to cover digital divide research in a more or less exhaustive manner.[184] We shall begin with the question which paved the way for

---

[180]For example, van Dijk (2006a, p. 223 and 230).
[181]van Dijk (2005, 2006a).
[182]van Dijk and van Deursen (2014, pp. 45–52).
[183]van Dijk (2000).
[184]For now, we shall set aside discursive analyses of the digital divide debate, as we shall revisit them in Chapter 6.

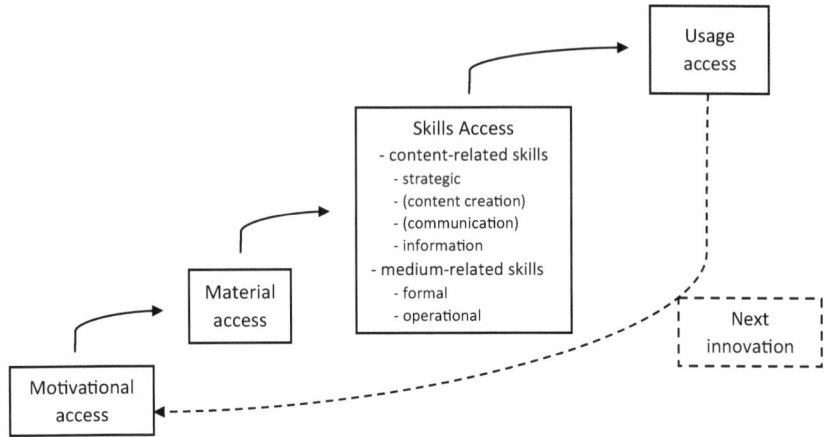

Fig. 4.14:   An Updated Version of van Dijk's Cumulative and Recursive
Model of Successive Types of Access to Digital Technology.
Source: Adapted from van Dijk (2005). Skills access was updated on the
basis of van Dijk and van Deursen (2014).

exploring the motivational component of access: if ICT is truly such an asset for
participation in society – why is it that some people do not adopt?

4.5.3 Motivation and Barriers to Access

In Section 4.1, we saw that probing into the reasons behind the non-use of ICT has
been an integral part of digital divide research since its inception. Investigating
the motivation and barriers to access plays a special role in digital divide research,
as the focus here lies mainly in that of non-users.[185] The primary research topics at
this level of access are differentiating types of people based on their relationship
to the technology, the problem of intermittent use, monitoring the dynamics of
non-use throughout the Internet diffusion process, reasons for non-use and lastly
an issue which is critical in relation to the digital divide thesis – the declared lack
of interest in ICT use by a select segment of the population. In this section, we
shall briefly examine each topic as it pertains to the digital divide thesis.

Early research on the motivation factor focused on the internal composition of non-users, categorized by the level of ICT awareness and declared interest in acquiring a personal computer or Internet connection in the near future.
Non-users with the lowest computer or Internet awareness and with the lowest
expressed intention of acquiring these technologies were predominantly identified as individuals with low educational attainment, low income, older individuals

---

[185]However, the question of motivation has recently cropped up in several studies focusing
on ICT users, monitoring the relationships between motivation, skills, usage and outcomes
(Courtois and Verdegem, 2016; Reisdorf and Groselj, 2017). We shall return to them in the
following sections.

and women.[186] According to these authors, a significant portion of non-users were thus faced with a 'dual digital divide'[187], as their problem was not merely one of lacking physical access, but lacking knowledge and motivation. The first of these barriers – that is, lack of awareness of computers and the Internet – is, at least in economically developed countries, a thing of the past. However, an issue which still remains is insufficient awareness of the usefulness of ICT and, by association, the existence of those who simply express no interest in using these key tools of the 'Information Age'. Efforts of bridging this dual digital divide, as opposed to the single physical access gap, should thus aim at mobilizing a wide range of substantially different strategies.

Efforts in generating a more detailed typology of the population that is not limited to non-users have resulted in a continuum between permanently connected heavy users equipped with the best technology, and non-users, whose odds of ICT use in the foreseeable future are slim – regardless of whether they have the minimum resources necessary or whether they would not acquire a personal computer or Internet connection at any cost. In 2003, a group of researchers from the Pew Internet & American Life Project dubbed this continuum 'a spectrum of access', identifying three types of users and three types of non-users: home broadband users, continuous users, intermittent users, dropouts (or drop-offs), net evaders and truly unconnected.[188] While this is certainly not the latest or most innovative typology for this continuum, it is particularly fitting when presenting the primary variations within the population of non-users and those teetering between use and non-use, as later, similarly targeted typologies[189] encapsulate the level of user access without paying much attention to the indistinct demarcation between users and non-users.

Intermittent users are those who have, at some point in the past, stopped using the Internet for an extended period of time. Such users often oscillate between this category and that of dropouts. It is difficult to ascertain the characteristics and growth rate of this group, as later typologies have geared their focus away from intermittent use towards sporadic (occasional, rare, low ...) use.[190] Painting a comprehensive picture thus requires compiling the relevant typologies together with qualitative studies which focus on fluctuations in ICT use.[191] This group's socio-demographic profile is not so well defined, though we often find its members to be individuals with tenuous positions in society, such as those from low-income households, ethnic minorities, individuals with unstable employment, single mothers and refugees. In addition, this group often exhibits a negative stance towards the Internet. It generally appears that the more the Internet is integrated into everyday life, the more positively it is perceived,

---

[186]Katz and Aspden (1997); Lenhart (2000); Reddick et al. (2000).

[187]A term employed by Reddick et al. (2000).

[188]Lenhart and Horrigan (2003); Lenhart et al. (2003).

[189]For an overview of other major user typologies pre-2010 see Brandtzæg (2010).

[190]See overview of typologies by Brandtzæg (2010) or Blank and Groselj (2014).

[191]Eynon and Geniets (2016); Gonzales (2016); Gonzales et al. (2016); Selwyn (2006); Selwyn, Gorard, and Furlong (2005).

with the most notable differences in perception being between non-users and low users and less so between different categories of users.[192] A significant advancement in explaining these attitudes has been made by Amy Gonzalez in a series of qualitative studies, highlighting the constant struggle for the sustainability and functionality of access (coining these practices *technology maintenance*) among the underprivileged population.[193] Gonzalez argues that access requires, in addition to motivation, the constant expenditure of time, money and energy. For the segment of the population with poor resources, 'using' digital media is thus a constant and relatively strenuous uphill battle, with poorly functioning or malfunctioning devices, lack of a household connection and disconnected services for extended periods of time. The interviews conducted with the respondents then suggest that their negative attitudes are rather a rational reflection of the low centrality of the Internet in their everyday lives, which is in turn suggestive of the social situations specific to individuals with poor resources. This implies that negative attitudes cannot be remedied solely via 'rationalization', that is, by explaining the benefits and usefulness of Internet use, as (some of) these attitudes reflect the individual's position within the complex system of social inequality. This drives Gonzales to the conclusion that digital divide policies, at the very least in economically developed countries, should divert their focus from physical access to that of facilitating sustainable access.[194]

'Sporadic use', that is, the occasional use of e-mail and similar basic online services, has been invoked to problematize conclusions of a narrowing digital divide, conclusions which result in the use of binary data (user x non-user), as seen in Section 4.3. Studies conducted by Norwegian researchers, for example, have undertaken to reanalyse user data from five well-connected European countries (Sweden, Norway, Austria, Great Britain and Spain) from the years 2004 to 2006, revealing that in these years, sporadic users comprised up to one-third of individuals who were otherwise categorized as 'users' in statistical reports. The authors cited the size of this group, along with that of non-users, as a testament to the 'alarming finding' of a 'large digital divide' in Europe.[195] A similar result would be obtained for these years if we were to consider those who do not fall under the 'regular users' category, as monitored by Eurostat.[196] However, more recent data on the frequency of Internet use in the EU indicates that even when defined in such terms, the gap appears to be closing nevertheless (despite notable differences based on education, age, gender and population density): while 64% of the European population was placed outside of the regular users category in 2004, this number dropped to 21% by 2016 (with a drop from 18% to 3% among users). The significance of this advancement for the digital divide thesis shall only

---

[192]Reisdorf and Groselj (2017).

[193]Gonzales (2014, 2016); Gonzales et al. (2016).

[194]Gonzales (2016).

[195]Brandtzæg, Heim, and Karahasanović (2011, p. 123); similarly, earlier by Selwyn (2006).

[196]Regular use is defined by Eurostat as using the Internet at least once a week, the remaining segment of the population falls into the category of 'not regular user' (DeMunter, 2006). The more recent data are courtesy of Eurostat (2017).

be assessed once the latest findings on the relationship between the intensity of use (hours per day/week), duration of use (years) and outcomes of use have been presented.

In terms of bridging the digital divide, dropouts, net evaders and the truly unconnected are far more critical groups to consider: they each problematize these efforts, albeit for different reasons.

Net Evaders make up a significant portion of non-users living in households where Internet access is a readily available commodity – the Internet is already being used by another member of the household and their social contacts are also Internet users. Lenhart's 2003 Pew Internet & American Life Project report came to the surprising conclusion that members of this group often included individuals who were otherwise highly predisposed to Internet use: young, wealthy, from larger households, cities, men, etc. Two-thirds of this group were parents of child users, with the rest being, for example, people in higher positions who always had someone on hand to delegate their online errands to, older women who enlisted another member of the household to perform certain online tasks, and those for whom Internet non-use was an intentional lifestyle choice.[197] Generally speaking, net evaders are not cut off from the Internet, as their online needs are tended to by others. The difficulty of deciphering this group's position apropos of the digital divide thesis is underscored by van Dijk's ambiguous assessment of this population's unconnected nature, putting forth the postulation that 'it appears to be a luxury problem, if it is a problem at all', while also entertaining the notion that it 'may also be a matter of cognitive dissonance and an easy escape from embarrassment'[198]. However, certain characteristics intrinsic to this group do not pose 'any problem at all' for maintaining the validity of the digital divide thesis – which is why we shall later revisit this group which seems to defy interpretation from a digital divide perspective. One might argue that growing user-friendliness, mobile Internet and the rising pressure of an increasingly informational society will gradually relegate this group to obscurity; however, this projection is out of line with data indicating a decrease in Internet diffusion rates across economically developed countries, the persistently stable number of net evaders in the United States and EU and the paucity of British net evaders expressing their intention to use the Internet.[199] This group is thus likely to continue existing well into the future.

Dropouts (also referred to as lapsed users or ex-users) became a topic of interest in digital divide research relatively early. As is the case with intermittent users, this category problematizes the idea that the ultimate aim of bridging the digital divide should be to facilitate the conditions under which non-users decide to acquire the necessary equipment and begin using it. This group was 'discovered' when Aspden and Katz, merely for the sake of completeness, included a question in their study on the number of ex-users.[200] The resulting figures were

---

[197]Lenhart et al. (2003); Selwyn (2006).
[198]van Dijk (2005, p. 34).
[199]Eurostat (2017); van Deursen and Helsper (2015, p. 178); Zickuhr (2013, p. 7).
[200]Wyatt et al. (2002, p. 31). The quotation marks are in reference to efforts of mapping intermittent use in DOI that date back to over 30 years ago.

unexpectedly high: in 1995, the number of users and ex-users in the United States was almost equal, amounting to 8%.[201] In the years 1996–2000, the number of dropouts increased slightly, sitting comfortably at approximately one-tenth of the US population, which in the years 1998 and 2000 equalled about four million households that no longer had Internet access.[202] At any rate, this number surpassed that of Canadian, Japanese and EU populations in the same year, where the number of dropouts was reported to be 6% of the population.[203] In the EU, this number gradually decreased to 4% of the population, that is, over one-fifth of non-users (data for the year 2016). The defining characteristics of dropouts in Sweden and the UK (as examples of the most connected countries) are social isolation, unemployment, low digital skills and low educational attainment (surprisingly, not age). Data from other countries corroborate these characteristics, which also include ethnicity, small household size and low income (factors correlated with social isolation and low qualifications).[204] Ten years ago, the majority of dropouts were more likely to fall into the intermittent use category, as they expressed an intention to resume Internet use. This categorization would be well in line with their socio-demographic profile as well as findings on the different reasons for non-use when compared to that of non-users, who declare financial or physical barriers (high costs or no access) less often than dropouts, reporting instead a lack of usefulness and lack of skills more often than dropouts.[205] The growing number of dropouts who justify their non-use with the answer 'not interested', and the gradually decreasing number of dropouts considering to resume Internet use, suggests that the majority of dropouts should instead be analysed in terms of being truly unconnected.

Truly unconnected is a term typically employed to define those who have never used the Internet and who live in households without Internet access. This group includes people in the oldest age brackets, with low educational attainment, from low-income households, the socially isolated, those highly exposed to traditional communication media and those with a social circle of other non-users.[206] The share of this group's members found in the non-user group can be partially explained by the finding that, over time, non-users become increasingly associated with characteristics typical of the socially excluded, with a growing percentage of non-users stating that they do not need the Internet, do not find it useful and do not intend to start using it.[207] An issue which may potentially

---

[201]Katz and Aspden (1997).

[202]Katz and Rice (2002); NTIA (2000).

[203]Thomas (2003). The European Union data were adopted from the Eurostat (2017) findings on the number of individuals who have not used the Internet in over three months.

[204]Crothers, Smith, Urale, and Bell (2016); Dutton, Blank, and Groselj (2014); Helsper and Reisdorf (2017); Katz and Aspden (1997); Katz and Rice (2002); Lenhart et al. (2003); NTIA (2000); Selwyn (2006); Thomas (2003).

[205]The statements made in this and the following sentence are also grounded in findings from the United Kingdom and Sweden, published by Dutton et al. (2013), Helsper and Reisdorf (2013, 2017) and Selwyn (2006).

[206]Fox (2005); Horrigan (2007); Lenhart et al. (2003); Reddick et al. (2000).

[207]Eurostat (2017); Helsper and Reisdorf (2017); see also below.

problematize the group of non-users further is that the expressed decision against acquiring a personal computer in the near future seems to have much higher predictive power than the expressed decision to become a user.[208] These two groups, that is, those who claim to have no interest in ever going online and those whose primary reason for non-use is the rejection of technology as a whole, deserve special attention in terms of the viability of the digital divide thesis – once again, any indication of this group's (or segment of this group's) legitimacy or rationality could potentially destabilize or even directly undermine the entire digital divide thesis.

The method of surveying the reasons for non-use emerged in the 1990s in the form of open questions and a wide range of possible answers.[209] Later efforts to synthesize this format by employing factor analysis and eliminating gross overlaps led to the use of a reduced list of reasons, summarized as follows:[210]

- lack of financial resources ('access costs are too high', 'do not have computer', 'too expensive' ...);
- lack of skills ('do not know how to use', 'too difficult to use' ...);
- lack of time;
- uneasy about use (privacy, security, pornography ...);
- no need or interest ('not interested', 'not useful' ...).

Insufficient financial resources are the most significant reason for non-use in scenarios where household income is low and where computer or Internet prices are high. This extends to economically developed countries, as a significant number of non-users list the above as reasons for non-use (approximately one-fourth of unconnected households in the EU in 2017), though this response has been on the decline over time. However, when observing other media expenses across households (mobile phone, cable television, satellite, etc.), the more likely rationale for non-use for a substantial percentage of these individuals is the low perceived added value of Internet use;[211] another notable factor is insufficient skills (four out of 10 unconnected EU households in 2017). Apprehension towards the use of technology is a less frequently selected response, with less than one-tenth of non-users citing this as their reason for non-use. Conversely, the most frequently cited reason for Internet non-use, one which increases together with the rise of Internet penetration, is 'I don't need it" or "not interested' – responses which are, as has already been suggested, the most problematic in terms of the digital divide thesis.[212]

---

[208]Venkatesh and Brown (2001).

[209]Katz and Aspden (1997); Lenhart et al. (2003); van Dijk (2005, p. 29).

[210]Based on Reddick et al. (2000), Lenhart et al. (2003), van Dijk (2005) and answer possibilities offered by Eurostat and the World Internet Project.

[211]Katz and Rice (2002); Selwyn (2006).

[212]Data on the prevalence and dynamics of reasons specified in this paragraph have been adopted primarily from Eurostat (2017) and the Center for the Digital Future at USC Annenberg (2010, 2012, 2016).

Given that respondents who answer 'I don't need it' perceive the usefulness and safety of the Internet to be much worse than users,[213] van Dijk accounts for their sweeping rejection of technology with three potential reasons:[214] the first is the lack of knowledge among non-users regarding the benefits of the technology and the disadvantages stemming from non-use; the second is a possible combination of 'cognitive dissonance, "sour grapes" reasoning, and plain ignorance of the Internet'[215]; the third and final reason is the failure of designers and creators of applications and online content to meet the needs of this population segment – a group of people who, as a result, do not see the Internet as a tool designed to meet their everyday needs. Their decision not to use the Internet therefore appears to be a rational act.

The rationality argument for Internet non-use is, however, either directly at odds with the model of the key argument, or needs to be explained in such a way that prevents this segment of non-users from being portrayed as an irrational, backwards group, ignorant to the benefits of Internet use. Van Dijk's primary objective here is not to combat the current state of the digital divide, but rather its very likely contribution to structural inequality; he thus champions the necessity of implementing a series of targeted interventions, which would – as clearly implied in his work – boost the appeal, usefulness and simplicity of Internet use in order to motivate this group to connect, preventing the rational behaviour of today from becoming a source of social exclusion tomorrow.

Such a solution can typically be seen in the form of proposed measures for overcoming the motivation factor of the digital divide – measures specifically tailored to the needs and values of the target (primarily lower-status) subpopulations: reducing socio-economic inequality, improving trust in the Internet, promoting its usefulness and status-specific benefits, striving for a more user-friendly design, developing applications and online services (for lower social strata) and supporting public access points and sustainability.[216]

4.5.4 Digital Skills

The computer literacy debate flared up at the turn of the 1970s and 1980s in response to the often unsuccessful efforts to computerize bureaucratic institutions, schools and businesses, and was also tangential to debates about media literacy and information literacy. By the time this topic gained traction in digital divide research, a wealth of concepts had already long been the subject of debate across a wide range of disciplines – pedagogy, sociology, communication studies and library and information science. The usage of various, often overlapping, terms such as digital literacy, informacy, ICT literacy, e-competence and

---

[213]Lenhart et al. (2003).
[214]van Dijk (2005). Similarly, also, e.g., Reddick et al. (2000); Reisdorf (2011); Selwyn (2003); Warschauer (2003).
[215]van Dijk (2005, p. 35). Similarly, e.g., Reisdorf (2011, p. 418).
[216]van Dijk (2005); Gonzales (2016); Reisdorf and Groselj (2017).

computer skills,[217] have remained characteristic of debates spanning various scientific disciplines and the domain of public policy.

One question that arises is whether or not we could simply employ an older concept of literacy, thereby questioning the necessity of creating a new concept targeted specifically at ICT use – has one ever heard of, for example, radio, television or telephone literacy? The answer is two-fold: first, despite the great advances made by designers and programmers, the technologies at play here are complex in that, unlike traditional media, using them efficiently and with ease requires a sufficient skillset and non-intuitive techniques which extend far beyond those of reading, writing and navigating static content with either slow or no feedback (i.e., in letters, paintings, telegraph, newspaper or radio).[218] Second, the core argument of the digital divide presupposes that intrinsic to ICT access, and thus also to digital skills, are certain special features absent in 'traditional' communication media – features which intertwine ICT use with the ability to move along the social ladder and which cannot be limited to the specific technical features of ICT (if that were the case, the benefits of ICT would be guaranteed at the level of material access).

The term digital skills is employed here not only because it appears in the four-tiered access model, but due to its scope and significance in digital divide research.[219] Van Dijk, later in cooperation with van Deursen, gradually came to differentiate two basic types of digital skills which were then further divided into subtypes.[220] The latest digital skills typology designed by these authors can be used as a 'grid', suitable for creating a compilation (similar to the types of access chart above) of typologies aimed at measuring ICT skills.

The basic set of skills required for working with online content are called *medium-related skills*. These include *operational skills*, that is, the ability to navigate hardware and software interfaces (e.g., using a mouse, finding and using the scrollbar, opening and saving different file types, etc.) as well as *formal skills*, which are a set of technical skills allowing the user to effectively, and without becoming disoriented, navigate the non-linear, fragmented and ever-changing architecture of the Internet, that is, hypertext, web browser, multimedia websites, search engines etc.

The second basic type of skills is *content-related skills*, consisting of two primary components – *information skills* and *strategic skills*. Information skills

---

[217]For an overview and brief description of the relevant concepts of ICT 'dexterity' see, e.g., Ala-Mutka (2011); Bunz (2004); van Dijk and van Deursen (2014); Warschauer (2003).

[218]For more on this argument see van Dijk and van Deursen (2014).

[219]See Scheerder, van Deursen, and van Dijk (2017).

[220]During this time, he also narrowed his focus on Internet skills to represent a specific type of digital skills. As older studies and other authors often include the technical aspect of computer or mobile phone use in the term 'skills', we shall, unless otherwise indicated, use a broader scope of the term to include ICT and digital media as such (i.e., devices connected to the Internet allowing its broader use for communication and information-related tasks). The different types of skills as outlined in the following two paragraphs are based on van Deursen and van Dijk (2009, 2010), van Dijk (2005), van Dijk and van Deursen (2014).

refer to the ability to find, sort, modify, combine, generalize, connect and critically assess information looked up for a specific purpose and from various sources. Like other authors, van Dijk originally employed the term information skills to cover the ability to work with information (which he transiently dubbed substantive information skills), as well as with the formal structure containing the online data. Later, however, van Dijk moved the formal component of information skills over to medium-related skills. Van Dijk's conception of (substantive) information skills is thus the closest approximation to the general concept of information literacy (used primarily in library and information science and in pedagogy), in which ICT is merely one of the possible interfaces for working with information.[221]

The two basic types of skills and subtypes are, akin to the levels of access, successive in that a user must first acquire the basic minimum level of operational skills and formal skills in order to work with information online. The skills-based level of access then culminates in *strategic skills* – a key mediating agent between other types of digital skills and social mobility. Strategic skills can be generally understood as the ability to use a wide range of available resources (knowledge, money, influence, social networks, rules and laws, traditions, technologies, etc.) 'as the means to achieving specific goals and for the general goal of improving one's position in society (in the labour market, in education, in households, and in social relationships)'[222]. Digital strategic skills are the most demanding and complex of digital skills, requiring analytical, critical and decisive thinking. The direct correlation between digital strategic skills and social mobility is symptomatic of the competitive advantage of employing strategic ICT use; this is in contrast to users with underdeveloped, lower-order skills and 'non-digital' strategies, who use less flexible and more resource-intensive means of communication, information processing and mobilization of resources. Van Dijk and van Deursen define the use of strategic skills as a four-step process: (a) navigating a rapidly changing environment, selecting an appropriate goal and maintaining focus on that goal in a highly distracting digital environment; (b) selecting and using available information sources effectively in order to achieve this goal; (c) decision-making using mobilized information sources; and finally, (d) converting the outcomes of this decision-making process into benefits of a personal, professional or financial nature.[223]

In recent years, this list has been expanded to include new digital skills such as communication skills, content creation skills and mobile skills.[224] The advantage of such an elaborated typology is a clearer correlation when modelling the relationship between skills and different types of online activities. The disadvantage of this typology, however, is its strain on the theoretical validity of the core

---

[221]See, e.g., Bawden (2008).
[222]van Dijk (2005, p. 74).
[223]van Deursen and van Dijk (2009); van Dijk and van Deursen (2014).
[224]Helsper and Eynon (2013); Van Deursen, Helsper, and Eynon (2014); van Dijk and van Deursen (2014).

argument and its theoretical footing. For example, the role of *content creation skills*, compared to information and strategic skills, as a precondition for maintaining or improving participation in society is highly debatable, thereby calling into question its standing within the core argument. These new types of skills also prove problematic in their categorization as digital skills, that is, to what extent their level and distribution in the population is merely a reflection of general (e.g., social or communication) skills independent of ICT use. This problem pertains to all content-related skills and is quite significant – if these skills were in large part not exclusive to ICT use, this digital skills divide would then be a reflection of another type of inequality, and bridging this divide would thus require substantial change on a broader social scale.[225] This would also corroborate the lacking impact of the duration and intensity of Internet use on the user's level of content-related skills (see below).

The issue of theoretical validity is least problematic where *communication skills* are concerned, as these skills demonstrate a high correlation with beneficial outcomes of Internet use.[226] The high potential that communication skills offer for future research on digital skills stems from the increasingly Internet-mediated nature of social communication, with expanding platforms for online communication and self-presentation. Van Dijk and van Deursen define *communication skills* as 'the ability to encode and decode messages to construct, understand, and exchange meaning in all interactive applications'[227] with other users and non-human artefacts (e.g., websites, search engines, AI assistants). The existing conceptualization must, however, reconcile with the highly normative and instrumental understanding of interpersonal communication and self-presentation in an online setting. Concerted efforts to 'attract attention online', aggressive online networking, the use of social networking sites and online gaming are not generally desirable activities (i.e., they are not based on generally accepted values) that would condition success in today's society, with failure to comply having an adverse impact on participation in society.[228]

ICT skills are measured using three basic methods:

The most accurate, but also most demanding of methods, and thus scarcely used in research,[229] is the direct observation of users as they perform a set of complex tasks in controlled environments. The fundamental problems with direct observation are the constraints of time, money and space. This is reflected in smaller sample sizes and a limited selection of standardized tasks. The risk that this measurement method thus poses is the generalizability of results, requiring

---

[225]Cf., e.g., van Deursen, Helsper, Eynon, and van Dijk (2017); van Dijk and van Deursen (2014).

[226]See Helsper, van Deursen, and Eynon (2015); van Deursen, Courtois, and van Dijk (2014). See also below.

[227]van Dijk and van Deursen (2014, p. 30).

[228]Compare with the composition of communication skills in van Dijk and van Deursen (2014, pp. 30–37).

[229]For example, Eshet-Alkalai and Amichai-Hamburger (2004); Hargittai and Shafer (2006); van Deursen, van Dijk, and Peters (2011).

an adequately justified selection from a wide range of possible computer functions, tasks and solutions.

The second measurement method, which also poses similar problems, consists of indirectly surveying users about their expertise/abilities. There are effectively three methods for measuring digital skills in this manner. A method scarcely employed in academic research involves verifying the user's skill level by testing the respondent's knowledge of terminology, possible solutions for given situations, synonyms, etc.[230] The second approach is to infer the user's skill level from (a number of) performed online activities. This method, employed, for example, by Eurostat, is, however, problematic in that it confuses skills for activities. While the two are very closely correlated, recent findings indicate that online activities cannot be used as indicators of skill level.[231] Simply put, the (frequent) use of a tool does not automatically equate to efficient use.

The third method is based on the respondent's self-assessment in a selected set of skills. Efforts of finding an optimal set of digital skill indicators must factor in the rapidly evolving world of ICT and the obsolescence of certain skills as a result (e.g., knowledge of DOS commands), as well as the greatly varied individual strategies for achieving certain goals in the complex environments of an operating system, the Internet and software tools:[232] for example, one can obtain information regarding government subsidies or pre-school for their child directly through the institution's website, by e-mailing the said institution, via Internet telephony, online forums, friends of friends on Facebook, etc. A CV can be formatted in a text editor 'manually' one parameter at a time, it can also be edited using presets, specialized websites or with a macro. Although it is rather simple to ascertain the difficulty level of each of these approaches, what remains problematic is the unspoken assumption that presupposes a correlation between the difficulty of the task (e.g., the use of macros as an indicator of advanced skills) and the effective use of the technology as a gateway towards improving one's quality of life or position in society.

The issue of selecting an adequate set of items using the simplest self-assessment measurement method ('In terms of your Internet skills, do you consider yourself to be…'[233]) becomes problematized when confronted with the respondents' idiosyncratic forms of self-expression and varying perceptions of difficulty. This is reflected primarily in the tendency to overestimate in young respondents and men and in the inverse tendency to underestimate in women and older respondents.[234] Although this bias is also present when inquiring about specific skills, the creation of a composite index using a number of suitable items predicts a realistic picture of expertise and efficiency far more reliably than a summative

---

[230]For example, Brandtweiner, Donat, and Kerschbaum (2010); Hatlevik, Guðmundsdóttir, and Loi (2015).
[231]For example, van Dijk and van Deursen (2014).
[232]Hargittai (2009); van Dijk (2005).
[233]Hargittai (2005, p. 377).
[234]Hargittai and Schafer (2006); van Deursen and van Dijk (2010).

self-assessment[235] – yet another reason why summative self-assessments are used so rarely.

There are two general research questions that have received the most attention when examining skills access: what are the differences in digital skills among the adult population and how are these skills acquired? While the first question is directed at the current state, development and determinants of the digital skills divide, the second strives to ascertain the relationship between skill level and the adoption of digital skills, that is, determining the most effective method of skill adoption. The most attention (for both research questions) has been paid to operational and formal skills, with minimal attention being paid to strategic skills. This can be attributed to the predominant measurement method used in indirect observation which tends to avoid skills that are more difficult to measure. Another contributing factor is the widespread notion that adequate Internet or computer use can be measured by observing only the technical and formal aspects of use, such as using the interface (mouse, keyboard), text editor, inbox, etc. Only recently has there been an upswing of studies examining the correlation between digital skills, other stages of access and outcomes of Internet use.[236]

The distribution of medium-related skills in economically developed countries reveals, with the exception of gender, similar features as the distribution of material access, with an overwhelming majority of users exhibiting a very low to medium skill level. From the baseline socio-demographic factors examined, age, followed by educational attainment and gender, had the highest impact on the distribution of operational skills (in reality, these differences will be less profound due to the effect of self-assessment for age and gender).[237] The duration (expressed in years) and intensity of use[238] also played a significant role, which can be accounted for due to the time-intensive nature of adopting medium-related skills, the age and educational composition of experienced and intensive users,[239] as well as the dynamics of user self-efficacy,[240] which increases as the innovation is integrated into everyday life. In terms of the user's skill level, income plays a substantially smaller role than in the case of the material and motivational stages of access, explicable due to the higher importance of cognitive and social resources when acquiring digital skills.[241]

A substantially lower level of medium-related skills – with the exception of gender – can be observed in the segment of the population that has already been

---

[235]Hargittai (2005).

[236]See the section on strategic skills below.

[237]DeMunter (2006); van Deursen et al. (2017, 2011); van Dijk (2005, 2009).

[238]Hargittai and Hinnant (2008); van Deursen et al. (2011).

[239]For van Deursen et al. (2011); the correlation between intensity and medium-related skills disappeared after controlling for socio-demographics, the impact of duration of Internet use decreased.

[240]The term self-efficacy refers to the personal assessment of one's own ability in a given area and appears in psychology-informed parts of digital divide research. Self-efficacy indicators are sometimes used as a proxy for skills as there is a correlation between self-efficacy and ability to perform a given task successfully.

[241]van Dijk and Hacker (2003); Helsper and Eynon (2013).

identified as having lower levels of motivational and material access in connection to economic instability, lower odds (or frequency) of use, poor-quality devices, etc. The applicability of this data as an *absolute* barometer of digital literacy is, however, problematic, and not only due to the rapid technological advances being made in the field of IT: The more difficult of a 'skill test' we employ, the fewer respondents will rank at the highest skill level. According to van Dijk, implementing a test with a broader range of operational skills would result in the 'IT elite' occupying the highest categories. Surprisingly, testing for relatively trivial operational skills lands the vast majority of users in the lower-skilled categories. However, if we do not retain a certain set of elementary digital skills for measurement and comparison purposes, aimed at a specific set of stable features of digital technology interfaces (as ludicrous as this may sound in the long run), we risk turning the amelioration of the digital skills divide into a perpetual struggle of vying for widespread expertise in ICT skills in the face of constantly evolving technology.

Studies that employ a broader understanding of information skills (i.e., those including the formal component) all reveal substantial differences in terms of how successfully and efficiently users can handle information, the most difficulty being exhibited by groups with lower educational attainment. The impact of age, intensity and duration of Internet use remains unclear (contrary to technical skills, gender has no impact with regard to information skills).[242] Studies on the efficient use of search engines hold a special place in research on information skills, placing an emphasis on ineffective word combinations, the failure to browse more pages of search results or to use Boolean operators – including in the seemingly proficient segments of the population (e.g., college students).[243] The impact of the afore-mentioned ambiguous variables on the distribution of information skills can perhaps be ascertained in studies based on performance tests, which make a clear distinction between information skills and formal skills.[244] These studies yield two main findings. First, educational attainment is the only one of the listed variables where higher values are demonstrably correlated with higher information skills. The direct impact of the duration and intensity of Internet use on the level of information skills has not been observed and the impact of age appears inverse when compared to medium-related skills: the older the user, the higher the success rate when completing tasks that explicitly require the use of information skills. Second, information skills are closely interlinked with the level of medium-related skills, thereby indirectly re-contextualizing the variables which impact these medium-related skills when examining information skills (similarly as seen below in strategic skills). The sophisticated methodology employed by these studies prevents these variables from being rejected in light of the exceptional nature of the findings: on the contrary,

---

[242]Hargittai (2002); Hargittai and Schafer (2006); Mossberger, Tolbert, and Stansbury (2003); van Dijk (2005, pp. 87–88).

[243]For example, Hargittai (2002); van Deursen and Van Diepen (2013); van Deursen and van Dijk (2009). For more details see van Dijk and van Deursen (2014).

[244]Eshet-Alkalai and Amichai-Hamburger (2004); Eshet-Alkalai and Chajut (2009); van Deursen and van Diepen (2013); van Deursen and van Dijk (2009, 2010); van Deursen et al. (2011).

their contribution lies in differentiating the measurement of information skills from skills in using search engines and processing and transmitting information.[245]

Van Dijk, as a salient voice of authority in the field, spoke of the paucity of research on digital skills in 2009, purporting that the only existing data 'are about the command of operational skills'[246]. This, however, was not as alarming for the digital divide thesis as his later assertion in 2014 that 'there is no research that explicitly addresses these [strategic – noted by PL] skills on an individual level'[247]. Van Dijk's 2005 book thus included a mere three pages on the concept of strategic skills crucial for the entire digital divide model, containing primarily general, factually unsupported data championing the strategic use of ICT in the network/information society.[248] The empirical evidence and attention paid to the different types of digital skills have long been grossly inconsistent with the significant role that ICT skills play in the core argument. These are generally alarming findings given the government policies on the expansion and use of digital media, which have underpinned the digital divide thesis for the last quarter of a century. While having a technical command of ICT is indeed a crucial asset, all data and international comparisons on operational skills become moot points for the digital divide issue if we cannot determine whether (and how) certain segments of the population utilize these technologies in order to gain 'a considerable advantage in social competition and educational or job careers'[249].

The number of studies mapping the strategic use of digital media and digital divide research can be counted on one hand. Empirically grounded argumentation on the impact of ICT use on one's quality of life or participation in society has been based merely on macroeconomic indicators measured against the level of ICT penetration, debates on the outcomes of Internet use in selected domains of social life (sociability, economic life, political participation, etc.) and on the subjective assessment of changes in efficiency stemming from Internet use in the workplace and other spheres of social life (e.g., establishing and maintaining social relationships, consumer behaviour, etc.). However, these findings alone are not sufficient in validating the digital divide thesis, which shall be demonstrated later in Chapter 5.

Data on the level and distribution of strategic skills can be obtained primarily from a set of performance tests courtesy of van Dijk and van Deursen[250] and from later surveys[251], aimed at mapping and explaining (tangible) outcomes of Internet use, which can serve as a testament to the application of strategic skills.

---

[245]However, the clear demarcation between formal and informal skills is still up for debate; van Deursen, Helsper and Eynon (2014) recently employed a factor analysis of indirect survey data, ultimately calling into question the very existence of formal skills.

[246]van Dijk (2009, p. 295).

[247]van Dijk and van Deursen (2014, p. 83). Earlier seen in DiMaggio, Hargittai, Celeste, and Shafer (2004) and Helsper (2008, 2012).

[248]See van Dijk (2005).

[249]van Dijk (2005, p. 88).

[250]For a more detailed presentation and summary of the applied methodology and results, see van Dijk and van Deursen (2014). For specific articles, see, e.g., van Deursen and van Dijk (2009, 2010, 2011); van Deursen and van Diepen (2013); van Deursen et al. (2011).

[251]Courtois and Verdegem (2016); Helsper et al. (2015).

However, these figures cannot be taken at face value, as they were all gleaned using similar methodologies from one of the world's most highly connected populations (approx. 95% of the population of the Netherlands uses the Internet).

Between the years 2007 and 2011, van Dijk and van Deursen implemented three waves of carefully designed performance tests, studying the strategic use of the Internet for making decisions of a political nature, obtaining government support for underpaid work, solving health issues and shopping and travelling.[252] One of the most important findings in terms of strategic skills was the very low success rate in executing the assigned tasks: in the first wave, one-half of respondents had no idea how to start the assignment, and another 20% were 'misled' during the execution of their assignment without even noticing; one-fourth of respondents used unverified and easily obtained information from unreliable websites and did not know how to efficiently apply this information to reach a satisfactory conclusion; two-thirds of participants made their decisions based on incomplete information and one-half of participants made erroneous decisions based on the (incomplete) information obtained. The successful completion of both assignments was recorded in approximately one-third of users in each of the three waves, with substantial differences in the quality of information obtained as well as the ability to work in a structured manner – for example, over two-thirds of participants did not obtain information step by step but rather by randomly browsing websites in an unstructured fashion.[253] A path-analysis was conducted on the data from all three waves, revealing a strong direct impact only for educational attainment and medium-related skills, along with a relatively striking positive correlation with age (as similarly observed in the case of information skills). After controlling for other variables, the direct impact of the duration and intensity of use disappeared entirely.[254] If this finding were to hold up, then claims of the digital divide being deepened by gaps in frequency of use would have no solid ground (cf. p. 100–101).

A follow-up online survey aimed at exploring the link between skills, uses and outcomes garnered two noteworthy findings in relation to the core argument.[255] First, it stressed the importance of distinguishing different domains of outcomes, as users who profited from Internet use in one domain (e.g., economy), did not necessarily profit in others (e.g., culture). Predictors were also domain-specific in that intra-domain uses and outcomes were generally correlated. However, certain types of online activities (primarily social and personal uses) also contributed to outcomes across several domains. The authors put forth the general assertion that 'characteristics traditionally associated with first- and second-level divides... stand at the beginning of the sequential digital deprivation process'[256]. However,

---

[252]van Deursen et al. (2011).

[253]van Deursen and van Dijk (2009).

[254]Similarly Courtois and Verdegem (2016).

[255]Based on Helsper et al. (2015); van Deursen and Helsper (2017); van Deursen et al. (2017).

[256]van Deursen et al. (2017, p. 469). General claims about predictors for different domains still need to be verified through additional studies and corroborated with domain-specific research on the outcomes of Internet use.

the problem with such a multidimensional core argument lies in the existence of individuals who would at once benefit from Internet use in one domain while being disadvantaged in another. The gravity of the digital divide would thus become domain-specific (i.e., highly contingent upon a certain context or situation), and poor-quality access would not necessarily indicate general social disadvantage. This entire issue is further problematized by the second finding: the necessity of differentiating achievements from satisfaction, which would indicate the need to distinguish between the impact of Internet use on participation in society (hinging more closely on the topic of social status and social inclusion) and the impact of Internet use on the quality of life (which is more of a psychology issue). In this regard, it is difficult to ignore that digital divide research has typically assumed that Internet use is beneficial, overlooking the proliferating mass of literature calling attention to the negative consequences of Internet use.[257]

If data on the different types of digital skills are scarce and limited to the select few most connected countries, then our understanding of the development of digital skills over time boils down to a single longitudinal study monitoring changes in digital skills across (Dutch) users from the years 2010–2013.[258] According to this study, there was an increase in all skill types, with the exception of information skills, which exhibit persisting gaps across education groups. In terms of medium-related skills, we can expect these gaps to narrow in the long term due to the presumed positive impact of duration and intensity of use on a user's command of ICT (which is also substantiated by Eurostat data). The future development of content-related skills remains unclear; van Dijk projects that differences across these types of skills, given their determinants, shall remain a long-term, structural matter.[259]

The significant differences found at the levels of motivational and material access are more or less reiterated here in the case of digital skills. This results in a cumulative effect – for example, elderly individuals, already disadvantaged due to lower odds of physical access to the Internet, present a significantly higher incidence of low motivation and low skills. The small fraction of the population presenting a combination of high skills, motivation, equipment, etc., is then put to the test when confronted with constantly evolving ICT innovations. These significant differences, which, by a similar logic, seep into ICT access on a user level (as we shall examine below), are considered by van Dijk to be a testament of the 'deepening divide'. This divide serves as the crux of van Dijk's argument, calling for intervention measures to thwart the trend of growing gaps in ICT access. The deepening divide thesis can be summarized in several points (see Fig. 4.15).

The combination of observed differences in skills across the various levels of access lends support to the argument that gaps – primarily among education and age groups – resulting from different uses of new media, are far more pronounced

---

[257]Cf. Scheerder et al. (2017) and the above-mentioned studies focusing on outcomes of Internet use.

[258]van Deursen, van Dijk, and ten Klooster (2015).

[259]van Deursen et al. (2015); van Dijk (2005, pp. 125–126, 2009, p. 297).

(1) Physical access to ICT (i.e., ownership or use) alone does not guarantee effective participation in the information society.

(2) Access to ICT is subject to the completion of several successive levels of access.

(3) There are currently significant access gaps at every one of these levels.

(4) Access gaps at these levels are characterized by considerable homology.

(5) Access gaps at these levels are of a cumulative nature.

(6) Cumulative gaps in ICT access have the tendency to widen.

(7) The validity of points 3–6 is constantly being reasserted through the implementation of new ICT innovations.

Fig. 4.15:   The Deepening Divide Thesis. *Source:* Author, based on van Dijk (2005).

than in the case of traditional media. It is thus crucial that more attention is paid to this issue both with respect to research as well as the implementation of adequate education programmes.[260]

The problem of digital skills gaps has become increasingly reflected in information policies through programmes aimed at bridging this aspect of the digital divide. The European Commission, for example, designated the promotion of digital literacy as one of its eight initiatives as a part of the Digital Agenda for Europe 2020 strategy, thereby ensuring the European population's command of ICT and motivating future generations to study computer science and related subjects.[261]

One issue which must be addressed by these intervention policies is the establishment of effective strategies for ameliorating the digital divide by refining the above-mentioned findings and comparing the efficiency of various skill acquisition resources.

Potential learning sources and methods can be divided into three categories: individual learning (trial and error), learning in informal communities and settings (friends, family members, peer groups, etc.) and formal learning (manuals, user guides, schooling and courses). Authors focusing on the adoption of digital skills, using this categorization, draw attention to ineffective measures striving to bridge gaps in digital skills through types of formal learning which largely neglect motivation, an individual approach and learning in informal settings.[262] Their critique is bolstered by findings obtained through reanalysing the measured (predominantly operational) skills with respect to the above-stated learning sources, revealing that

[260]van Deursen et al. (2011); van Dijk and van Deursen (2014).
[261]European Commission (2010).
[262]van Dijk (2005); Warschauer (2003).

groups of users with the highest measured skills and widest portfolio of online activities obtained these skills through a wider range of learning sources, primarily hands-on practice, trial and error and through the support of formal and informal social ties (i.e., utilizing cognitive and social sources).[263] This is further corroborated by the finding that the ability to utilize social ties (measured as social support availability and use, social skills or communication skills) is one of the most important mediators between social inequality and the benefits of Internet use – bearing the potential of supplanting insufficient digital skills, for example, in the case of information skills.[264] Groups of users with lower skills and lower declared benefits from Internet use exhibit a higher dependence on informal social ties (friends and family), thereby circumventing the issue of insufficient skills. The benefits of these social ties are, however, lower than for users with higher social status due to social homophily (i.e., comparable skill levels across the entire social group).[265]

In order to bridge the digital skills divide, van Dijk and van Deursen thus recommend implementing a locally tailored mix of the following measures: encouraging ICT designers and investors to increase their focus on groups with low medium-related skills; the implementation of search engine algorithms that prioritize the quality and validity of search results; establishing support systems targeted at the strategic use of ICT, extending educational curriculums to cover information and strategic skills and incorporating these skills across all subjects taught; extending curriculums of ICT courses to include content-related skills for various types of new media; greater emphasis on creating higher-quality educational software; motivational support for teachers to adopt better digital skills as educators; providing more digital literacy learning opportunities for older age groups; modifying the content of educational courses to meet the specific needs of different, primarily digitally excluded, groups; and finally, creating courses which combine the options of e-learning, home learning and learning in attractive local environments.[266]

Before we bring this section to a close, allow us to briefly examine a concept which is closely related to the distribution of digital skills and which problematizes how the current state and development of digital skills is perceived by the general as well as a sizeable portion of the scholarly public.

4.5.5 Intermezzo: The Myth of the Digital Generation

The Internet boom of the late 1990s sparked a debate in the United States over whether the growing ubiquity of digital technology is also 'digitizing' children and their thought processes. This debate has continued to thrive in the media

---

[263]See Brandtweiner et al. (2010); Kraut et al. (2002); Lei et al. (2008); Selwyn (2004); van Dijk and Hacker (2003); van Dijk and van Deursen (2014).

[264]Courtois and Verdegem (2016); van Deursen, Courtois et al. (2014); van Deursen et al. (2017).

[265]Courtois and Verdegem (2016); Eynon and Geniets (2016); Fieseler, Meckel, and Müller (2014); Helsper and Deursen (2017).

[266]For details, see van Dijk (2005); van Dijk and van Deursen (2014).

as well as the humanities and social sciences. The perceived ease with which the youngest generation uses ICT is often regarded as a fact in today's world, and is based on two arguments. First, many of us have first-hand experience in witnessing children use a mouse and keyboard with almost alarming ease. The second argument is founded in age-based statistics on ICT use, revealing that in contrast to preceding generations, nearly all adolescents use the Internet and mobile phones. American author Don Tapscott rooted his 1998 book *Growing up digital: The rise of the net generation* in these very two arguments, catalysing the entire debate on the issue. The book became a bestseller: it landed a spot on the leading e-commerce website amazon.com as the highest selling book in the non-fiction category and has been translated into 20 languages. Tapscott's labels 'N-Gen' and 'digital generation' were soon accompanied by other terms, such as digital natives, homo-zappiens, I-Kids, digitally born, generation I, generation Z, M, C, V, … .[267]

Tapscott gained acclaim for being one of the first to elaborate the notion that traditional power relations within the family are being disrupted by children teaching their parents how to navigate the digital sphere and not vice versa (in contrast to the television, automobile, etc.):

> For the first time in history, children are more comfortable, knowledgeable, and literate than their parents about an innovation central to society. And it is through the use of the digital media that the N-Generation will develop and superimpose its culture on the rest of society…Already these kids are learning, playing, communicating, working, and creating communities very differently than their parents. They are a force for social transformation.[268]

According to Tapscott, it is the responsibility of parents, teachers, advertisers, journalists and politicians to alter their approach to this emergent generation in order to maintain relevance in these new conditions and to gain their attention and purchasing power (the generation intended by Tapscot here includes those born between 1977 and 1997).

Tapscott's ideas were elaborated upon in 2001 by 'internationally-acclaimed speaker, author, and "practical visionary" in the field of education,'[269] Marc Prensky, in his differentiation between the generation he dubs 'digital natives' and 'digital immigrants'. The key defining criterion here is age, in relation to the user's relationship to ICT and coupled with a new way of thinking and relating to the world: according to Prensky, computer games, Internet, e-mail and IM are no less natural to today's youth than trees, the sun or roads. As a result, digital natives 'are used to receiving information really fast. They like to parallel process and multi-task'[270]. When Prensky and his successors speak

---

[267]For an overview of these concepts see Selwyn (2009).
[268]Tapscott (1998, pp. 1–2).
[269]Prensky (2017).
[270]Prensky (2001, p. 2).

of the digital generation's (regardless of the label they use) use of ICT, they make use of adjectives such as 'immersed', 'surrounded', 'plugged into' and 'bathed in bits'. In his estimation, the youth of today do not differ so greatly in terms of new values or ways of life, but rather in that they 'think and process information fundamentally differently from their predecessors'[271]. Digital immigrants, in contrast

> typically have very little appreciation for these new skills that the Natives have acquired and perfected through years of interaction and practice. These skills are almost totally foreign to the Immigrants, who themselves learned…slowly, step-by-step, one thing at a time, individually, and above all, seriously.[272]

Authors associated with the concept of the digital generation are thus among the leading proponents of abandoning 'outdated' traditional, individualized and demotivating teaching methods.[273] These should instead be supplanted by digitalized classrooms, interconnecting playing and learning, and making the learning process an interactive one. The digital generation thesis can be summarized thus: young generations are socialized while being engulfed in digital technology, thereby organically adopting high-level ICT skills which are then reflected in their different thought, learning and information-related processes. It is then of no surprise that the focus of subsequent academic debates has been in the field of pedagogy and in overlapping matters in closely related disciplines.

Prensky and Talcott's ideas have become very influential and many researchers and commentators draw on their work uncritically.[274] Efforts to lend empirical validity to these ideas have relegated their work to popular myth status, among which the strongest arguments are:

- Multitasking is generally associated with lower efficiency of the activities being performed and even with lower study performance in situations which lead to cognitive overload. Psychologists and neurologists who study the ability to perform several activities in parallel have discovered that this ability, coupled with the ability to remain focused despite the presence of simultaneous distractions, is not fully developed in children, peaking at around the age of 20 years and then gradually declining. Moreover, the self-assessment of young people as having excellent multitasking abilities is out of line with reality once these abilities are actually put to the test.[275]

---

[271]Prensky (2001, p. 1).
[272]Prensky (2001, p. 2).
[273]See a summary of thus oriented approaches in Bennett, Maton, and Kervin (2008).
[274]See literature overviews in Bennett et al. (2008) and Jones, Ramanau, Cross, and Healing (2010).
[275]Courage, Bakhtiar, Fitzpatrick, Kenny, and Brandeau (2015).

- In the age distribution of digital skills, there is no break which would reflect the existence of a digital generation.[276] Furthermore, it remains unclear where such a break should lie, as according to Tapscott's original definition, the digital generation includes the generation which is now over 40.
- When compared to older generations, we do not find that teenagers exhibit significantly higher information skills;[277] the relationship between the level of strategic skills and age is also not a clearly negative one, as we have seen above.
- The youngest generation exhibits a high intensity of use, but of a relatively narrow range of entertainment and communication functions (photo sharing and communication via social networking sites, instant communication, gaming, watching videos and listening to music online).[278]
- The most expectedly connected and experienced subpopulation of college students is very highly differentiated in terms of digital skill level.[279]

4.5.5 Gaps in Internet Usage

Internet use is incomplete without a certain set of online activities, which, according to the model, is where Internet access reaches its peak. While use itself is preconditioned by the preceding levels of access (certain motivating factors for ICT use and related goals, the minimum level of digital skills required, technological availability and the context in which the technology is used), it is not entirely determined by them: the dynamics and distribution of usage are unique in that they constitute their own distinct aspect of the digital divide. Consider for instance a promising individual with the sufficient motivational prerequisites, access and basic skills who entirely neglects services and products which are expected to bolster social participation (e.g., online banking or social networking sites) and instead redirects his potential, for example, towards solitary gaming.

Socio-scientific studies on Internet use present a wide array of research topics, each of which can be justifiably applied to the digital divide issue. Hypothetically speaking, and presupposing the validity of the core argument, the assertion of Internet use as a gateway towards participation in society can be interpreted in relation to any observed differences in Internet use. In order to avoid conceptual ambiguity and an extensive (albeit unnecessary) reconstruction of this entire field of research,[280] the concept of Internet usage shall thus be applied here in a more narrow sense, as observed in the model outlining the four successive types of access: that is, Internet usage as a level of access defined by authors of digital divide texts as containing several basic parameters (and their variations) from which distinctive sources of inequality arise. The three most often used parameters of Internet usage are the

---

[276]Helsper and Eynon (2010).

[277]See, e.g., Eshet-Alkalai and Chajut (2009); van Deursen et al. (2011).

[278]Findahl (2014); Selwyn (2009); see also the following section.

[279]Hargittai (2010); Jones et al. (2010).

[280]The empirical footing of claims championing the benefits of Internet use must nevertheless be examined, which is something we shall revisit in Chapter 5.

properties of the used ICT, time devoted to Internet use (intensity and duration) and the breadth, quality and frequency of the performed online activities.[281]

The particular design of the innovation does not only influence the odds of adoption itself, but also the scope and purpose of use. Certain properties can, in comparison to previous technologies, enable a wider range of use; other properties, on the other hand, may have restrictive or deterring effects, when considering the possibilities of use.[282] The technical properties of ICT which significantly impact the intensity and quality of use include the following:[283]

- interactivity (increases the appeal and use value of ICT via fast feedback and flexibility in terms of both form and content, though it also requires a higher degree of user engagement and greater cognitive faculties);
- the network factor (applies primarily to products which exhibit a network effect);
- multimediality (sound, text, databases, static images, video, etc., are integrated in a single environment);
- multifunctionality (ICT can be used as a communication tool, source of knowledge, means of production, transaction tool, source of entertainment, etc.),
- selectivity (ICT enables and often even requires the user to make a selection from a large number of options);
- complexity of use (different interfaces and functions presuppose the adoption of special skillsets);
- openness (a vast amount of information is available at a low cost; conversely, the design of certain types of ICT can restrict access due to language, paid licenses, legal regulations, organizational jurisdiction, geographic location, etc.);
- capacity for data transmission (for the majority of ICT, the cost of obtaining a large number of data is relatively low, though a high capacity may also produce information overload and disorientation).

The combination of the above-mentioned features results in highly varied hardware and software across users. There is, however, also a financial element to such variedness: due to the successful commercialization of the online environment and escalating pressure to increase performance and multifunctionality, there are significant financial costs to be borne on a usage access level in terms of updating and maintaining hardware, Internet access

---

[281]Adapted from Blank and Groselj (2014), Brandtzæg (2010), DiMaggio et al. (2004) and van Dijk (2005, 2009). The fourth, frequently observed dimension could be the creativity of use (e.g., Blank, 2013; Hargittai and Walejko, 2008; Newhagen and Bucy, 2004), which is, however, often classified under types of use.

[282]See, e.g., comparisons of Internet usage across different interfaces in Mossberger, Tolbert, and Anderson (2017) and Pearce and Rice (2013).

[283]This list is not intended to be an exhaustive one; it is rather a selection of the typical features of ICT or new media which unequivocally impact usage according to Castells (2000b), McQuail (1994), Rogers (1986) and van Dijk (2005).

and software.[284] In Section 4.4.3, we examined the persisting number of users using low-speed Internet connections as well as the impact of connection speed on Internet use. In Section 4.5.3, we then observed how the need to maintain functional equipment plays a significant role in the motivation and resulting use of ICT. What is more, given that efforts of programmers and investment strategies are targeted more heavily towards the financially well-situated and skilled segment of the population, the use value of available programmes and online environments thus varies greatly for users across different cultures and social strata. Laura Robinson, in her qualitative study nestled in a Bourdieuan interpretive framework, points out the root of how various forms of an 'information habitus' have developed and stabilized for users with varying quality Internet connections.[285] According to the results of the study, time-space constraints associated with the quality of Internet access on a material scale (speed, availability, openness, etc.) translate to the development of different user orientations and strategies, which for users with low-quality Internet connections means developing a 'taste for the necessary', resulting in a limited portfolio of adopted skills, which in turn further reinforces the skills gap among users.[286]

In terms of time spent online, we can make a distinction between duration (expressed in years) and intensity of Internet use (the amount of time spent online over a given period of time). Intensity is most often determined via indirect surveys inquiring about the frequency of Internet use or time spent online over a given period of time (usually in terms of the average or previous week). However, the first method does not allow for much detail and the second is not particularly valid – when providing estimates, respondents have the tendency to overestimate the actual amount of time they spend online,[287] while some respondents simply state their online availability – understandable, given the increasingly continuous use of always-on smartphones and tablets. The most reliable methods are thus the diary method and tracking software, installed with the respondent's permission onto their connected device. The usage of special tracking software in an academic context is ethically, methodologically and technologically problematic (this tool must, for example, reconcile with the fact that one device may be used by more people and that a single user may access the Internet from multiple locations using multiple devices) and is thus scarcely used. However, given the rapidly evolving commercial solutions for the above-mentioned problems and problems inherent in other methods, its potential will surely not go untapped. As the socio-demographic traits of subpopulations, as defined by duration of use in years, can be gleaned from the data provided in Section 4.3.1, we shall now briefly examine the observed differences in intensity.

---

[284]For a more detailed account in relation to the digital divide on a usage access level see van Dijk (2005).
[285]Similarly also Zillien and Hargittai (2009).
[286]Robinson (2009).
[287]Greenberg et al. (2005).

Studies which focus on the differences in time spent online yield relatively consistent results.[288] It is fully evident that time being spent online is constantly on the rise – just over the last ten years, this number has more than doubled all over the world, due in large part to the proliferation of mobile Internet. It can further be stipulated that time spent online significantly decreases as age increases, with the steepest year-on-year increases in time spent online in the younger age groups. Women spend verifiably less time on the Internet than their male counterparts, though this difference is not as striking as in the case of other variables. This difference can be attributed to the enduring modern iteration of the patriarchal distribution of household chores and the resulting imbalance in available leisure time.

The impact of income and educational attainment here depends on how time spent online is defined, that is, whether we focus on time spent on the Internet in leisure time or on the total time spent online, including Internet use at work. While data on the total time spent online indicate a positive relationship between education and income, studies focusing on leisure time, however, indicate an inverse relationship: the higher a user's educational attainment and income, the less time they spend online (the nature of this relationship, however, varies in the case of education, which is why I use income alone to illustrate the negative correlation). This discrepancy can be accounted for due to the identified correlation between Internet use at work and educational attainment and income. The segment of the population with the biggest differences when comparing at-home Internet use and total time are the financially active, for whom Internet use is an integral part of their work. This is associated with the significant impact of higher educational attainment when monitoring the amount of time spent online at work, as well as the notable impact of duration of use in years[289] and the respondent's working age. How then can we reconcile the indirect correlation between income and time spent online during leisure time? Studies using e-tracking data provide at least three possible explanations that are not mutually exclusive: The first explanation, rooted in the economic concept of opportunity costs, posits the higher value of leisure time among higher-income individuals in order to account for this negative relationship.[290] The second explanation is based on the assumption that individuals with higher income partially saturate their Internet-related needs at work, thereby gaining the advantage of having more time to spend on offline activities outside of working hours. However, as more detailed analyses do not

---

[288]Information in this and the following two paragraphs has been synthesized from the findings of Findahl (2014), Goldfarb and Prince (2008), Jackson et al. (2004), Lupač, Chrobáková, and Sládek (2015), Pantea and Martens (2014), the Center for the Digital Future at USC Annenberg (2014), van Deursen and van Dijk (2014), van Dijk (2005) and World Internet Project Poland (2011). Interpretations regarding observed differences in Internet use are the author's own.

[289]The significant impact of duration of Internet use in years can be partially explained due to the specific socio-demographic makeup of adopters in the first stages of Internet diffusion.

[290]Goldfarb and Prince (2008).

lend support to these explanations,[291] a third explanation presents itself, rooted in the perceived status-specific benefits of Internet use. Individuals with higher social status generally lead more culturally and socially richer lives that require a greater expenditure of time. A wider range of opportunities and, by association, busy lifestyle can then be reflected in lower levels of leisurely Internet use.[292] This would be well in line with the finding that higher-income individuals often cite time saving as an incentive for online purchasing.[293] Conversely, fewer opportunities (more characteristic of lower-income individuals) can be associated with the higher perceived added value of Internet use (e.g., as a mediator of social interactions and status-specific cultural activities) which can in turn be reflected in the higher total time spent online.[294]

The hypothesis postulating the impact of a busy lifestyle holds up even when controlling for social status and household composition. Higher values in (leisure) time spent online can be found in students, singles, smaller households, households without dependents, individuals with lower educational attainment and the unemployed, that is, in groups that frequently exhibit poor ICT skills or lower odds of Internet use. The intensity of Internet use (in leisure time or at home) is thus clearly highly contingent upon the amount of free time available. However, these findings also indicate that the idea of a linear correlation between time spent online and the user's position in the digital divide is ill conceived.

Users exhibiting highly intensive Internet use may nonetheless be carrying out only a very limited number of online activities, which either prove irrelevant or only marginally influential in terms of social mobility. In order to obtain a more illustrative picture of the usage gap, we must assess differences in the intensity of Internet use in tandem with information regarding online activities. Studies oriented in this manner almost exclusively use indirectly (i.e., using questionnaires) obtained data to ascertain the types of online activities being performed. The studied online activities can be divided into several basic categories: social interaction, searching for and verifying information, online finance management and financial transactions, education, entertainment and creation of content. Answers to questions regarding the performance of the given activities with a certain frequency or within a designated timeframe (yesterday, in the last week, etc.) can then be used to generate a 'profile' of online activities for every studied subpopulation, that is, to ascertain which activities are more or less characteristic of a given subpopulation. However, utilizing international comparisons in order to make generalizations regarding online activities seems to be grossly problematic – not only due to linguistic and cultural differences, but also due to differences in Internet architecture (e.g., the Chinese Internet experience varies greatly from the Euro-American experience in terms of interface and, by association, user

---

[291]The negative correlation remained even when controlling for Internet use at work in Pantea and Martens (2014) and when controlling for hourly wage in Chapela (2016).
[292]Chapela (2016).
[293]Punj (2012).
[294]Pantea and Martens (2014).

practices). The key to resolving this issue seems to lie not in comparing individual items, but rather in the types of activities, as well as employing methodological sensitivity when categorizing the said activities.[295] In terms of the digital divide thesis, particular significance is attributed to gaps in online activities that are seen as relevant for maintaining or increasing the user's social, financial and political capital (sometimes referred to as capital-enhancing activities).[296]

Virtually all Internet users communicate via e-mail, browse the Internet and follow the news online.[297] Studies focusing on differences in online activities agree that age negatively impacts (the frequency of) use in almost all of the observed types of online activities. The higher a user's age, the lower the breadth of Internet use (measured by the number of activities performed). The youngest age groups exhibit a broad portfolio of online activities, with the most frequently performed being entertainment and communication activities. When observing everyday use in the youngest age groups, it is the use of instant messaging applications and social networking sites which proves to be most prominent. In this respect, one of the most striking traits of the youngest generation is the higher preference of online communication over offline communication when compared with older age brackets.[298] The transition into a working adult also bears higher odds of health and finance-related use. In the male population, larger amounts of time spent online are reflected in a wider range of online activities, with the most significant differences being observed in entertainment activities, such as looking up jokes, visiting erotic websites, gambling, surfing, online gaming, watching videos and listening to music or the radio. In the female population, demonstrably higher values can be observed only in the case of health information seeking. The higher proportion of information activities in the male population can be attributed to the tendency of men to rely on themselves and use social support to a lesser extent than women when using the Internet for problem solving.[299] Unsurprisingly, the absolute magnitude of differences differs from analysis to analysis, though the relative differences between men and women, viewed in conjunction with time spent online and differences in types of online activities, are nonetheless very similar. Gaps in time spent online observed across different income groups are mostly reflected in entertainment activities such as chatting, online gaming, etc., with no perceptible decrease in the frequency of finance-related activities in

---

[295]For further detail see, e.g., Helsper and Gerber (2012); Büchi, Just, and Latzer (2016).

[296]See, e.g., DiMaggio and Hargittai (2001, p. 12), Katz and Rice (2002); Mossberger et al. (2008); van Deursen and van Dijk (2014, p. 55).

[297]The arguments presented in this paragraph regarding gaps in Internet use are based on Blank and Groselj (2014), Büchi et al. (2016), Fallows (2005), Goldfarb and Prince (2008), Haight et al. (2014), Helsper and Gerber (2012), Howard, Rainie, and Jones (2002), Ono and Zavodny (2003), Pantea and Martens (2014), Purcell (2011), the Center for the Digital Future at USC Annenberg (2010, 2012), van Deursen et al. (2017, 2015), van Deursen and van Dijk (2014) and van Dijk (2005).

[298]Lupač et al. (2015).

[299]Courtois and Verdegem (2016); van Deursen, Courtois et al. (2014).

higher-income individuals (further evidence that time, if considered in isolation, is likely an irrelevant indicator in terms of the social benefits of Internet use).

At the level of usage access, the main differences used to support the core argument are those found when observing the correlation between the user's online activity profile and educational attainment as an indicator of social status. The segment of the population with lower formal education performs substantially less finance- and information-related activities than more educated groups, that is, activities which have a higher perceived potential in increasing participation in society (e.g., online banking, online shopping, targeted searches and verifying information, following the news). Congruent findings from the United States, European Union, Australia, South Kora and Switzerland[300] have been interpreted in debates on gaps in Internet use with reference to the *knowledge gap hypothesis*, coined by a group of authors from the University of Minnesota (Tichenor, Donohue and Olien) in 1970:

> as the infusion of mass media information into a social system increases, segments of the population with higher socioeconomic status tend to acquire this information at a faster rate than the lower status segments, so that the gap in knowledge between these segments tends to increase rather than decrease.[301]

A more in-depth elaboration of the knowledge gap can be observed in the work of van Dijk, who has been working with his own concept of the 'usage gap' since the 1990s. This concept strives to exceed the narrow scope of the knowledge gap, limited to the proliferation and absorption of information in a mass media-centric society – only scarcely applicable to ICT, the use of which requires a much more active approach, interaction and command of special skills. The usage gap thus includes not only knowledge but also behaviour, interpreted in terms of different user practices – referring primarily to gaps in the use of computer and Internet applications 'in all spheres of daily life'.[302]

Although van Dijk lacks the sufficient data to allow for multiple time comparisons to substantiate his claim of a widening usage gap[303], he nonetheless predicts that this gap will continue to widen and gradually 'cement itself' as one of the main structural forms of inequality in the information/network society. This projection, also meant to reassert the gravity of the digital divide, has been primarily rooted in the observed differences in user profiles based on educational

---

[300]Bonfadelli (2002); Eynon (2009); Jansen (2010); Mason and Hacker (2003); Nguyen and Western (2007); Robinson, DiMaggio, and Hargittai (2003); van Deursen and van Dijk (2014); van Dijk (2000, 2005, 2006a, 2009); Wei and Hindman (2011).

[301]Tichenor, Donohue, and Olien (1970, pp. 159–160).

[302]van Dijk (2005, p. 126, 2006a, p. 183, 2009, p. 299); van Dijk and van Deursen (2014, p. 55).

[303]van Dijk (2005). Recently only van Deursen et al. (2015) have supported this claim based on studies monitoring the development of online activities across users in the Netherlands in 2010–2013, which is, nonetheless, weak empirical evidence.

attainment and socio-economic status, three broader social tendencies contributing to the gradual differentiation in quality of access,[304] the specific properties of ICT which contribute to the differentiation of user practices, financially predetermined differences in hardware and software across users, the growing centralization of the social relations structure based on the scale-free networks theory[305] and the growing indispensability of computer and Internet use. The further proliferation of the Internet would, under the current conditions, spur an increase in the usage gap and thus also magnify differences in 'participation in all relevant fields of contemporary and future society'[306]. In such a scenario, the Internet would become an increasingly polarizing technological infrastructure, stratifying the social structure of the information society into that of the information elite, the participating majority and the marginalized segment of the unconnected and ostracized, thereby reaffirming the Matthew effect ('For to those who have, more will be given; and from those who have nothing, even what they have will be taken away.'[307]) as the governing principle of resource distribution in late-capitalist societies.[308]

However, according to van Dijk, the observed trajectory of the digital divide as becoming a new form of structural inequality can still be reversed: the appropriate measures, in terms of usage and ICT design, should primarily include the support of lifelong learning and the command of complex applications and functions, supporting the user-oriented development of special hardware and software targeted towards groups typically overlooked by developers (i.e., those with poor motivation, low income, disabilities, etc.), open access to scientific, public and cultural information and finally the 'full integration of ICTs into social and user environments', taking into account the specific needs of users.[309]

However, when pitted against a research tradition growing around the knowledge gap hypothesis, van Dijk's conception of the usage gap and the subsequently purported Matthew effect of the Internet may prove simplistic and misleading. Let us set aside the significant supportive role of the information society theory for a moment and revisit the crux of this theory's empirical footing and its subsequent interpretations.

The theory of a growing usage gap consists of two components: the (I) hypothesis of the determining impact of an individual's socio-economic status when explaining preferences in online activities and the (II) hypothesis of a causal relationship between the performance of a certain type of online activity and social status. The use of advanced applications and performance of 'serious' activities

---

[304]van Dijk (2005) lists continuing social differentiation and individualization, global increases in income gaps, and the commercialization of information sources leading to increasingly restricted access to information sources.

[305]The scale-free networks theory defines centralization as the basic parameter of any network with non-randomly interconnected nodes. See Barabási (2002).

[306]van Dijk (2006a, p. 184).

[307]Mar 4:25 *New Revised Standard Version*.

[308]van Dijk (2005, pp. 125–126, 2006a, pp. 185–186); Hampton (2010).

[309]Summarized from van Dijk (2005).

(working with information, following the news, financially relevant activities) are expected to have a positive impact on social status, while simpler applications and entertainment-based activities are expected to have zero or negative impact on the user's social status. The intensive use of advanced applications and serious activities in individuals with high socio-economic status thus furnish us with the only logical conclusion, that is, the increasing polarization of the social structure in line with the Matthew effect. Fig. 4.16 presents a graphic depiction of the *growing usage gap thesis*.

If the first hypothesis were invalid but the second retained its validity, Internet use would serve as a new channel of social mobility, disrupting the current mechanisms of social reproduction and also negating the Matthew effect as a guiding principle behind the transformation of the social structure, as induced by informatization. Are there any reasons to doubt the impact of socio-economic status as the most significant predictor of online activities? While the mentioned studies[310] see education as the most salient differentiator between serious and entertainment activities, the aim of these studies is primarily to confirm differences across education groups; what is more, they employ a limited number of independent variables (socio-demographic traits). A possible explanation for this may be the framing of this issue using a simplified interpretation method in the first and oldest branch of knowledge gap research, the beginnings of which can be traced back to the Minnesota Team. In reality, knowledge gap research has been far more diverse and much less clear-cut when validating the hypothesis and its variants.[311] One of the key topics of the entire debate has been ascertaining the primary predictor of the observed differences. But why? The answer can be found in early knowledge gap research: its significance and contribution lay primarily in its critique of the notion of mass media as a set of knowledge-dissemination and educational tools, projected to ameliorate gaps in knowledge – that is, an essential asset in decision making and exerting agency in modern society. The practical overlap thus lays in imparting knowledge for the management of information campaigns, the outcome of which would be a highly knowledgeable population. The almost exclusive orientation of knowledge gap researchers towards scientific and political knowledge can then be explained as the logical consequence of research limited to that of the unequal distribution of information relevant to the modernization of the social system and facilitating feedback between political

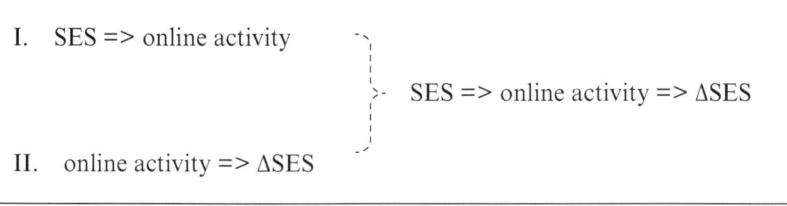

Fig. 4.16:   Thesis of the Growing Usage Gap. *Source*: Author

---

[310]See Chapter 4 footnote 300.
[311]Gaziano (1983, 1995).

institutions and their populations in a democratic setting. The roots of knowledge gap research thus lie in a normative framework that is closely tied to cybernetics, functionalism and modernization.[312]

Responses to this approach from the late 1970s tried to reconcile the often contradictory research results espousing the significant impact of SES (or education) by finding a more suitable explanatory model. The difference model, which explains the knowledge gap via context-specific motivation and interest, garnered a great deal of attention and strong empirical backing, along with the later contingency model, targeted towards the impact of the interaction between education and motivation.[313] Internet use has not yet been su.fficiently incorporated into knowledge gap research, which explains the paucity of such studies. Nevertheless, the available multiple regression results problematize the purported deciding impact of education. Markus Prior, based on a multiple regression analysis of data from the United States for the years 2002 and 2003, discovered that 'in a high-choice environment, people's content preferences become better predictors of political learning than even their level of education'[314], coming to the same conclusion upon analysing predictors of real political behaviour (during elections). Similarly, Mossberger, Tolbert and McNeal, using data from the United States from 2000 to 2004, revealed the significant impact of the user's political interest, gender, national TV watching habits and political affiliation on online news reading behaviour.[315] Minsun Shim focused on the seeking of specific health-related information (about cancer) online and the level of subsequently obtained knowledge in her analysis of US data from 2003. The study indicates that the predictive power of education is, in the case of seeking cancer information online, similar to situationally determined motivation (family history of cancer and age), the quality of the Internet connection and gender, with the most cogent predictor being interest (scanning for cancer-related information in mass media). In terms of the level of obtained knowledge, interest was approximately as important of a predictor as educational attainment, followed by age and gender.[316] Similarly, Dobransky and Hargittai, based on an analysis of predictors of health information seeking, discovered that interest in health/fitness was the strongest predictor, while the family's socio-economic status did not play any determining role.[317] How can these findings be interpreted in terms of ascertaining the validity of the first hypothesis? History seems to be repeating itself here: as observed in the critique of the original conception of the knowledge gap, the usage gap is confronted with a similar issue, that is, the discovered impact of contextual factors (interest and motivation) problematizes the determining impact of socio-economic status on online activities.

---

[312]Gaziano and Gaziano (2009).
[313]Kwak (1999); Bonfadelli (2002).
[314]Prior (2005, p. 583).
[315]Mossberger et al. (2008).
[316]Shim (2008).
[317]Dobransky and Hargittai (2012).

If we were to retain the validity of the second hypothesis, the Matthew effect would then be called into question, that is, Internet use would not spur the deepening of social inequalities based on the rich-get-richer principle, but would instead result in a specific transformation of the social structure, in which Internet use, mediated by motivation, would (at least for a part of the population) serve as a new conduit for upward social mobility. A possible reason as to why the rich-get-richer explanation is the more popular choice in this context, in addition to the use of a limited number of socio-demographic traits, may be the over-reliance on differences in averages and on predictors which are unjustifiably generalized into universal principles, potentially causing certain tendencies or patterns, pertinent only to a certain segment of the population, to be overlooked. In order to gain clearer insight into a given segment of the population, new variables must be considered, as observed in the case of motivation.

Determining the validity of the second hypothesis should not be mistaken for the more general issue of ascertaining the positive impact of Internet use on social participation or quality of life (we shall revisit this issue in the following chapter). Claims purporting a causal correlation between the (frequent or regular) performance of certain online activities and social mobility can be, in an empirically justifiable manner, problematized for at least three of the following reasons:

First, the very concept of the knowledge gap refers to gaps in knowledgeability caused by differences in the consumption of a particular type of media. The application of this approach to Internet use, however, does not focus on differences in knowledge obtained as a result of Internet use, but rather on gaps in the performance of certain activities.[318] This is akin to asking newspaper readers whether they read the 'Economy', 'Politics' and 'Celebrity' sections of the newspaper and subsequently interpreting the results as indicators of their knowledge and efficient command of the respective economic, political and tabloid information. When interpreting differences in online activity profiles, this shortcut is clearly discernible in the implicit presupposition of a direct correlation between the performance of a certain online activity (e.g., reading the news, online banking, etc.) and the associated capital gains or losses: serious types of online activities are perceived as profitable, while others (entertainment) are perceived as unprofitable.[319] Once again, we can observe a parallel here with the progression of the knowledge gap debate: in the Minnesota Team's original model, the same level of relevance was attributed to the studied information (e.g., political) in all parts of the social system. Later constructivist approaches, however, were influential in recognizing a user's decision to neither follow nor seek certain types of information as a rational act stemming from specific structures of relevance informed by a certain social environment, social experience and opportunities based on available resources.[320]

---

[318]See studies listed in Chapter 4 footnote 300.

[319]This hypothesis is made explicitly evident in the concept of capital enhancing activities, see, e.g., Hargittai and Hinnant (2008); van Dijk and van Deursen (2014); van Dijk et al. (2015); Zillien and Hargitai (2009).

[320]See Bonfadelli's (2002) summarized critique of the concept of knowledge employed in knowledge gap research.

Similarly, the normative distinction between 'better' and 'worse' online activities assumes that certain activities are consistently beneficial in terms of social participation and quality of life, regardless of their context. However, digital divide research continues to avoid addressing the direct correlation between certain activities and upward social mobility.[321] Recent studies on the outcomes of Internet use do not even support the idea that certain online activities produce certain outcomes: even though uses and outcomes can be demonstrably connected within a certain domain, it has also been found that different types of uses predict outcomes across multiple domains.[322] By analogy then, in a constructivist critique of the original approach to the knowledge gap issue, we could further interpret status-specific gaps in certain online activities as rational differences stemming from specific needs that are informed by a certain (socio-economic) situation.[323] For instance, online banking or online investments can have a different added value and benefit potential for an individual with higher income (and higher financial literacy) than for someone living pay check to pay check. This would be in keeping with the analytical distinction of skills and activities, implying the need to interpret information about online activities as information which is, to a certain extent, irrelevant in terms of its standalone impact on a user's participation in society. In this respect, the benefits of Internet use do not refer to the online activity itself (regardless of the identified correlation between the performed activity and respective skills), but rather to the user's ability to use this activity to successfully achieve a designated goal and then capitalize on the results with the intention of increasing participation in society. The deciding factor here should thus be (strategic) digital skills, as it is exactly these skills which 'determine the overall outcomes of Internet use'[324]. Even the act of compulsively looking up and reading jokes online, an activity viewed under a negative light in digital divide research, can be strategically utilized to increase one's social standing in a community that values humour and comedic individuals. Such a person can, even in our own cultural milieu, increase his/her participation in society (in the words of the core argument) by launching a career in the entertainment industry. Another, similar example could be a career in sports.

The second reason for the tenuous correlation between observed differences in online activity profiles and social mobility is the relatively even distribution and high incidence of communication activities, the content of which, and thus even their potential impact on the accumulation of different forms of capital, can scarcely be deduced from data on the frequency or intensity of use. For example, interpreting findings on differences in online activity profiles across generations in terms of the financial, health- and travel-related benefits in older age groups[325] can be a misguided endeavour, as we cannot ascertain the nature of the content

---

[321]Explicitly reflected, e.g., in van Deursen and van Dijk (2014).

[322]van Deursen and Helsper (2017); van Deursen et al. (2017).

[323]Cf. Helsper (2017b, 2017a) and above, as already mentioned in this context by Goldfab and Pearce (2008) and Gonzales (2015).

[324]van Dijk and van Deursen (2014, p. 83).

[325]van Dijk (2009, p. 299).

hidden under the empty label of 'online communication' (e-mail, social networking sites, skype, chatting ...). On a similar note, we could read the possession of cultural capital, accumulated as a result of using various online 'entertainment' functions, as facilitating access to cultural commodities of a varied quality (film, music, literature). Claims purporting the significant impact of communication (and to a slightly lesser extent entertainment and information) activities only recently garnered empirical support, furnished by analyses of predictors of outcomes, which suggest that communication activities significantly inform outcomes of use across different domains.[326] When considering the online activities of the youngest age groups then, entertainment, cultural and communication activities may indeed produce socializing effects, though there is no long-term data available which would indicate the potential impact of this group's user preferences on future socio-economic status, social behaviour, school performance, intergenerational mobility, etc.[327] Similarly, the added value of communication activities in the lives of older users may be higher than for younger individuals.[328]

One explanation as to why the potentially crucial function of the Internet as an interpersonal communication tool has been neglected is the highly individualized understanding of Internet use, which largely overlooks the social, relational nature of online communication activities. The presupposed correlation between online activities and upward social mobility is rooted in the idea of the individual perception and use of information as an isolated endeavour, with any potential for social mobility being limited to that particular user (we shall revisit this notion as it pertains to the validity of the digital divide thesis in the following chapter). In reality, however, communication environments have differently arranged communication and information structures. Online communication networks with a dense and decentralized distribution of interpersonal communication produce what are called 'learning communities', which foster their own distinct group identities, norms and group status distribution.[329] Learning communities allow for mutual learning between members (hence the name), indicating that the declared performance of any communication activity in this (or similar) communication structure (with a dense network of interpersonal communications) can be associated with an increase in a certain type of knowledge which then translates to a boost in opportunities, skills, participation, understanding or certain form of capital in offline decision-making and activities.[330] The benefits of Internet use for users who efficiently obtain advice, financially relevant information, information from the sphere of culture or interpretations of news items via online

---

[326]van Deursen and Helsper (2017).

[327]Livingstone and Helsper (2007); Boonaert and Vettenburg (2011).

[328]Loges and Jung (2001).

[329]Kidane and Gloor (2007). See also the critique of the implicit concept of learning in research on Internet use in children by Boonaert and Vettenburg (2011) and findings from an associated research tradition and the closely related concept of communities of practice (van Dijk 2005, p. 91).

[330]Cf. Hampton (2010); van Deursen, Courtois et al. (2014).

communication cannot be fully captured by data depicting the communication activities of a single individual.

The presented critiques call into question the currently most widespread form of argumentation for the social gravity of the digital divide at a user level. These critiques can also serve to conclude our presentation of the internal composition of the various arguments and evidence furnished by digital divide research, structured around Jan van Dijk's four-tiered digital divide model. As has been made evident from the presented materials, empirical research on the digital divide has only recently begun systematically tackling issues that are central to the validity of the digital divide thesis, that is, the raison d'être of the entire research tradition is being empirically validated in retrospect. The argumentative framework contains several questionable reductionist interpretations, the empirical footing of the argument is, in certain respects, unconvincing, and the validity of the information society theory in terms of preserving the digital divide thesis proves crucial as this chapter comes to a close. We have seen that in Castells' version of the information society theory, the possibility of bridging the digital divide bears significant implications for contextualizing positive social change in an information society and for utilizing the positive potential of ICT when addressing the major issues of social development and social inequality in our society. Exactly how valid is the digital divide thesis and which adjustments or restrictions would have to be made, presupposing the sustainability of the basic tenets of digital divide research? What should then be the focus of the social sciences in this field and which policies would be most effective, should the validity of the thesis be affirmed? Can the resulting findings be fruitfully applied in a further elaboration of the information society theory? These questions will be tackled in the following chapters in an analysis of the information presented thus far.

Chapter 5

Tenuous Assumptions in Digital Divide Research

Regardless of how one measures it, the digital divide exists and is wide.[1]
United Nations

The reconstruction of digital divide research has repeatedly resulted in the unearthing of certain constants in terms of how this area of research, as a whole, has been approaching the object of its interest. By constants I am not referring to a certain phraseology, established forms of empirical measurement or other characteristics pertinent to any specific field of research. The constants I am referring to here are those arising from certain, often tacit, assumptions or biases, which, together with empirical evidence and theoretical backing, form an interconnected cluster in support of the digital divide thesis. As with any generalization, this cannot be applied, without exception, across the board to every single case – it is instead intended to illuminate the prototypical traits and articulations of the said discourse. These assumptions and biases are particularly characteristic of government and corporate reports and earlier digital divide research, and have been recently brought to light by up-to-date research in an attempt to establish empirical adequacy. None of these assumptions has gone unnoticed, whether in the form of a passing remark or elaborated objection; however, they have neither been examined collectively, pitted against available empirical evidence, considered in relation to one another, nor has their persisting nature been called into question in order to shed light on and move beyond our current understanding of the digital divide.

The purpose of this chapter is thus to identify and re-examine the basic set of assumptions and biases inherent in defences of the digital divide thesis and which form the empirical and theoretical core of its legitimacy. Upon verifying the above and making the necessary adjustments, we will finally be able to ascertain the validity of the digital divide thesis as a pressing and central issue in the

---

[1]UN (2006, p. 7).

---

transition into an information society. The impetus of this chapter is thus not a destructive one, that is, to make a negative critique of the latest research efforts, but rather to illuminate the often-present limitations which obscure our path towards moving closer to the truth behind the digital divide, thereby allowing us to transcend these limitations.[2]

5.1 The Reduction of Information and Communication (Technologies) to that of the Internet

The question of what exactly can be considered an information technology, or rather, which technological artefact in particular possesses the revolutionary potential of information technology, is a concern which has long resounded in discussions on the technology-centric definition of the information society.[3] As we have observed in Chapter 3, Castells considers information technologies to be the central artefact of our times,[4] with increasing attention being paid to the Internet as the technological backbone of a new, bourgeoning type of society.[5]

A similar question can be made out to digital divide research. The materials we have examined thus far make it abundantly clear that digital divide research reduces the category of ICT to that of the Internet – the common denominator of multiple, albeit scarcely studied, technologies such as the modem, e-mail, search engines, broadband Internet, etc. While digital divide authors speak about ICT at the level of general models and theoretical footing, almost all of the empirical evidence, argumentation and proposed intervention measures are nonetheless limited to (the quality of) Internet access or online activities.[6] In this regard, digital divide research remains consistent with the latest developments in the information society theory. Is the reduction of ICT to the Internet, however, sufficiently exhaustive, that is, does it not gloss over certain ICTs which could significantly impact the validity of the digital divide thesis?

In Section 4.4.3, digital divide research was scrutinized for its lack of effort in terms of integrating mobile phone use into analyses of the digital divide in economically developed countries – surprising, given discussions on the digital divide which attest to the significant role of the mobile phone as a potential conduit towards bridging the digital divide in Third World countries. Let us also consider the fact that the mobile phone is, due to its character, also used by those who are most vulnerable to digital exclusion. Why then is the mobile phone virtually non-existent in research on the digital divide in developed countries and

---

[2]Their relevance for the whole field of Internet studies is an open question which will not be addressed here.
[3]Webster (2006, p. 11).
[4]Castells (1989, 2000b).
[5]Castells (2001b, 2004a).
[6]Critical exceptions, such as Selwyn (2004) and Gunkel (2003), insist on reading the digital divide as a multifaceted phenomenon, present in every major component of the entire technological system that is the Internet.

how would recognizing its impact subsequently affect our understanding of the digital divide?

The absence of the mobile phone in early digital divide discourse can be explained by the mass Internet craze at the time, initially low computing capacities and the absence of the mobile phone in information society theory. Subsequent advisories stressing the need to include the mobile phone in digital divide analyses,[7] however, have been almost exclusively limited to research on the impact of mobile communication on sociability[8] and analyses of the digital divide in developing countries. It is thus highly unlikely that the transformations in technology observed by digital divide research are symptomatic of a natural adaptation to technological change.[9] Could all of this be chalked up to the difficulty of incorporating the mobile phone into the digital divide thesis or even that doing so would jeopardize the validity of the thesis?

The significantly greater proliferation of the mobile phone compared to that of the Internet opens up the question of mobile phones being used for beneficial activities that are typically ascribed to the Internet in digital divide research. The primary significance of the mobile phone lies in facilitating immediate access to one's social network, both in terms of synchronous (voice call) and asynchronous (SMS) communication,[10] which can bear crucial implications in terms of the observed impact of communication on outcomes of Internet use (see Chapter 4). The mobile phone also facilitates access to basic information and news services in the form of SMS-based services and help and information lines. As we have already observed (Section 4.4.3), the poorest nations have been experiencing the dynamic development of locally adapted mobile phone infrastructures, resulting in an increase in connectivity and information, banking and health services; what is more, in economically developed countries, the mobile phone has surpassed the Internet as the most indispensable medium. Research on the interaction between both Internet and mobile phone use in digital divide research has not yielded many results as of late, and the situation has shown no signs of progression due to the shifted focus towards smartphones as Internet connection conduits.[11] So far, we know that the ultimate decision to use either a mobile phone or the Internet is heavily influenced by the geographic distance between the user and communication partner, the complexity of the information being communicated, the nature of the relationship, culture and the perceived cost of using an alternative communication channel.[12] The role of the Internet as a communication tool is

---

[7]For example, Katz and Rice (2002); Rice and Katz (2003).

[8]See, e.g., Rainie and Wellman (2012) and the studies in Chapter 5 footnote 12.

[9]Cf. Gunkel (2003, pp. 503–504).

[10]See, e.g., Ferras, Garcia, and Pose (2013); Rainie and Wellman (2012).

[11]In order to aptly illustrate the problem of reducing the issue to the Internet, we must differentiate between the mobile phone as a medium for voice and text services and the smartphone as a facilitator of Internet access.

[12]Boase, Horrigan, Wellman, and Rainie (2006); K. Brown et al. (2011); Ferras et al. (2013); Hampton, Sessions, Her, and Rainie (2009); Liu and Yang (2016); Mesch and Talmud (2008); Quan-Haase, Wellman, Witte, and Hampton (2002).

thus grossly overvalued if we fail to consider other communication channels (in this case, the mobile phone), as the added use value of the Internet is limited and context-specific. The impact of the Internet has most likely been so overvalued due to the Internet-centric focus of researchers on the outcomes of a given technology and not on the user practices and variables specific to the various domains of social life (e.g., civic participation, sociability and information consumption):[13] 'When holding a hammer, everything seems to be a nail; when focusing on new media, everything seems to be related to new media.'[14]

If we were to read the Internet as a source of information, we could also consider other information sources which are either overlooked or marginalized. When, for example, van Dijk speaks of political intervention as a necessary measure for bridging the digital divide, he bolsters his argument using the concept of information as a primary good, claiming that 'every human being has the right to this particular minimum level in that society'[15]. We can then ask why such an assertion should imply the need for universal Internet use – provided that we recognize the possibility of obtaining this minimum level via other information sources. Knowledge gap research has already revealed that education, context and the topic's position within a personal structure of relevance are salient predictors for navigating a particular issue, undoubtedly of greater relevance than the accessibility of information via an available information channel (e.g., the Internet). Is it then possible that even today, a certain segment of the population may be exceptionally informed in a certain area of interest due to personal motivation, social status, the use of 'old' media (e.g., books), or soliciting their social contacts, without having to use the Internet (skilfully or otherwise)? An affirmative response would mean destabilizing the validity of another significant assumption of the digital divide thesis, that is, that Internet use is becoming a prerequisite for maintaining or improving one's social standing (or quality of life) across all domains of social existence. If this hypothesis did not apply, then the Internet would just be one of many tools, which would in turn subvert the validity of the digital divide thesis as well as the prevailing technological definition of the information society.

5.2. The Assumption of Universal Impact: Proportional, Positive and Constant Outcomes

The symbiotic link between society's technologically induced structural change, as posited in information society theory and the digital divide thesis, explains the strong tendency towards presupposing 'universal impact' in order to maintain the validity of this thesis. The assertion of universal impact is explicitly perceptible in the introductory and concluding sections of expert texts where ICT is consistently referred to as an unprecedented force, permeating 'every aspect

---

[13]Haythorntwaite and Wellman (2002, p. 5); Macek, Macková, and Kotišová (2015).
[14]Macek et al. (2015, p. 69).
[15]van Dijk (2005, p. 137).

of our lives' or all 'spheres of social existence'.[16] In digital divide research, the assumption of universal impact is accompanied by three additional interconnected aspects. First, the impact of ICT use must be a *positive* one – if the impact were negative, efforts of bridging the digital divide via ICT expansion would not be unequivocally desirable. The lack of negative outcomes of Internet use is well discernible, for example, in arguments advocating for the need to bridge the digital divide[17] and in research on outcomes of Internet use as presented in Section 4.5.4. The purported positive impact is further understood as being *directly proportional* to the user's degree of digital inclusion, that is, benefits of use should increase alongside digital skills, intensity of use, the quantity and quality of ICT being used, breadth and variability of online activities, etc. If this direct proportion did not exist, it would significantly problematize our reading of the observed differences across users, as quantity would not always mean quality (e.g., better participation). Furthermore, impact is considered *constant* in the sense that the indispensability of ICT use in maintaining or increasing participation in society applies across the board. This indispensability bears significant implications for the gravity of the digital divide: higher indispensability indicates fewer opportunities for social participation via alternative routes, which in turn serves as a testament to the gravity of the digital divide, meaning higher risk of social exclusion as a result of non-use or inadequate use. If this indispensability and thus the added value of Internet use were context-specific (an interpretation we have already encountered), it could present itself as being very low, non-existent or even negative, depending on the context. General, decontextualized arguments attesting to the gravity of the digital divide would not hold in this case.

In this section, the validity of the universal impact argument shall be assessed using two domains of social existence often referenced in digital divide research: economy and social life.

The assumption that successful participation in the economic domain is preconditioned by having sufficient access to the ICT infrastructure is a notion closely tied to the economic/occupational definition of the information society.[18] Three arguments in particular are often employed in support of this hypothesis:

The first is the argument purporting the positive impact of informatization and ICT investments on economic development and productivity growth.[19] In conjunction with increased efficiency stemming from the informatization of production and distribution processes, this argument anticipates the reduction of production, transport and transaction costs, which are to be subsequently

---

[16]For example, Alvarez (2003, pp. 102–103); Castells (2001b, p. 275); Gourova et al. (2001, p. 16); Hoffman, Novak, and Venkatesh (2004, p. 37); McKenzie (2007, pp. 17–18); Nie, Hillygus, and Ebring (2002, p. 216); O'Hara and Stevens (2006, pp. xi, 86–88); Quan-Haase et al. (2002, p. 292); van Dijk (2005, pp. 131–143, 182–183). For reference to other texts which explicitly work with this assumption, see, e.g., Weaver, Zorn, and Richardson (2010).

[17]Cf., e.g., van Dijk and van Deursen (2014, pp. 45–52).

[18]Cf. Warschauer (2003, p. 13); Mason and Hacker (2003).

[19]For example, Campbell (2001); van Ark, Gupta, and Erumban (2011); van Deursen and van Dijk (2012); Vinaja (2003).

reflected in lower final prices for consumers, resulting in an increase in real wages and competitiveness. The second argument is the significant contribution of the IT sector in creating new jobs.[20] Upon conducting a more thorough assessment of the employed empirical support when pitted against the three facets of the universal impact argument, its applicability proves problematic: (a) the impact of ICT investments on productivity growth is too often applied only to a select few economically developed countries (primarily United States in the 1990s) and fails to consider the significantly lower or even non-existent impact in other countries; (b) the monitored impact of IT investments on local development is generally not examined in conjunction with the effects of possible alternative non-IT invest-ments, such as education, health care or basic pipeline and power systems (hydro, electricity, sewage); (c) instead of focusing on an increase in production output volumes as a result of IT investments, we should consider the impact of these investments in terms of organizational change – their added value is highly dif-ferentiated depending on the sector of the economy and reorganizational capaci-ties of the given location; and lastly (d), the increase of a company's 'economic participation' on a business and production scale is not fundamentally sympto-matic of the Internet but only partially so, as the Internet only supplements other, non-virtual social interactions and operations (business negotiations, persuasion, exertion of influence, etc.).[21]

What is more, the past three decades of economic development have not instilled us with much faith in the generally purported positive impact of infor-matization on economic stability, job security or a more equal distribution of generated wealth: although the average net income has seen an increase during this period, income inequality has increased alongside it; the increased efficiency and speed of economic processes, induced by informatization, has spurred high volatility in financial markets with grossly disproportionate impact in terms of geographic location and social stratification; the labour market continues to exhibit increasing education and skill demands; and lastly, increasing uncertainty and redundancy have been looming over the low-qualified segment of the popula-tion, which, according to certain estimates, amounts to approximately one-third of the population in economically developed countries.[22]

Even if we did not question the validity of the arguments of increased national productivity and the creation of new jobs (this debate is far from being con-cluded), these arguments are still based on aggregated data which may fail to reveal the internal, and for our purposes potentially illuminating, differences in the impact of Internet use on economic success or autonomy. In this respect, it would be more fitting to examine intrapopulation differences in the impact of

---

[20]For example, O'Hara and Stevens (2006, p. 80); Warschauer and Matuchniak (2010, pp. 180–181).
[21]For (a) see Garnham (2000); Moodley (2005) and van Ark et al. (2011); for (b) see Leye (2007) and Section 4.2.2; for (c) see Avgerou (1998) and van Ark et al. (2011) and for (d) see Graham (2011).
[22]Castells (1989, 2001b); Fuchs (2009); Heeks (2010); Mossberger et al. (2008, 2003); O'Hara and Stevens (2006); Sassen (2014); Warschauer (2003). See also Section 3.4.3.

Internet use on productivity and employability and analyses exploring the impact of computer or Internet use on financial remuneration.

When asking individuals who use the Internet at work whether or to what extent Internet use has affected their job performance or productivity, a positive answer was obtained from about two-thirds of respondents, with approximately 5% indicating a decrease in productivity.[23] However, given that positive responses may be associated with job positions that are more Internet-intensive, this finding may not necessarily indicate lower productivity or occupational success in job positions which do not necessitate Internet use or more advanced digital skills. This can first be corroborated with reference to a comprehensive set of findings from a PIAAC study of 13 European countries, out of which 92% of respondents expressed confidence when asked if they had the sufficient computer skills required to perform well at work, with only 5% providing an affirmative response to the question 'Has a lack of computer skills affected your chances of being hired for a job or getting a promotion or pay raise?'[24] Educational attainment was not a significant predictor for the questions asked, with only 9% of less-educated respondents providing an affirmative answer to the second question. Furthermore, a recent study by Gang Peng using US data has revealed that 'the impact of computer skills on reemployment is stronger for employees with higher education'[25] and that neither computer skills nor the use of computers in the workplace bears significant statistical impact on reemployment for individuals in the agriculture, service and manufacturing sectors (such an impact was observed only for management and professional jobs).

Studies focusing on the impact of computer and Internet use on financial remuneration indicate a 10–15% increase in wage premiums when considering constant job positions, age and education. Job positions with a lower standing in the labour market, such as those occupied by the less-educated or minorities, exhibit a similar average absolute wage premium; given the lower average wages in these groups, this indicates that workplace ICT use is more beneficial for these positions than for those with a higher standing in the labour market.[26] However, can it be inferred from these findings that today, for the sake of 'equal justice', 'everyone in the United States has…to develop the digital and educational skills. . .needed to prosper in the information economy, and that it matters most for those on the bottom of the economic ladder'?[27] Not if we take a closer look at the bigger picture. The lowest differences in wages have been observed across job positions for which computer or Internet use[28] at work has become an absolute necessity. The added value of ICT use can be attributed to a combination of the

[23]Madden (2006); the Center for the Digital Future at USC Annenberg (2009, 2010).

[24]Pellizzari, Biagi, and Brecko (2016, p. 33). Data are from the years 2011–2012.

[25]Peng (2017, p. 29)

[26]Mossberger et al. (2008, pp. 27–45).

[27]Mossberger et al. (2008, pp. 46, 142).

[28]The term ICT from here on in exclusively refers to these two technologies and not, for example, digital cash-desks.

increasing demand for highly skilled workers in the labour market, the uniqueness of a certain skill (in our case, ICT proficiency) in a given segment, and also likely due to the fact that ICT is first adopted by employees with empirically hard-to-define qualities.[29] The impact of a skill's uniqueness is further corroborated by the finding that wage premiums are higher in less-educated and minority groups and decrease depending on the diffusion of ICT in the given segment. In a hypothetical scenario in which all job applicants possess the same digital skills for a certain position, the value of such a skillset sinks to zero.[30] It can further be argued that the number of job positions necessitating a command of ICT is limited, with higher wage premiums being awarded to individuals in lower-paid positions that typically require lower qualifications; ICT-related jobs are then associated with a different workload and different level of responsibility.

In today's world, only few would take on the fruitless cause of defending the universally positive impact of 'more ICT' in the economy domain. The aim of the previous few paragraphs has instead been to use the economic dimension of the digital divide to illustrate how easily all three facets of the second assumption can be problematized. There are three crucial findings to consider going forward: First, the labour market exhibits substantial gaps in the importance and necessity of possessing a command of ICT for securing and performing a job, that is, the required level of ICT proficiency is relatively low or even non-existent for certain positions that enable adequate participation in the economic system. Second, proficient ICT use (on an individual level) or implementation (on an organizational or national level) are neither the only nor the primary factors for successful economic participation. While they do play a crucial role in bolstering competitiveness, serving as a new channel of upward social mobility (see p. 128) and potentially leading to financial savings or a better job placement, Internet use or ICT investments alone do not guarantee positive economic outcomes. Third, we are presented with the finding that the added value of ICT use in a given segment of the labour market is contingent upon its uniqueness. At the same time, the more common the use of ICT (or command of a particular set of digital skills) in a given segment, the greater the need for use (or required skillset), in terms of the expected standard. In this case, use (or skillset) alone would not serve as a perceptible advantage in the labour market, though non-use could be a notable disadvantage here. This would paradoxically suggest that the digital divide thesis would be *of higher validity* in a scenario where almost all individuals exhibit a (high) command of ICT, that is, in an environment where, according to existing information policies and digital divide research, the digital divide has virtually already been bridged.

The assumption that Internet use functions as a gateway towards maintaining or improving social relations has already been examined in Section 3.4.2.

---

[29]DiMaggio et al. (2004); Michaels, Natraj, and van Reenen (2014); Mossberger et al. (2008, pp. 27–45).
[30]Similarly, Fountain (2005) concludes that the minor observed impact of ICT use on finding employment is only perceptible if we entertain the notion that the majority of unemployed individuals do not use ICT.

The purported transformation of sociability towards an increasingly individual-ized and self-centric form has yielded only a very general answer, indicating a structurally induced and thus universal effect. Does this mean that (proficient) Internet use is truly a precondition for maintaining one's social life? Both *The Internet Galaxy* and the core argument seem to agree, though the above-outlined problematization of the first assumption has paved the way for an alternative, more complex answer.

The original popular debate from the early 1990s between those champion-ing the utopian scenario of universal communication as spawning the end of isolation and those forewarning of a dystopian, digitized mass society, in which isolated individuals sit alone in front of their flickering computer screens,[31] was fairly quickly addressed in the call for a scientifically accurate and data-sup-ported 'syntopic' response.[32] While literature addressing this issue may seem to have faltered in reaching a unified interpretation, we now have sufficient evidence to unambiguously assess the claim presupposing the universal impact of Internet use on sociability. The numerous findings generated by research on the Internet's impact on sociability offer up several basic hypotheses which could, if validated, provide answers to two fundamental questions: (1) If and in what manner does Internet use enrich or degrade a user's social life? (2) How are the benefits of Internet use as a medium for interpersonal communication distributed among the population?

Three main responses have come to the forefront regarding the first ques-tion, dominating existing research on the matter: the displacement (or hydraulic) hypothesis, increase hypothesis and supplement hypothesis.

The displacement hypothesis is rooted in the scarcely debatable postulation that there are only 24 hours in a day, and that time being allocated to Internet use must then be done so at the expense of other activities, which, in this case, primar-ily means spending time with friends and family. This hypothesis has been cor-roborated using (conveniently) selected excerpts on the Internet's impact on social capital from Putnam's work *Bowling Alone* from 2000, findings from the HomeNet study from 1998 (also referred to as the Kraut or Pittsburgh study) about the dete-riorating quality of life of users, and a comparative analysis of longitudinal data from the late 1990s, most commonly associated with Stanford sociologist Norman Nie.[33] Later revisions elaborated on this hypothesis by continuing to probe into differences in time spent with friends and family. However, the results are incon-clusive in terms of the validity of the displacement hypothesis:[34] the observed

---

[31]For specific examples see J. Q. Anderson (2005), Katz and Rice (2002) or Putnam (2000, pp. 171–172).

[32]For example, Castells (2001b); DiMaggio et al. (2001); Katz and Rice (2002), who have also employed the term 'syntopia' to describe the real impact of informatization on society.

[33]Kraut et al. (1998); Nie (2001); Nie and Hillygus (2002); Nie et al. (2002); Putnam (2000).

[34]This summary is based on findings presented in DiMaggio et al. (2001), Kennedy et al. (2008), Lee (2009), Robinson and de Haan (2006), Robinson et al. (2003), Stepanikova, Nie, and He (2010) and the Center for the Digital Future at USC Annenberg (2010).

decrease appears to be primarily in relation to time spent with family and not friends, with a significant decrease in television watching serving as the biggest drop in terms of non-social activities. Moreover, there is a lack of consensus on the often-referenced decreases in time spent on food preparation, household chores and sleep. There are four more arguments to consider which contest the validity of the displacement hypothesis: First, time spent online is understood here as an individual activity, with social life being reduced to direct social interactions, thus ignoring new forms of mediated social interaction and failing to recognize their comparability. Second, Internet-mediated communication is perceived as having lower informative value and being less rewarding than face-to-face contact.[35] This argument is compromised when pitted against the finding that the Internet is primarily used to communicate with individuals whom the user knows well, bolstering the social relationship due to the intensive and frequent mutual exchange of information.[36] Third, the hypothesis posits that the quality of time spent with others corresponds to the amount of time allocated to it, leaving no room for the possibility that a decrease in time spent on direct communication with friends and family may be offset by an improved use of time or wider circle of contacts.[37] Fourth, when directly asked about a possible change in contact or time spent with friends or family as a result of Internet use, the majority of respondents replied 'stayed the same' (it should nonetheless be noted that these answers are probably culturally conditioned, as evidenced by the different distribution of responses from Arab countries).[38] It is also important to consider that the remaining respondents exhibited a tendency to declare a negative impact on time spent with friends and family, but a positive impact on change in contact – both for friends and family. The exclusive focus on time thus distorts the reality behind the ongoing changes in social behaviour.

The increase hypothesis is rooted in an understanding of the Internet as a tool for fostering and forming social relationships, which produces – depending on the measurement method employed – a positive impact on social capital, the size and diversity of one's social network and time spent with friends or social contact.[39] It is precisely this hypothesis which must be accepted, in pertinence to the domain of social life, if we are to maintain the validity of the core argument. While this hypothesis has, unlike the displacement hypothesis, garnered support from a plethora of studies, both are nonetheless permutations of the argument indicating a sweeping negative or positive impact of the Internet on sociability. Critiques of the validity of the increase hypothesis may then mirror those directed at the displacement hypothesis: we already know that a large number of respondents do

---

[35]See Turkle (2011) for more elaborated argumentation.

[36]This argument is courtesy of Rainie and Wellman (2012, p. 120), see also below.

[37]Cf. Haddon (2004, pp. 66–67, 79–81); Lee (2009); Hampton and Ling (2013).

[38]Kennedy et al. (2008); the Center for the Digital Future at USC Annenberg (2010, 2012, 2013, 2016).

[39]For example, Albert et al. (2008); Boase et al. (2006); Hampton et al. (2009); Rainie, Lenhart, Fox, Spooner, and Horrigan (2000). For an overview of other studies championing this hypothesis see Lee (2009) and Wang and Wellman (2010).

not report any significant changes as a result of Internet use in terms of social contact or time spent with others. Similarly, in 2004, over half of (American) teenagers and parents expressed their disagreement with the notion that the Internet can help improve the social lives of teenagers.[40] Furthermore, several later studies have also failed to observe any significant differences in the social lives or the number of friends between users and non-users or between users exhibiting varying intensities of use.[41] The relationship between Internet use and sociability appears to be closely interconnected with the user's profile of online activities – users who primarily engage in solitary activities (reading e-mails, online banking, watching videos, etc.) exhibit lower sociability, while the average active user either does not exhibit any change, or exhibits certain signs of improvement – an effect attributed to Internet use in general in the increase hypothesis. A decrease in sociability is also exhibited by users who excessively engage in online communication, possibly due to the lack of remaining time.[42]

The observed multidimensionality of the core argument from pages 112–113 ('Those who achieve outcomes in one domain do not necessarily achieve outcomes in another domain.'[43]) can aid in explaining these differences, as it reflects the general unfeasibility of investing a limited amount of time – 24 hours a day – into the intensive accumulation of all possible forms of capital: due to time constraints and individual preferences, the Internet cannot possibly increase participation in all domains, as the overly intensive use of one function is offset by non-existent benefits or negative outcomes from other functions. This multidimensional interpretation thus corroborates the finding that heavy Internet use can lead to poor school grades, a distorted perception of reality, decrease in work efficiency, Internet addiction, etc. In terms of the user's social life, we can thus posit *a threshold hypothesis*: the positive correlation between time spent on online communication and participation in society then inverts into a negative one once a certain threshold is exceeded.

Is there any singular explanation which could adequately reconcile the findings ascribed to both the increase hypothesis and the displacement hypothesis, including their less cogent grounds? The supplement hypothesis presents itself here (with its main proponent, Barry Wellman) as a tool for reading the ongoing changes in sociability without needing to fall back on a unilateral, revolutionary understanding of the Internet.

The supplement hypothesis reads the Internet as an *additional* communication and information tool which people have incorporated into their lives to supplement other communication and information channels – akin to the role of the telephone in the past. This is fully in line with critiques scrutinizing the reduction of ICT to that of the Internet and with attempts to incorporate Internet use into a more general framework when studying the evolution of sociability in modern society (see Section 3.4.2).

---

[40]Lenhart, Madden, and Hitlin (2005), similarly, Kennedy et al. (2008).
[41]Kennedy et al. (2008); Wang and Wellman (2010).
[42]Quan-Haase et al. (2002); Warschauer (2003, pp. 159–160); S. Zhao (2006).
[43]van Deursen et al. (2017, p. 468).

According to the findings that give credence to the supplement hypothesis, the Internet is more often used for maintaining existing social relationships rather than forming new ones.[44] A significant advantage of the supplement hypothesis is the lack of tunnel vision, preventing the entire category of ICT from being erroneously reduced to that of the Internet and ensuring that other, frequently used means of communication (such as the telephone) are not left by the wayside. Rainie and Wellman illustrate this clearly in their general assertion (one that, given the context of the information discussed, cannot be dismissed) that people 'are organizing their communications based on the context of their contact. People use multiple media to communicate and can choose the one that is most suitable for the moment.'[45] This raises the question of what exactly informs one's decision to choose the Internet over other available communication channels. First, the added value of the Internet lies in fast response times and relatively low communication costs, especially for long-distance communication. The once considerable drawbacks of low portability (especially for laptops and desktop computers) have become a moot point today, given the proliferation of mobile Internet, especially for people with lower social status and those living in areas with poorly developed traditional telecommunication infrastructures.[46] On the other hand, choosing the Internet as a communication tool is associated with lower information density (primarily for written forms of online communication) and lower reactivity when using asynchronous forms of online communication (e-mail, discussion forums, etc.). In this respect, it is understandable why the telephone and direct communication are used more often than the Internet for communicating matters of a serious and personal nature and for communicating with people who live in close proximity; it also explains why the added value of the Internet lies primarily in maintaining contact with acquaintances and increasing the volume of long-distance communication.[47] The confrontation of empirical evidence with the three stated hypotheses can thus tentatively be concluded by inferring that the added value of Internet use in the domain of social life is not universally demonstrable; the impact of ICT should thus not be considered in terms of a universal increase or decrease, but instead as a non-exclusive component of the transformation of social life, in which the indispensability and added value of ICT fluctuates depending on the context. The arguments posed above thus speak in favour of the supplement hypothesis.

To a certain extent, the supplement hypothesis also answers the question: who benefits most from Internet use? Three possible answers have come into fruition: The first, compatible with the increase hypothesis, is crucial for maintaining the validity of the assumption that all users reap the same benefits from (a certain quality of) Internet use, indicating that technology has an inherent, constant added

---

[44]Gross, 2004); Haddon (2004); Kennedy et al. (2008); Quan-Haase et al. (2002); Wellman, Haase, Witte, and Hampton (2001).
[45]Rainie and Wellman (2012, p. 97).
[46]De Lanerolle (2012); Livingston et al. (2009).
[47]Boase et al. (2006); Hampton et al. (2009); Hampton and Wellman (2002); Lenhart et al. (2005); Liu and Yang (2016); Quan-Haase et al. (2002).

value, which also extends to its impact on sociability.[48] The second answer, formulated as the social-compensation hypothesis, is based on the premise that the added value of the Internet is not as apparent in the socially adept as it is in the more introverted, shy or socially excluded, for whom the Internet helps overcome the initial barriers of shyness, communication difficulties and prejudice. According to existing research, the Internet's potential for anonymity and lower initial communication costs make it easier for lonely, shy and socially anxious individuals to establish and maintain relationships: these groups exhibit an increase in openness, support and pleasant communication experiences as a result of Internet use when compared to the average Internet user or more sociable users.

However, the notion of compensation here is problematic for the following three reasons: first, a higher increase than in the socially adept population is accounted for due to the lower initial absolute value; second, only a minority of users with low sociability make significant use of online communication tools; and third, the positive outcomes for these users remain limited to the domain of online communication and do not translate to improved social interactions offline, associated instead with increased self-presentation on the Internet, persisting isolation, greater odds of excessive and problematic Internet use, lower quality of life and slight increase in depression.[49] The socially excluded will then not necessarily reap any benefits from ICT access, as demonstrated by Claire Bure in her study on Internet and mobile phone use among Scotland's homeless population. According to her findings, the socially excluded paradoxically 'appropriate and domesticate technologies in ways that reinforce the patterns and practices of everyday lives, and therefore ICT access and capability alone will not change an individual's situation'[50].

The most convincing, and also most compatible with the supplement hypothesis, then seems to be the *rich-get-richer hypothesis*, empirically grounded in a series of findings revealing that the main predictors of sociability change (as a result of Internet use) are pre-existing social skills and the size of the user's social network, with the Internet itself possessing minimal or zero added value.[51] Similar findings from the domain of economy reveal that the distribution of benefits from Internet use in a given population is highly dependent on the distribution of relevant resources prior to and extrinsic to the proliferation and use of the Internet. In terms of the global digital divide, the validity of this conclusion is further corroborated by the finding that 'the already rich, competitive and democratic countries and companies with high status are the most likely beneficiaries of the benefits produced by the proliferation of new media'[52]. However, as demonstrated in the case of user knowledgeability in Section 4.5.5, the

---

[48]See Lee (2009) for more detail.
[49]Amichai-Hamburger, Wainapel, and Fox (2002); Baker and Oswald (2010); Caplan (2007); J. Kim, LaRose, and Peng (2009); Kraut et al. (2002); Morahan-Martin and Schumacher (2003); Weidman et al. (2012).
[50]Bure (2005, p. 123).
[51]Lee (2009); Matei and Ball-Rokeach (2002).
[52]Guillén and Suaréz (2005, p. 697).

rich-get-richer theory may be misleading, with similar indications in the domain of sociability. This can be observed in findings from Hampton and Ling, who compared changes in sociability in the Ukraine, United States and Norway and found that outcomes of Internet use vary based on the type of social life typically attributed to different social strata (as similarly observed in the case of economy): in less prosperous countries, more frequent face-to-face interactions reduce the Internet's impact on the size of the user's social network and 'face-to-face contact is displaced when email is adopted for use within core networks among those of lower SES, whereas the opposite is experienced by those of higher SES'[53]. The authors attribute these findings to the fact that individuals with lower SES generally have smaller social networks and spend more time with members of their core network, leading to online communication being mostly conducted with members of these core networks, thus resulting in less in-person contact. The distribution of benefits from ICT use must then not be defined in terms of the universal impact of an independent force, stemming from the inherent properties of a given technology, but rather as the product of the context-specific interactions of ICT affordances[54] and the user's characteristics. The implications of the above-outlined findings from the spheres of social and economic life, vis-à-vis the various facets of the universal impact argument, can be summarized as follows:

When examined in relation to the domains of economy and social relations,[55] the validity of the assumption of Internet access as a precondition for maintaining or increasing participation in all domains of social life remains unsubstantiated: ICT should be treated as a new factor which determines 'success' in certain segments of economic and social life rather than as an absolute prerequisite for maintaining or increasing participation in economic or social life as a whole. Digital factors explaining outcomes of Internet use should then be examined in conjunction with an analysis of the conditions which render Internet use a prerequisite for success or participation; furthermore, the specific situations or contexts in which Internet non-use or poor digital skills are *not* inhibiting factors should be identified.

The positive universal impact argument is an unsustainable one, primarily with regard to the observed multidimensionality of the Internet's impact, where

---

[53]Hampton and Ling (2013, p. 582).

[54]The affordances of the Internet in the domain of sociability is summarized by Boase and Wellman (2006, pp. 710–711).

[55]The third frequently examined domain, which I do not examine in greater detail here, is the domain of politics and civic engagement; similarly to the two domains presented in this book, the Internet has been responsible for significantly transforming only certain aspects of politics, functioning instead as an intensifier of status- and interest-based civic engagement rather than a universal amplifier of political activity (Hindman 2008; Wellman et al. 2001). What is more, instead of serving as a radical new communication tool, contributing to the technology-induced amelioration of the relationship between the political and public sphere, the Internet here serves instead as a specific component of the evolving media mix framed by the political climate of the given country (Castells 2009; Macek et al. 2015).

Internet use, even within a single domain, takes on various qualitatively different forms, depending on the context of use and variability of potential outcomes. A user may thus exhibit a certain level of Internet use which is at once correlated with positive outcomes in one domain and negative or non-existent outcomes in another. Another problem is the considerable number of users for whom Internet use does not produce any notable changes (though this could be ascribed to underdeveloped digital skills). Ascertaining the (positive) nature of the Internet's impact is further complicated by inconsistencies in the observed types of outcomes (not domains). Greater efforts should thus be made in conceptualizing gaps in Internet use vis-à-vis the different types of outcomes, which have been identified as, for example, participation, quality of life, satisfaction and achievements.[56]

The above-mentioned findings (the impact of context on outcome types, multidimensionality, varying degrees of relevance) are of value when examining the claim of a directly proportional relationship between digital inclusion and positive impact; the threshold hypothesis, the applicability of which extends beyond sociability research, is also worth mentioning – applicable, for example, in analyses on the correlation between ICT investment volumes and increased quality of life in developing countries. Future digital divide research would, also with regard to potential negative outcomes, benefit greatly from modelling this correlation.

The aforementioned issues also point to the unsustainability of the argument positing the constant necessity of ICT use, or rather, the constant relationship between a certain level of use and participation. We have reached a rather interesting counterintuitive paradox here: a higher presence of (skilled) users in a studied population can indicate the existence of a greater rather than smaller digital divide. Until now, increasing the number of users in a given population has been seen as the cure for bridging the digital divide. The need to employ a context-specific approach in ascertaining the validity of the digital divide thesis is made apparent in the insufficiently elaborated assertion that 'in developed countries, computer use has become less a lifestyle option; it has more and more become an everyday necessity'[57]. Does this mean that the digital divide issue is not as significant in developing countries, that is, is there a limit to the validity of the digital divide thesis? If the indispensability of Internet access varied and was, for example, dependent on the 'level of economic development', then the validity of the information society theory – one which is logically tied to the structurally induced necessity of ICT access – would also vary (see Chapter 3).

5.3 The Assumption of the Universal Necessity of Internet Use

If we were to accept that ICT use is but one of several factors that determines 'success' only in certain domains of economic and social life, then we could also safely

---

[56]A good starting point would be the study by van Deursen and Helsper (2017).

[57]van Dijk and van Deursen (2014, p. 45). Similarly, e.g., Castells (2001b).

assume that there are certain individuals or social environments where Internet non-use or 'inadequate' use are not catalysts for social, cultural or economic disadvantage. A user's decision not to use the Internet could then be validated with empirical data as a rational act, and the answer 'I don't need it' could be interpreted as reflecting the needs of an individual in a certain social situation. Senior citizens typically exhibit needs and preferences which do not mirror the needs and preferences that lead to Internet use, rendering certain efforts to promote Internet use among the elderly as counterproductive.[58] Lynette Kvasny, in her study on the cultural reproduction of digital gaps in American inner cities, describes her unsuccessful attempt at trying to promote the 'benefits' of using the popular sales portal amazon.com to a group of elderly Afro-Americans: 'Neither man was interested in making a purchase online. They told me that there is nothing like going to the local store, chatting with the regulars and browsing in person.'[59] In the Czech Republic, approximately three-quarters of non-users claimed that not using the Internet has no impact on their lives (for better or worse) in the 11 domains of life indicated; and in Great Britain, a mere 5% of non-users agreed with the claim: 'I could perform daily tasks better if I used the Internet.'[60] The objection that these individuals cannot adequately assess the Internet due to their non-use can be countered by the significant percentage of net evaders categorized as non-users (see p. 101) as well as the finding that approximately half of former users do not claim to be in any way deprived due to non-use.[61]

Despite opinions positing the decision not to use the Internet as a rational act,[62] digital divide research has been dominated by a construction which could be described as the universal necessity of Internet use. This construction is a logical one – the digital divide thesis cannot reconcile the idea of a segment of the population which objectively possesses no need for the Internet (or exhibits no need for frequent or skilful use) without sabotaging its very own validity. This assumption can be found in allegations deeming non-users a truly deprived segment of the population[63] who are in dire *need* of Internet access or in most need of access support[64]; this approach is also perceptible in empirical research employing permutations of the question: 'Non-users: will you logon soon?' and 'Non-users: why not online?'[65] as well as in arguments championing information and access to information (i.e., Internet access) as a primary good, positional

[58]Loges and Jung (2001); Weaver, Zorn, and Richardson (2010).
[59]Kvasny (2006, p. 174).
[60]Dutton et al. (2013); Dutton, Helsper, and Gerber (2009); Lupač et al. (2015).
[61]Dutton et al. (2013, p. 57); the Center for the Digital Future at USC Annenberg (2004, p. 42).
[62]See, e.g., Bonfadelli (2002); Compaine and Weinraub (2001); Eynon and Geniets (2016); Gonzales (2016); Satchell and Dourish (2009); Selwyn (2003); Wyatt et al. (2002).
[63]See, e.g., van Dijk (2005, p. 35).
[64]See, e.g., Alampay (2006, p. 13); Helsper (2008, p. 48); Hoffman and Novak (1998, p. 9); Holloway (2005, p. 175); Lenhart et al. (2003, p. 25); Warschauer (2002, 2003, p. 199).
[65]The Center for the Digital Future at USC Annenberg (2004, pp. 40, 43). This is noted by, e.g., Satchell and Dourish (2009, p. 10).

good, basic human right, civil right, universal access right, etc.[66] One can also observe the manner in which digital divide research addresses the answer 'I don't need it' and how reasons for non-use are determined: this answer is either assessed as an irrational one (the user's failure to understand the benefits of ICT use or as a scapegoat for the real reasons behind non-use), or as a rational act under current conditions (limited potential for Internet use), though not under the conditions of the growing necessity of ICT use.[67] Two additional approaches associated with this construct can be defined as generalization and psychologization. Generalization is employed when interpreting the observed socio-demographic makeup of users and non-users: descriptions of non-users often gloss over the presence – albeit marginal at times – of college students and young and socially successful users, thereby eliminating the problem of addressing the rationality of non-users with higher social status. In a similar vein, the category of experienced users often excludes or undermines – though also often a marginal group – the presence of seniors, women and the unemployed. The digital generation thesis presented in Section 4.5.5 can serve as a prime example here. The second approach could be labelled as the psychologization of non-users, which makes use of definitions such as technophobia and computer anxiety, seeking rationale for non-use in the form of psychological deficits, problems and deviations.[68]

A by-product of the universal necessity construct is the interpretation of non-use as a sign of irrationality, the consequence of unfortunate circumstances, backwardness and social or psychological deviations. There is still one more argument which needs to be integrated into the contention that there is a certain segment of the population that truly does not need the Internet or does not require high Internet proficiency; in order to do so however, we must return to p. 84 regarding the implications of the correlation between DOI and digital divide research and pick up where we left off.

Diffusion of innovations research exhibits four problematic shortcomings which have been criticized since the 1970s: (a) the individual-blame bias, (b) the pro-innovation bias, (c) the recall problem, that is, the respondent's retroactive effort of recalling the moment when he/she first adopted the innovation and (d) insufficient attention paid to the impact of DOI on socio-economic inequality. Rogers ascribes the persistence of these shortcomings to the 'trained incapacity' of researchers to see certain aspects of the examined reality, an integral by-product of being professionalized within a particular paradigm. This imposes notable limitations on the research issues being examined, which in turn thwarts the further development of fruitful DOI research.[69] If we know that digital divide research and diffusion research both engage with the diffusion of an innovation in society and that the notion of ICT diffusion in digital divide research is well

---

[66]See, e.g., R. H. Anderson et al. (1995); Fuchs (2008); Mossberger et al. (2008); O'Hara and Stevens (2006), Steyaert (2002); van Dijk (2005); Shneiderman (2004).
[67]See conclusion of Section 4.5.3.
[68]See, e.g., Beckers, Schmidt, and Wicherts (2008); Finn and Korukonda (2004).
[69]Rogers (2003, p. 106).

in line with the arguments of the DOI model, can we then expect digital divide research to exhibit similarly problematic qualities? Given that retroactively recalling the moment of adoption is more of a methodological issue of measurement accuracy and because the very existence of digital divide research can be seen as a gateway towards solving the fourth problem, we shall not attempt to resolve these two shortcomings of DOI research within the scope of this book. The following two sections shall focus on the remaining two issues and their applicability to digital divide research, as, surprisingly, these sources of inspiration have remained untapped in digital divide research.

5.4. Individual-blame Bias: The Assumption of Isolated Users

The individual-blame bias can be described as the 'tendency to hold an individual responsible for his or her problems, rather than the system of which the individual is a part'[70]. Upon first glance, this tendency is not a ubiquitous feature of digital divide research, as we can find indications of a contrasting approach, that is, researchers looking for the root of the problem on a systemic level via interpretations which implicate ICT manufacturers in the issue of non-use, attribute insufficient ICT diffusion to poorly configured information policies and the assertion that the digital divide cannot be bridged unless we address social inequality as such (primarily in terms of income and education gaps). However, in the quantitative, survey-based analyses which dominate the field of digital divide research, the individual-blame bias holds a very strong position. We have observed this tendency in the above-mentioned line of reasoning, according to which the failure to adopt a technology is the fault of the non-user (failure to grasp the benefits of use, low educational attainment, lacking motivation, etc.). Such a tendency is also well perceptible in the prevailing approach, which ascribes determinants of Internet adoption to individual characteristics rather than the social environment (as observed on p. 65), views Internet use as an activity shaped solely by the user's own abilities and (digital) skills and finally, champions the notion that benefits of use can only be accounted for in terms of the qualities and abilities of the (isolated) user (see Section 4.5.4) or the personal ownership of certain ICT devices.[71] Will consolidating these indications in any way enrich our understanding of the digital divide?

A positive answer would mean abandoning the notion that ICT use and the associated benefits are strictly limited to the user as an isolated, statistical unit.

---

[70]Rogers (2003, pp. 118–119).

[71]On a similar note, we can consider the tendency towards an individualized diffusion of ICT in terms of the global digital divide, where the causes and benefits of informatization are attributed to the internal qualities of the studied countries and not the system of global economic dependence and, by association, inequalities in technological and social development, where the responsibility and implementation of information policies and development of information infrastructures falls to the governments, though their actions are limited by the system of international law, the decisions of multinational organizations, globally defined prices and the global geography of the ICT infrastructure.

While this idea is not exactly a novel one in digital divide discourse,[72] it is not entirely compatible with the digital divide thesis. Is there any way then to corroborate its validity? On page 65, we already established the crucial role of the respondent's social network as an important communication channel, informing the user of the innovation and significantly influencing the user's odds of adoption. Upon presenting strategic skills and outcomes of social/communication uses, we were confronted with the finding that using the Internet as a communication tool can generate benefits across various domains (p. 112). The benefit of increased participation in society here is contingent not only upon the user's communication and strategic skills and the correlated uses (e.g., looking up and using a specialized discussion forum to resolve an issue), but also on the parameters of the user's social network. We have also already examined the role of social support in Internet use (p. 115).

It is also possible that non-users may benefit from the adoption of ICT by other individuals in their social circles, in the same way that individuals who do not drive reap the benefits of having access to a car through friends and family.[73] This notion of proxy use (or intermediaries) has been cropping up in studies focusing on intermediated use in developing countries and in qualitative research on non-users and low-skilled users.[74] Thanks to these studies, we now know that the most unconnected segments of the population, such as senior citizens or non-users from poor countries, use contacts in their social networks to process online requests, for online communication with bureaucratic institutions, looking up information, etc. Quantitative surveys monitoring proxy use have only recently begun to gain traction. These studies have confirmed that proxy use of the Internet is fairly common practice both among users and non-users.[75] No significant differences in the availability and use of proxy users have been observed across different socio-demographic groups. Most non-users know someone who they could turn to if they needed to have something arranged online (9 out of 10 of surveyed drop-offs in Britain) – this contact usually being a friend or family member. Approximately one half of non-users make use of this option, though proxy use is also standard practice among Internet users. The relevance of proxy and assisted Internet use is further validated (in addition to the above-mentioned findings) by studies on the (substantial) number of users who have been able to use the Internet to help someone with a serious illness or health condition[76] and studies on the use of delegated or assisted access for patients with diabetes.[77]

---

[72]Can be explicitly found in older texts such as Castells (2001b, p. 285), DiMaggio et al. (2004, pp. 378–379) and Newhagen and Bucy (2004, p. 19).

[73]Metaphor adopted from Wyatt et al. (2002).

[74]De Souza e Silva, Sutko, Salis, and de Souza e Silva (2011); Heeks (1999); James (2005, 2007); Selwyn (2006); Warschauer (2003); Wu, Ware, Damnée, Kerhervé, and Rigaud (2015).

[75]Crothers et al. (2016); Dutton et al. (2009, 2013); Helsper and Deursen (2017); Lupač et al. (2015); Zickuhr (2013).

[76]Horrigan and Rainie (2006); Fox and Duggan (2013).

[77]Mayberry, Kripalani, Rothman, and Osborn (2011).

Intermediaries who act as go-betweens between non-users (or less experienced users) and the Network significantly problematize the assumed benefits of ICT use that are attributed to direct ownership or use. This could have far-reaching implications for our understanding of a given population's access to the information infrastructure in international comparisons, as it would be skewed in favour of cultures with collective user practices and higher interconnectedness. In reports conducted by multinational institutions, the issue of the statistical representation of shared access is a recurring one[78] and can be observed in the 2005 UN report on the digital divide, in which the number of users in countries with lacking data are estimated based on the assumed rate of collective Internet use (e.g., eight users per account in Egypt, 25 in the case of Iraq).[79] In his 2011 study *Sharing Mobile Phones in Developing Countries*, Jeffrey James provided an empirically grounded overview of the culture of sharing and its implications, using international digital divide statistics based on mobile phone use.[80]

The category of intermediaries thus provides a concise and logical explanation as to why a certain segment of the population is not deprived as a result of non-use or poor digital skills. If we were to include delegated and assisted use in the category of ICT users in economically developed countries and interpreted the results using the supplement hypothesis, we would be left with a much less dramatic depiction of the digital divide: the 'truly unconnected' category would then shrink drastically, reduced to a minority of individuals whose primary problem would then be social isolation and/or poverty.[81] In order to gain more adequate insight into the state of the digital divide, we would always have to consider the category of users with respect to the availability, use and level of social support in the user's social circles.

Digital divide research has downplayed the significance of social support and proxy use on the basis of two arguments: The first argument is based on the finding that people with low social status and poor digital skills are more likely to turn to informal social support, the quality of which is presumed to be similarly low due to social homophily (see p. 115). A closely related claim then is that digital skills do not improve when a user with low skills relies on social support as opposed to attempting to resolve the issue alone.[82]

However, these claims cannot be used to refute the significant role of proxy or assisted Internet use in the context of the digital divide for the three following reasons:

First, qualitative studies compellingly demonstrate the significance of social support in its subjective added value. Despite the presumed lack of quality in low-skilled users, social support clearly moderates the association between the dimensions of Internet access and diversity in positive outcomes.[83] What is more,

---

[78]See UNDP (1999, pp. 64–65); UN (2006, p. 46); ITU (2016, p. 160).
[79]UN (2005).
[80]James (2011).
[81]Cf. Lüders and Gjevjon (2017); van Deursen and Helsper (2015).
[82]Eynon and Geniets (2016); Helsper and Deursen (2017).
[83]Courtois and Verdegem (2016).

Section 5.2 suggests that the required skill level may be lower in these groups, indicating that the skill level of available social support may be sufficient; if it were inadequate, then it seems unlikely that such a large number of users and non-users would repeatedly turn to this group for assistance. Purported 'gaps' in social support must then be reassessed using this interpretive framework. Moreover, in the case of developing countries, proxy or assisted use is often the most effective option due to cultural restrictions (e.g., for women), insufficient financial resources or illiteracy. In economically developed countries, proxy use and social support plays an unparalleled role for disabled individuals, the elderly and the socio-economically underprivileged.

Second, the empirical footing of the first argument is not very compelling in this context, as it plays off of the characteristics of certain types and thus creates the impression of largely homogeneous social networks – an assertion that has been scarcely validated in pertinence to social support.

Third, in economically developed countries, motivation proves to have a higher impact than socio-economic characteristics and social support perceptibly bolsters an individual's motivation to use the Internet or to keep trying to utilize the Internet for a given purpose (e.g., in the case of the unemployed).[84] This third argument is rooted in the purported universal necessity of ICT use: 'in the twenty-first century, *every* individual of a particular age needs a basic level of digital skills or literacy to perform in society'[85]. In addition to the presumed universal necessity, this normative argument also suggests the inevitability of further informatization – let us take a closer look.

5.5. Pro-Innovation Bias and the Presupposed Inevitability of Further Informatization

The tendency to individualize the problem of ICT diffusion in society is, in the prevailing problematization of the digital divide, inextricably linked to the *pro-innovation bias*, that is, the belief that 'an innovation should be diffused and adopted by all members of a social system, that it should be diffused more rapidly, and that the innovation should be neither re-invented nor rejected'[86]. These two DOI issues should then not be seen as mutually exclusive when it comes to digital divide research: if an innovation is to be adopted by all members of the system, the required solution is always in the hands of the society of users. The rationalization and value neutralization of the pro-ICT bias is supported, in addition to the above-mentioned assumptions, by the notion that further informatization is inevitable. This can be observed when modelling non-decreasing S-curves for ICT diffusion (see, e.g., Fig. 4.12), in interpretations of the digital divide as a transitional period, claims that the digital divide is already being bridged in terms of physical access (necessitating a shift in focus to differences across users), as

---

[84]Fieseler et al. (2014); Reisdorf and Groselj (2017).
[85]van Dijk and van Deursen (2014, pp. 56–57). Italics PL.
[86]Rogers (2003, p. 106).

well as in claims that without any intervention, the gravity of the digital divide and the social benefits of Internet use will increase along with further informatization.[87] In theoretical terms, this argument is rooted in an understanding of the current situation as merely the initial phase of the information society, one which will take full shape in the coming years due to continuing informatization.[88] The informatization of society presents itself here as a form of natural evolution, the impetus behind the current phase of social development and a universally accepted historical necessity from which there is no way out, rendering the refusal to use ICT a futile effort.[89]

5.6. The Presupposed Feasibility of Closing the Digital Divide

The purported need for political intervention in the digital divide issue presupposes that such a gap can even be closed, that is, it is rooted in an understanding of the digital divide as a (potentially) temporary deviation in the development of the information society. Explicit advisories calling for the need to bridge the digital divide very rarely delve into further detail, while more meticulously thought-out deliberations (vis-à-vis increasing social inequality) often lead to more cautious appeals to prevent or at least mitigate the further expansion of the divide. The need to maintain the validity of the digital divide thesis by adhering to the above-mentioned assumptions does not allow for much wiggle room. An illustrative example here is van Dijk's attempt at recognizing the impossibility of completely closing the divide while simultaneously striving to find a remedy for the digital divide as a new source of social inequality. Van Dijk is aware that 'in principle [i.e., given the trend of a deepening divide – noted by PL] and for more practical reasons, it is impossible to close the divide completely'[90]. He thus redefines the issue of bridging the digital divide as the threat of structural inequality in ICT access, catalysing the formation of second- and third-class citizens.[91] Given that unequal access to ICT stems from the systemic unequal distribution of scarce resources, he goes on to acknowledge that ameliorating this divide requires implementing general measures aimed at addressing economic, educational, cultural and political inequalities.[92] The shifted focus towards eradicating 'structural inequalities' in ICT access may however re-invoke the claim that 'such a conclusion would be very unsatisfactory after the detailed analysis...It is not justified either. Concrete policies for confronting the digital divide are possible.'[93]

---

[87]See, e.g., Castells (2001b, p. 271); Dewan and Riggins (2005, p. 299); Hoffman (2012, p. 202); Martin and Robinson (2007, p. 18); Norris (2001, p. 71); O'Hara and Stevens (2006, pp. 87–88); van Dijk (2005).

[88]For example, Reddick et al. (2000, p. 46).

[89]Explicitly, e.g., O'Hara and Stevens (2006, p. 166). Cf. Castells' information society theory in Section 3.4.

[90]van Dijk (2005, p. 205).

[91]Similarly also Norris (2001) and Martin and Robinson (2007, p. 18).

[92]Also, e.g., van Dijk and van Deursen (2014).

[93]van Dijk (2005, p. 206).

Trying to identify the threshold of this presupposed transformation is a futile endeavour, as is trying to identify how political measures aimed at closing the digital divide differ from political measures aimed at preventing the digital divide from becoming a new layer of structural inequality. However, such a threshold does not seem to even exist here – the feasibility of ameliorating the digital divide is backed by advisories indicating the need to thwart a certain societal transition, which, according to the core argument, has already taken place.

According to the core argument and the afore mentioned measures for bridging the digital divide, the promotion of ICT diffusion and proficient use are projected to reduce other social inequalities which will, in turn, result in decreased gaps in ICT diffusion and use. The authors using this combination of assumptions, that is, the feasibility of bridging the digital divide and the universally positive impact of ICT,[94] are then caught in a tautological trap: while continuing informatization is on the one hand legitimized as a cure for economic stagnation, rising social inequality, waning social cohesion and democratic deficit, it is the (revolutionary) treatment of precisely these issues which serves as a precondition for bridging the digital divide. This tautology only makes sense if we entertain the notion that the design of ICT itself serves as a tool of positive social change, a miraculous remedy for social ailments which can be promoted at a sufficiently quick pace together with an instructive leaflet on the conditions of satisfactory use. As we already know, such a hypothesis is not a valid one, forcing us to put an end to this vicious cycle and call into question the very idea of closing the digital divide – regardless of the implications it may impose.

Let us first consider which arguments opposing the feasibility of closing the digital divide can be salvaged if we are to retain the remaining assumptions of the digital divide thesis (i.e., without having to incorporate new observations from the above-mentioned critiques).

First, the argument purporting the feasibility of closing the divide implies the need for the universal proliferation of a particular lifestyle which breeds the same pro-innovation preferences and values across the entire population; closing the digital divide would then require substantial cultural homogeneity. Countries with the highest percentage of users also exhibit a decrease in the rate of new adopters; in the United States for example, the percentage of users has been stagnating for years, creating a scenario equivalent to the stratification model.[95] The diffusion ceiling for the Internet is lower than that of, for example, the telephone due to its higher complexity and, by association, higher operational difficulty. We can then expect a certain segment of the population to remain unconnected and for a significant percentage of users to continue using certain basic functions without any anticipated impact on participation. The assumption that the unequal distribution of digital skills resources will prove problematic when considering the likely non-existent correlation between intensity or duration of Internet

---

[94]This tautology can be observed, e.g., in Castells (2001b, pp. 247–271) and van Dijk (2005).
[95]Martin and Robinson (2007); Perrin and Duggan (2015). For the stratification model, see Fig 4.12.

use and level of strategic skills (see p. 112). Van Dijk sees social status and the associated stock of knowledge, intellectual capacity and work requirements as catalysts of the differential acquisition of digital skills, meaning that individuals with higher social status adopt skills with higher added value and higher strategic potential than individuals with lower social status, which, according to van Dijk, bolsters the existing trend of rising social inequality.[96] We must also bear in mind that the social distribution of knowledge, closely interlinked with social status, is also the social distribution of strategically useful knowledge. Today, this social distribution also indicates a certain permeability of 'cyberspace',[97] that is, to a certain extent, dictated by status. If we look at the dynamics of global gaps in bandwidth quality, the combination of continuous technological development and uneven diffusion then lead to the persistence (or even expansion) of this aspect of the digital divide.[98] Guillén and Suárez, in their 2005 study *Explaining the Global Digital Divide*, came to the conclusion that international differences in ICT adoption are not simply the by-product of poorly configured internal information politics, but rather,

> the result of the fundamental economic, political and social gap that separates the advanced from the less developed countries, which to a certain degree is due to unequal power relations, as indicated by dependency and world-system status.[99]

Efforts of ameliorating international differences in ICT adoption would then presuppose a radical transformation of the entire socio-economic system of global relations. To summarize, the differences in ICT use are inextricably correlated with other inequalities in society,[100] the eradication of which is not feasible in today's (if at all in any) social system. When maintaining the assumptions intrinsic to the digital divide thesis, we can expect the divide to continue deepening, with even a possible reversal of the current increase in users in light of the ongoing crisis and privatization of the social state, rising social inequality, instability spurred by climate fluctuations, anticipated spikes in food prices and depletion of non-renewable resources. The segment of the population that is currently most vulnerable to producing the highest number of drop-offs is the low-income segment, a group already struggling to maintain at least some form of access to ICT.[101]

In this case, we should take non-use or poor use seriously as a starting point in tackling the problem of the digital divide and not fall prey to the notion that

---

[96]van Dijk (2005, pp. 140–143), similarly, Jansen (2010).

[97]Sassen (1998b); Graham (2011).

[98]Hilbert (2016).

[99]Guillén and Suárez (2005, p. 697).

[100]This is hardly a breakthrough finding given the practice of intertwining social inequality and gaps in Internet use (e. g., Helsper, 2008, 2012), though it takes on a new meaning in this context.

[101]See the concept of technology maintenance on p. 100.

the only possible solution lies in teaching the entire population how to use the Internet well (and thus also intensively).

The above-critiqued validity of the arguments backing the digital divide thesis, and which are also crucial for the core argument, leaves us with no other choice than to interpret the core argument as an incomplete construction. Does this also mean that we should entirely resist reading the uneven proliferation of ICT (and thus gaps in ICT use) as a new dimension of social inequality? And if not, how can the severity of the digital divide be assessed after such a critique and what recourse can be taken now? Also, let us not forget – what implications would these answers impose on the information society theory?

In order to answer these questions, we must first revisit all of the problems and shortcomings in digital divide research that we have discussed thus far, and which we have addressed in this chapter, by identifying the basic assumptions of the digital divide thesis and conducting a critical assessment of their validity.

Chapter 6

Understanding Indispensability: Contexts, Networks and Discourses

> The effect on the few who remain technologically disconnected
> has never been more profound — especially for the teens, like DJ,
> who are part of the most digitally defined generation in human
> history. Almost everything they need exists in cyberspace.[1]
>
> *Washington Post*

The notion that inadequate Internet access always leads to social disadvantage is not fully in line with existing knowledge on the matter. The validity of this correlation is problematized in light of the findings that (1) 'high-profile' Internet use does not generate benefits across all domains and can even produce negative outcomes in the case of excessive use, (2) Internet use is but one of several factors which determine 'success' and does so only in certain situations and contexts, indicating that (3) non-use or weak use is not necessarily an indicator of social disadvantage or decreased quality of life, and that (4) certain Internet functions can be performed using alternative communication and information channels, which is why incorporating other communication and information channels into analyses could paint a substantially less extreme, and possibly less grave, picture of the digital divide. This critique does not, however, refute claims of the Internet's positive impact on participation or quality of life with a broad stroke. Such a refutation would only replace the construction of universal indispensability with an unsustainable construction of universal dispensability, which would scarcely hold up when pitted against the aforementioned evidence, including (1) findings revealing the Internet's significant role for respondents experiencing major life moments;[2] (2) attestations by Internet users of the Internet's positive impact on

---

[1] Gibson (2016)
[2] Horrigan and Rainie (2006).

---

their hobbies, work efficiency, knowledgeability and social life;[3] and (3) the reality that Internet use is an indispensable facet of certain segments of the labour force[4] (e.g., the IT sector, academia and public administration).

In Chapters 4 and 5, we witnessed the futility of resolving this incongruity using an interpretive framework that is inextricably tied to the assumptions critiqued therein. The heterogeneity of the findings generated by digital divide research and the unsustainability of the presented assumptions compel us to seek a more adequate interpretive framework to house existing findings on the digital divide. Context and indispensability, as guidelines for specifying these factors, have repeatedly cropped up in critical evaluations of the existing findings. We can then assume that if the Internet truly functions as a source of inequality, its use must be indispensable in a certain context in terms of securing exclusive access to resources or participation in society. The inability to (effectively) use this tool in such a context would hinder the attainment of the said resources and thus also the ability to fully participate in the given domain of life in the (given segment of) society.

6.1 Contexts and Networks

What, then, are the contexts which render ICT use an absolute necessity – that is, where does it serve as the demarcation between participation and exclusion, between the ability and inability to obtain or find information or complete an assigned task? It seems that answering this question would require abandoning the identified assumptions and existing analysis scales, which also means abandoning the notion of the digital divide as a population-wide issue (referring to national, regional or global populations).[5]

We can tentatively identify several basic levels of context here, defined based on their proximity to the observed situation or individual: social network, organizational and structural. On a social network level, the indispensability of ICT use is dependent upon the quality of the individual's social network (in terms of size, heterogeneity, number of bridging ties, share of users, etc.), which impacts the use value and quality of proxy use or, for users lacking digital skills, social support. A social network parameter that is worth mentioning separately is ICT-specific network capital, that is, the share of users or digital skills in a social network.

---

[3] Helsper et al. (2015); Hoffman et al. (2004); Lupač et al. (2015); Madden (2006). See also Section 5.2.

[4] Horrigan (2011, p. 22) referred to the (no longer available) 2010 analysis *The Economic Impact of Digital Exclusion* from the Digital Impact Group and Econsult Corporation, according to which 80% of the 500 most profitable US companies (according to *Fortune* magazine) offered their job applications exclusively online. Burning Glass Technologies (2015) stated that in the United States, two-thirds of new middle-skill jobs require a command of office or business software such as Oracle or SAP.

[5] This also brings us back to open-ended question C on p. 71 regarding the possibility of interpreting the digital divide using scales other than those which have dominated digital divide research.

Social networks should not be understood only as a set of informal contacts – formal social support, in the form of IT specialists and IT-savvy colleagues, plays a substantial role in corporate organizational structures. On an organizational level, indispensability is informed by the level of informatization in the organizations that the individual interacts with, and possibly also the pressure that such informatization puts on participating individuals, that is, the demand for certain digital skills in a given labour market segment, the digitization of schooling, online ticket sales, online appointment scheduling and electronic communication as the preferred method of bureaucratic institutions. Organizations may, however, even act as facilitators of the digital divide depending on whether they act as intermediaries for online services (in such fields as financial consulting and tourism) or retain multiple communication channels. On a structural level, we can consider influences which transcend individuals or particular organizations and are associated with population-wide effects of Internet diffusion. These include, for example, the impact of culture on user practices and the implications of Internet use, the impact of digitization on the labour market and price levels[6], and so on.

Based on this brief overview, we can infer two general aspects which impact the indispensability of Internet use across all levels of context.

The first aspect is the level of embeddedness[7] of a given ICT in social institutions and everyday routines.[8] This refers to the real process of certain communication infrastructures becoming more entrenched in social institutions, that is, the standard ways in which type X individuals perform type Y activities. An example of indispensability as conditioned by infrastructure is the informatization of such areas as journalism, science and certain labour market segments. Embeddedness as an indispensability factor does not necessarily have to extend to the entire institution or population – such indispensability can be strictly location-specific, such as when the use of one particular channel becomes routine in a particular social group or social setting. Higher embeddedness in a given setting turns Internet use into a social norm and a form of common sense, which may lead to the decreased use of other channels and thus also to non-users being excluded from communication.

The second general aspect thus stems from opening the purported correlation between social disadvantage and the indispensability of Internet use to include other alternatives. The level of disadvantage for non-users or weak users in a given context thus hinges upon (1) the availability of alternative information or communication channels (or tools), and (2) differences in the cost–outcome ratio when compared to Internet use (where ICT proficiency is also a factor).

If, for example, a bureaucratic institution issues an electronic version of an official form or offers the option to submit online, the individual's position as a disadvantaged citizen is contingent upon the possibility of obtaining or submitting the form via alternative means, such as directly at the institution, through an authorized individual, or at the post office. Another illustrative example is a case

---

[6] See e.g., Jensen (2007).
[7] This concept is inspired by its uses in Sassen (2006).
[8] Cf. Hoffman et al. (2004).

study on the impact of mobile phones on cloth-weaving microenterprises in Nigeria, where the relatively high cost of face-to-face communication (due to the physical demands of travelling) and mobile phone acquisition became a competitive disadvantage in the wake of the diffusion of mobile phones within these supply-chain networks – something which allowed for time- and cost-effective coordination and also meant that 'those without [access to – noted by PL] mobile phones were losing orders and income'[9]. This perspective can also provide a rationale for those who have little use for the Internet, such as alternative subcultures, manual workers and those in communities where the majority of communication is either direct or conducted over the phone and where Internet access is often available by way of proxy use (e.g., in the case of senior citizens). This, of course, would no longer hold true upon the arrival of an externally imposed necessity to communicate with no option other than online communication.

This leads us to consider what happens to the indispensability hypothesis when we read the Internet as a communication tool. The value that network communication technologies offer their users has been explained for over two decades using Metcalfe's Law, which is the application of the network effect in telecommunications. According to this law, the value of being connected to a communication network is proportional to the square of the number of its nodes (the value is derived from the number of possible combinations of the nodes in the network).[10] Those who are among the first Internet users in the world will reap only minimal benefits from its use. The more people connect to the Internet and the more information is made available online, however, the higher the use value for all involved. This law has understandably gained significant traction among programmers and those investing into such social networking platforms as Myspace, Facebook and LinkedIn; the founder of every new project in this sector must come to terms with the low initial added value for new users, a reality stemming from the low initial number of possible connections. We can follow a similar principle in the use of mobile networks, online gaming, text document formats and countless other examples.[11] In terms of a contextual approach to the digital divide, the most interesting aspect of Metcalfe's Law is its other side: What implications does the increasing number of users in a network have on its non-users? Let us consider a hypothetical example where e-mail begins to take traction in a society where communication had been conducted solely via landline telephones. The greater the number of people who switch from landline to e-mail, the higher the value of e-mail use and the more excluded telephone users will become in terms of communication. In such a hypothetical scenario, the last landline user will be relegated to complete social isolation with his/her defunct telephone device.

---

[9] Jagun, Heeks, and Whalley (2008, p. 60).

[10] In relation to the digital divide, see, e.g., O'Hara and Stevens (2006, pp. 38–40).

[11] Similar concepts include positive network externality and critical mass. Metcalfe's Law is a specific modification of these two in that it focuses exclusively on intranetwork added value (positive network externalities are not restricted) and does not place much emphasis on the threshold which, once exceeded, results in accelerated diffusion (as is the case in the concept of critical mass). See Rogers (2003) for more details.

Note that the rate of exclusion for non-users is determined here, in addition to the ratio of telephone and e-mail communication network sizes, by the extent to which e-mail is used as a replacement rather than supplemental communication technology (for such reasons as time and money constraints). In addition, due to economies of scale, the cost of participation in a network decreases as the number of users increases, meaning that the user of a marginalized communication device will be at a disadvantage due to rising communication costs. The level of disadvantage can then be ascertained using the impact of the interaction between the ratio of differences in communication network sizes and differences in communication costs when using alternative communication channels.

The flip side of Metcalfe's Law was modelled in a notable study of the same name by Rahul Tongia and Ernest Wilson.[12] According to these authors, when considering the population as a whole, participation in a new communication network is associated with the comparative benefit of lower communication costs only up to a certain optimal point, beyond which the disadvantages for non-users increase exponentially faster than the added use value for new users. This point is purported to be somewhere around the 50% mark, which resonates with the DOI model, where once the 50% diffusion threshold has been exceeded, the use of an innovation starts to become a social norm, making non-users increasingly more likely to adopt it due to external pressure.[13] The authors also note that the current application of Metcalfe's Law places too much emphasis on the expansion of a communication network as catalysing an increase in value for the user population,[14] disregarding the repercussions of rising costs, which impact the entire population due to the concomitant formation of an excluded subpopulation. As an example, they cite the high costs borne by the US healthcare system due to the uninsured segment of the population and the security costs for the majority of computer users with more advanced operating systems stemming from decreased security support for older systems, which renders the entire computer network vulnerable. Similarly, the rising number of high-speed Internet users leads to increasing demand for fast website connection speeds, which decreases the value of Internet use for those lagging behind with slower (e.g., dial-up) connections. According to the authors, the flip side of Metcalfe's Law is also present in non-network technologies due to secondary or complementary effects catalysed by the formation of associated network infrastructures. For example, the rising number of cars leads to an increase in investments in road infrastructure and supermarket chains, which in turn cuts costs for car owners due to economies of scale. I would only add that after a certain point, investments into alternative forms of transportation, such as public transport infrastructure, cycling trails and pedestrian crossings, become less profitable, leaving non-drivers at a growing disadvantage.

---

[12] Tongia and Wilson (2011).

[13] Brown and Venkatesh (2003); Rogers (2003).

[14] See, e.g., the assumption of a universal positive impact. This limitation also applies to the concept of critical mass, cf., e.g., Markus (1987).

What implications does the flip side of Metcalfe's Law then have for our understanding of the digital divide?

The flip side of Metcalfe's Law corroborates the idea that the validity of the digital divide thesis is directly proportional to the indispensability of ICT use in a given social setting, that is, that it is directly proportional to both the proliferation of the observed ICT and the extent to which the said ICT cannot be replaced by alternative communication mediums. This suggests that the digital divide poses the greatest threat – and places the greatest pressure on the remaining non-users to connect – in the most highly connected subpopulations in which ICT is the exclusive work tool or communication channel (in accordance with DOI and the conclusions made in Section 5.2). Greater indispensability of Internet use in settings with higher ICT embeddedness is perceptible when observing the distribution of declared indispensability in the domains of economic life and sociability: greater indispensability of Internet use for maintaining the user's social life was recorded for younger age groups, and the indispensability of Internet use for performing work-related tasks was recorded as higher among those with higher educational attainment, who occupy labour market segments with intensive ICT use.[15] An example is the highly connected population of students, with an Internet penetration rate in excess of 90% in economically developed countries. If, for example, 9 out of 10 students in a class use Facebook for chatting and planning leisure activities, the remaining student can face exclusion from a number of group activities if the content being communicated via Facebook is not relayed in person or by mobile phone. This illustrates just how essential it is to maintain parallel communication or information networks in order to preserve social cohesion (or, inversely, to prevent social exclusion).

The more ICT becomes an *exclusive* communication and information infrastructure, the more of a disadvantage this poses for non-users and weak users.[16] This paradox of the digital divide bears significant implications for information policies, future digital divide research and the information society theory. The information policies based on the principle of 'total inclusion' that have been promoted in digital divide research (with only minor exceptions[17]) do not aid in

---

[15] Lupač et al. (2015).

[16] This is explicitly mentioned in Loges and Jung (2001, p. 559), Valentine et al. (2002, p. 298) and Livingstone and Helsper (2007, p. 692). However, these authors, akin to those explicitly reacting to Tongia and Wilson's study, maintained the assumptions of the digital divide thesis (primarily a pro-innovation bias, universal indispensability and universal impact) and fail to consider the implications that this paradox poses for the digital divide itself, information policies and the social role of academic digital divide discourse. Horrigan (2011, p. 29) therefore repeatedly espoused the need to tackle the digital divide using a combination of availability and attractiveness and the promotion of digital skills, while Donna Hoffman (2012) spoke of 'the Internet's inexorable march toward ubiquity' (p. 193), presenting Internet use as a mechanism for increasing one's social capital and personal fulfilment and automatically regarding the failure to engage in online communication as a catalyst for social disadvantage.

[17] For example, Reddick et al. (2000) advocated for the necessity to maintain parallel information and communication channels.

thwarting the digital divide, but may instead prove instrumental in catalysing its formation.

Functional policies for bridging or circumventing the digital divide should not limit their focus to the support of Internet diffusion and the universal promotion of digital literacy; they should also consider the context-dependent nature of the digital divide, including repercussions arising from alternative channels that have been made defunct or less viable. Strategies aimed at promoting digital skills with a more context-sensitive approach should then be rooted in approaches, measures and educational opportunities that focus on the development of logically related sets of digital skills and their relevance for the target individual or group and, at the same time, promote the strategic use value of these skills in solving problems in everyday private or professional life. Such policies require a context-sensitive analysis of the necessity and indispensability of possessing digital skills for the target population (e.g., specific labour market segments).

Additionally, functional policies for bridging the digital divide should focus on (i) monitoring the availability of alternative communication and information channels (including support for social cohesion), and (ii) the regulation of gaps in communication costs associated with the use of alternative communication and information channels. Attention should also be paid to the creation and maintenance of adequate 'translation' mechanisms for those on the cusp between user and non-user, that is, mechanisms which would secure the flow of information and communication across different communication networks, such as by promoting the tailored institutionalization of delegated or assisted access.[18]

Surprisingly, although maintaining parallel communication channels is, in varying forms and to various degrees of 'discrimination' towards non-users, a part of official administrative practices, general propositions for ameliorating the digital divide put forth in academic research typically gloss over this issue and instead advocate for a sweeping increase in informatization.

6.2. Contextualizing the (Research on the) Digital Divide

The mechanism of the digital divide paradox is not so striking in itself, as it may by now seem obvious and relatively easily inferable. What is striking here is the fact that, despite continually emerging criticism of certain assumptions as well as the possibility of approaching the data from different angles (e.g., recognizing the response 'I don't need it' as a rational act) and numerous other indications, digital divide research has largely clung to a singular interpretation, employing virtually the same logic used to legitimize informatization in the political, investment and media spheres which has been permeating the public arena since the 1970s.

---

[18] An explicit formulation of this requirement as a problem-solving tool, based on an analysis of small economic players in developing countries, can be found in, e.g., Duncombe and Heeks (2002). Britain's "Assisted digital support" initiative can serve as an example of good practice (see https://www.gov.uk/service-manual/helping-people-to-use-your-service).

One may possibly find cause for alarm in this book's treatment of digital divide research as a monolithic whole, where the search for truth takes the shape of a formulaic effort to uphold the validity of the digital divide thesis using the identified set of assumptions. Such an assessment is unfortunately not so far removed from the truth – something which becomes apparent after examining the digital divide research presented in this book (one of the more prominent approaches we have not yet touched upon is a discursive analysis of digital divide research, which is presented below). Given the volume of statements being generated on this issue, the amount of criticism of the digital divide thesis is negligible, and noteworthy studies examining the validity of key parts of the core argument (the backbone of the entire research tradition) have only begun to surface over the past decade, that is, ex post. This is well evidenced by the fact that a short-lived critique that came to light over 15 years ago (see Section 4.2) did not pave the way for any noteworthy schools of thought or research traditions with an alternative approach in defiance of the mainstream assumptions (the binary and multidimensional conceptions of the digital divide are both part of the same research tradition).[19] What is then behind the constant reproduction of the assumptions circling around the digital divide thesis and the resulting rigidity with which research questions are approached? And what can then be said about the critical function of the social sciences?

In order to answer these questions, we must 'disengage' from digital divide research and approach it as a particular set of social practices generating knowledge in a broader social context.

The first explanation can be found in the shared qualities of digital divide researchers. This hypothesis is based on the notion that researchers constantly experience the high added value and required effective use of ICT first-hand in their professional and personal lives due to the high level of innovativeness and ICT embeddedness in their everyday routines. Other relevant qualities associated with reaping the high added value of ICT use include increased social engagement, knowledgeability, sociability and geographic mobility. In a context-based understanding of the digital divide, it can be said that digital divide researchers truly live in information society settings. This experience is then reaffirmed in interactions with habitually similar individuals and serves as the source of an intersubjective consensus about the positive universal transformation of everyday life. The resulting viewpoint is unconsciously projected onto the entire population and is legitimized by way of specifically crafted, technical diction. We could then infer, with a grain of salt, that when the homogeneity of the social environment is disrupted (e.g., when researchers are working on qualitative studies examining purportedly disadvantaged segments of the population), the scientific discourse finds itself confronted with findings that prove incompatible with the digital divide thesis (findings on proxy use and the rationality of non-use or weak use have entered the debate primarily via qualitative studies). However, limiting ourselves to this explanation would mean undermining the intellectual faculties

---

[19] Cf. Yu (2006).

and heterogeneity of researchers' social environments while simultaneously over-valuing the impact of the everyday on research efforts.

We can turn to Rogers for inspiration regarding the second explanation, as he partially attributed the pro-innovation and individual-blame bias tendencies of DOI researchers to the bias of the given study's sponsor.[20] Sponsorship bias does not, however, seem to serve as a satisfactory explanation for studies conducted by authors from all over the world and a wide range of institutions, predominantly universities. A less conspiratorial and more likely explanation is the impact of influences which exceed the scope of bureaucratic and direct institutional influence, influences which permeate the scientific community, and which are defined by a shared presumption of the social relevance of unequal ICT diffusion.

The influences at play within the scientific community can be defined as internal or external. Internal influences arise out of shared scientific practices, while external influences, which preserve certain areas of problematization and interpretation methods, primarily comprise the theoretical framework housing the associated assumptions (i.e., the information society theory) and information policies, which serve as a referential framework for establishing the social relevance of the issues studied in digital divide research.

An endogenous explanation for the scientific community's inertia can be found using the most widely known conception of the term 'paradigm', elaborated by Thomas Kuhn in his book *The Structure of Scientific Revolutions.*[21] While Kuhn himself did not view the concept of paradigms as relevant to all social sciences (e.g., sociology), it was later applied to different 'research traditions', comparable to digital divide research. In what way can digital divide research be read through the lens of a paradigm? Digital divide research is rooted in the generally accepted model of a causal relationship between ICT use and participation in society (the digital divide thesis) in which the core of the thesis is not problematized but rather further elaborated and empirically validated (see Chapter 4). This initial model is associated with a coherent set of assumptions, specific optics, a limited field of problematization (see pp. 91–94 and Chapter 5), a certain method of data interpretation, and a relatively small number of frequently cited key studies[22] and key figures associated with significant shifts in digital divide research. Incompatible findings or interpretations pose no threat to the paradigm as they offer no alternative interpretations of the problem addressed by the original model and thus provide no new answers to the initial question of the relationship between social inequality and ICT use. They also receive scant attention in digital divide research as they fail to respect the 'rules of the game' dictated by the stock of knowledge produced within the paradigm's framework and the theory based on research

---

[20] Rogers (2003, pp. 122–125).

[21] Kuhn (1970).

[22] The foundational and still most frequently referenced studies are the NTIA reports initiated by the Clinton administration. Warschauer (2003) described them as 'the most authoritative studies on the issue to date' (p. 54). Burgeoning academic discourse effectively glosses over similarly oriented digital divide research from the Unites States, Sweden, Norway and Canada (see chapter 4, footnote 9) and makes no effort to remedy this oversight.

furnished by the initial model. Special attention is, however, paid to groups of 'digital divide refuters' and 'physical access reductionists', with this attention typically serving to establish the relevance of research questions (see p. 91–94). The sense of disconnect exhibited by the paradigm can be partially explained by the low level of interaction between digital divide research and neighbouring research traditions (e.g., DOI and knowledge gap research) as well as the systematic overlooking of ICT access gaps as articulated in critiques of the information society theory.[23] Why, then, in the context of the social sciences, home to a multiplicity of theoretical perspectives and common sense criticism, has there been no sign of an alternative interpretive framework for the correlation between ICT and social inequality in which the assumptions presented in the Chapter 5 do not play such a (determining) role? If we decide against sweeping this issue under the rug and chalking the whole problem up to the short span of the entire research tradition, we must examine the external factors responsible for the rigidity of digital divide research.

The digital divide is not only a rewarding subject for researchers studying the changing structure of ICT access gaps, it is also a powerful legitimizing trope, reflected all around the world in the form of hefty private and government investments in the order of billions of (US) dollars.[24] These investments require a certain legal, economic and *symbolic* framework, implemented with the aid of corporate and government information policies.[25] In order to better grasp the relationship between the inertia of digital divide research and this framework, we shall employ the concept of ideology. Here, ideology is not intended in the Marxist sense, that is, as the temporary pathological product of a small powerful group masking the relationships from which its power stems. The term 'ideology' is employed here in its later understanding as a certain set of beliefs and ideas based on a mix of false and true assumptions, reflecting certain interests, and legitimizing the (power) positions of institutions associated with the development, operation and use of ICT infrastructures.

Ideology in this sense is thus not a purely negative force and does not need to be exerted by way of coercion and suppression but rather via the distortion, identification and/or formation of needs and desires.[26] The tool traditionally used in the social sciences when analysing the ideological aspect of socio-scientific theory is the reconstruction of its implicit normativity. The normativity inherent in the espousal of the digital divide thesis can be detected relatively easily by identifying the desired state of future development based on the assumptions characteristic of digital divide research.

If we were to maintain the validity of the presupposed universal indispensability of ICT use, the call to bridge the digital divide would then boil down to the

---

[23] For example, Roszak (1994); Schiller (1996); Webster (1995, 2002, 2006).

[24] Graham (2011).

[25] In general terms, see Sassen (2006), specifically regarding investments into mitigating the digital divide, see below.

[26] Cf. different concepts of ideology as presented by Freeden (2003).

project of implementing a fully informatized society in which every individual would own ICT and devote sufficient time to ICT use, accruing new digital skills and staying informed about the latest ICT innovations (cf. Section 4.5). The individual-blame bias and the call to bridge the digital divide via continuing efforts to informatize the population imply an individual-oriented understanding of the project: intensive and experienced users are, in the eyes of digital divide research, the desirable norm, while non-users are assessed as dysfunctional, disadvantaged deviations.[27] On a global scale, the normativity of the digital divide is reflected in the ranking of a country's progress based on its degree of informatization and in recommendations for development that adopt a global version of the digital divide thesis.

A group of researchers from the University of Waikato in New Zealand conducted a narrative analysis of interviews with unconnected senior citizens, illuminating how older non-users interpret their situation through optics rooted in a normativity that has proved to be out of sync with their everyday life, experiences and needs.[28] The disparity between the everyday lives of these seniors and their narrative of the indispensability of ICT use beautifully illustrates the imaginary relationship between an individual and the actual conditions of his/her existence, that is, the product of ideology as reflected in the individual's interpretation of himself/herself in the world. This narrative, combining elements of unmet Internet needs, disadvantages and stagnation in non-users, can thus be seen as part of a broader ideological sphere of influence of which digital divide research is also a part. Here, the advanced user is seen as a cultural paragon, a pragmatic source of inspiration for the rest of the population.[29] If the benefits of use were not context-specific, this type of influence would appear generally favourable. As it is not rooted in valid and value-neutral assumptions, however, the effort to informatize the entire population can be seen as an ideologically framed act, one which is part of the current system of social inequality at play. Such a sphere of influence does not refer to the propagation of a specific, for example, American, culture, but to the proliferation of practices related to ICT use, which, in a very specific manner, transform the cultural behavioural patterns associated with communication and the social distribution of knowledge, as demonstrated, for example, by Inge Kral in an ethnographic study on changes related to the proliferation of ICT in Indigenous Australian communities.[30]

The discovery that digital divide research bears the signs of a broader, clearly ideological scope of influence allows us to make room for findings from discursive analyses of political statements and documents on the relationship between informatization and social development. These analyses can be divided into two larger groups:

---

[27] Selwyn (2003, 2006) made similar observations regarding normativity, as did Sims (2013).

[28] Weaver et al. (2010).

[29] This perspective was also shared by Dervin (2003) and appeared later in a critical analysis of children's Internet use by Boonaert and Vettenburg (2011).

[30] Kral (2014).

The first group of analyses, spearheaded by Lynette Kvasny, turns its focus towards national or local political discourse on the digital divide in the United States, subsequent implementation measures via specific informatization programmes, their reception and cultural barriers for the socially marginalized.[31] The authors of these studies seek solutions to the digital divide primarily in adapting informatization programmes to meet the needs of the socially marginalized and expanding the scope of these programmes beyond the binary division of users/ non-users (in keeping with the logic presented in Chapter 4). Their aim is thus to shed light on the flawed parts of the discourse in order to outline an effective roadmap towards digital inclusion which is in line with the digital divide thesis. Although it is a discursive analysis which delves into such aspects as the language of information policies as a form of symbolic violence and which allies itself with the tradition of critical discourse analysis,[32] it does not exceed the scope of problematization arising from the acceptance of the assumptions which form the building blocks of unequal informatization discourse.

The second, more prominent and thematically expansive group consists of analyses of political statements and documents framing unequal informatization with the issue of uneven global development.[33] These analyses provide a perspective which can scarcely be found in mainstream digital divide research. These studies support the hypothesis that political discourse on global informatization is rooted in the very same or similar assumptions that have been identified in digital divide research: technical development by way of informatization is perceived as an unstoppable force penetrating all aspects of social life, where resistance means facing adversity and stagnation; informatization is not viewed as a partially political or cultural project, as ICT's positive impact on development is perceived as an inherent feature of technology; and the category of the information poor is defined by reducing information access to Internet access, thereby devaluing local knowledge and other communication and information systems. There is a tendency here to individualize the benefits of and responsibility for use, accompanied by the prevailing premise that the information society is a new stage of historical development into which society can leapfrog without having to first go through the 'lower' stages of development.[34]

---

[31] Kvasny (2005); Kvasny and Trauth (2003); Kvasny and Truex (2001); Tapia, Kvasny, and Ortiz (2011).

[32] Critical discourse analysis treats texts as constituent elements of social practice, see, e.g., Fairclough (2003). According to Bourdieu (2001), the concept of symbolic violence refers to the mechanism of maintaining an unequal relationship in that the dominated subject only has access to the same tools of perception as the dominator, making the relationship appear natural to the dominated subject.

[33] Carpentier (2003), Hwang (2006), Thompson (2004) and Wilson (2002) focused on documents from prominent international institutions and statements made by their proponents; Chigona, Pollock, and Roode (2010) and Moodley (2005) analysed government documents and statements made by African politicians; Stevenson (2009) analysed US government documents.

[34] Chigona et al. (2010); Hwang (2006), Leye (2007); Moodley (2005); Stevenson (2009); Thompson (2004); Wilson et al. (2003).

Such a framing of informatization has become emblematic of modernization: the terms 'informatization' and 'modernization' are virtually interchangeable in political proclamations, strategic documents and political speeches. When compared to the treatment of technological innovations in twentieth century discourse on development, the present political approach to informatization takes the form of a new strategy: a long-term cultural process where the problem of social development is reduced to technological and economic solutions.[35] Which label will be next once the discursive power of the 'information society' fades away?

This modern-informational connection impedes efforts to integrate local knowledge and features and the needs of the local population into local political development. What we continue to see instead are international advisors and experts from national and global bureaucratic institutions carrying briefcases with instruction manuals for progress which cannot be realized using local resources.[36] This creates a new layer of technological dependence, contributing to the global system of inequality (those IT industry segments with the highest added value are localized in the most economically developed countries). The concepts 'digital divide' and 'information society' thus need to be recognized as providing IT companies with great opportunities to create and capitalize on new markets. It is of no surprise that there is such a striking parallel between the arenas of private business and politics with initiatives under the motto 'we are closing the digital divide' and private philanthropists such as Google, Microsoft and Facebook who pay 'out of pocket' for the informatization of the 'underdeveloped' and 'information poor'.[37] The convenient by-product of such efforts is the creation of new markets for their products, a cultivated dependence on these products and the establishment of license-only software as a local norm due to the network effect.

In this regard, it seems to be no coincidence that deregulation measures have been at the forefront of information policies and that informatization has gone hand in hand with economic neoliberalism in terms of specific political practices.[38] For example, the creation of a 'unified digital market', 'the deregulation of the telecommunications market' and 'the eradication of trade barriers' are to this day the main pillars of European information policies.[39] Depolitization and the pretence of universal interest then secure information society discourse as an unavoidable apolitical process, yielding benefits for all, as do subversive discursive strategies, such as the use of the pronoun 'we' when endeavouring to subtly persuade the reader that we all live in the 'Internet galaxy'.[40]

The concept of the digital divide has been used as a new source of legitimacy, both by major global institutions (the UN, ITU, World Bank, OECD) during their strategic shifts in focus[41] and on a national level. Let us not forget that research on

---

[35] Hwang (2006); Leye (2007); Moodley (2005); Wilson (2002).

[36] See, e.g., Steeves and Kwami (2017).

[37] De Miranda (2009); Leye (2007); Stevenson (2009).

[38] De Miranda (2009); Leye (2007); Hwang (2006); Stevenson (2009).

[39] See European Committee (2010).

[40] Hwang (2006); cf. the use of 'we' in Castells (2001a) and Fuchs (2008).

[41] Thompson (2004).

unequal informatization has been closely interwoven with national interests and information policies from the very outset – in the United States, where the first reports on the digital divide served as support for Clinton and Gore's National Information Infrastructure programme; in the formulation of a specific theory of informatization and its measurement in the context of governmental institutions in Japan (see p. 14–15); and in the European Union and its sophisticated system of feedback between informatization research and the articulation of initiatives as a part of 10-year informatization plans. The use of the digital divide as a source of legitimization for the state apparatus has been elucidated in *Digital divide: A discursive move away from the real inequities* by Siobhan Stevenson, who adopted the dual state theory elaborated at the beginning of the 1970s by economist James O'Connor. According to O'Connor, the state must always fulfil two opposing functions simultaneously:

> On the one hand, the state must create an environment conducive to capital accumulation. On the other hand, it must also create or be perceived to be creating policies and programmes that address the social needs and welfare of the population as citizens, workers, and consumers.[42]

Stevenson employed this theory in order to illustrate how the American administration managed to use the digital divide trope to simultaneously promote the development of the IT industry and legitimize the state as a facilitator of the transition into the Information Age. The notions of a general interest in bridging the digital divide and of informatization as an unavoidable, strictly technological (i.e., apolitical, culturally non-specific) process are then subverted by the interests of a particular set of players, such as the IT industry, financial markets and population segments in which Internet use has become indispensable.[43]

The purpose of this critique, within the context of the present work, is not to paint informatization as a partial, ill-conceived process, as this would not even be possible in light of the conducted analysis. In terms of research on unequal Internet access, the added value lies in the perspective that the research objectives of certain studies have proved to be of a more institutional nature, pertaining more to the R&D departments of the respective corporations. A failure to clearly demarcate the line between interests associated with intensifying ICT use and scientific interests can pose a problem once these objectives start being postulated as generally favourable and generally applicable (cf. the issue of defining communication skills

---

[42] Stevenson (2009, p. 3), adopted from O'Connor, J. (1973). *The Fiscal Crisis of the State.* New York, NY: St. Martin's Press, and Harris, M. H., Hannah, S. A., and Harris, P. C. (1998). *Into the Future: The Foundations of Library and Information Services in the Post-Industrial Era* (2nd ed.). Greenwich, Conn.: Ablex.

[43] A similar conclusion was also reached by Garnham (2000, 2004), although he inferred the ideological aspect of information society theory through its disconnect from reality.

on p. 107). A prime example can be found in studies using the socio-demographic distribution of Facebook use as an indicator of the digital divide.[44]

Digital divide research, the information society theory and information policies could then also be analysed as ideological tools for maintaining hegemony[45] rooted in the creation, maintenance and masking of a relatively stable system of mutual interests associated with the proliferation of the technological infrastructure of ICT.

However, striving to understand the relationship between informatization and social inequality would be a dead end if we were to interpret this correlation through the optics of restriction, masking and the negative influence of groups with specific power-based interests. The rigid use of assumptions in the face of available counterarguments and empirical evidence indicates that the scientific practices of digital divide research should instead be read as an attempt at establishing a certain type of truth, the manifestation of a discourse which intentionally produces a specific, limited scope of knowledge.[46]

This intentionality is also perceptible in the majority of the aforementioned discursive analyses, which, in keeping with an ICT-centric standpoint, offer up such solutions as supporting the open-source software movement;[47] shifting the focus from creating passive ICT consumers to promoting the active, creative use of ICT;[48] and adapting ICT to the needs and issues of local inhabitants.[49] The ICT-development connection thus does not furnish us with solutions outside the technological progressivism framework, with the only alternative being backwardness and social decline. We can only exceed the scope of this framework by refuting the all-or-nothing logic inherent in the assumptions outlined in Chapter 5.

This last layer in explaining the inertia of digital divide research thus hinges upon the broader institutional setting: the boundaries which inform digital divide research are kept intact by this institutionalized imperative, which results in the disassociation from a politically shaped (and at times overlooked) and specifically articulated problem. Researchers of unequal informatization are thus relegated to seeking solutions to serious and long-standing social issues within the confines of these imposed boundaries.

---

[44] Cf. Wentrup, Ström, and Nakamura (2016).

[45] The concept of hegemony, elaborated by Gramsci, emphasizes the influence of ideology in the domain of common sense, where culture plays a significant role. The unproblematic reading of hegemony is attributed to its treatment as a seemingly natural occurrence.

[46] According to Foucault (1981), the will to know is the first of the three basic 'systems of exclusion' which societies lay out to prevent uncontrolled, unabashed speech. This 'prodigious machinery designed to exclude' is a coercive disposition (i.e., a specific set of ties between power and knowledge which produces coercive effects), which does not operate based on the principles of prohibition, taboo or rejection, but rather through the constant incitement to speak about an object which is systematically formed by a set of statements forming the discourse.

[47] Leye (2007); Stevenson (2009).

[48] Carpentier (2003).

[49] Chigona et al. (2010); Hwang (2006, pp. 190–197); Moodley (2005, p. 241).

Chapter 7

Conclusion: Towards a New Theory of Information Society

> The irony of this *dispositif* lies in having us believe that it shall lead to our 'liberation'.[1]
>
> Michel Foucault

There is still one big question which remains unanswered: What role has the information society theory played in the informatization process, that is, how can we assess the latest theory of the information society in light of the presented findings with regard to its validity and performative[2] function?

The first issue which problematizes the sustainability of Castells' theory of the information society is its totalizing nature, which paints a picture of the digital divide as a sweeping societal issue which can only be remedied via total informatization. American post-structuralist Mark Poster, in his critique of Bell's theory of post-industrial society, claimed, 'General theory becomes totalizing when it claims to include within its field all social phenomena, or the "essence" of society, in sum, when it marginalizes those perspectives or experiences that are not within its domain.'[3] Such a totalizing tendency is, however, more of a general issue when forming any theory of society rather than one characteristic of Castells' theory specifically. Castells' theory of society has several points which lend a totalizing tendency to his system as a whole, which are problematized due to the occasional presence of contradictory statements. Let us consider three such points. First, with regard to the notion that technology permeates all three levels of the social structure, Castells posits that ICT affects all life in society (see pp. 27–28) and is thus

---

[1] Foucault (1976, p. 211), transl. PL. The term *'dispositif'* is used by Foucault to indicate a specific configuration of knowledge and power.

[2] The term 'performativity' refers to the power of language to act upon social reality.

[3] Poster (1990, p. 22). Castells' totalizing tendency is also mentioned in Garnham (2004, p. 168), though he elaborates on the problematic validity of a selection of Castells' concepts and arguments and not the totalizing source in Castells' theory of society. I address these sources later in this chapter.

Beyond the Digital Divide: Contextualizing the Information Society, 175–180
Copyright © Petr Lupač
All rights of reproduction in any form reserved
doi:10.1108/978-1-78756-547-020181011

the 'fabric of our lives'.[4] Second, out of keeping with his own theoretical system, Castells often reduces human agency to communication ('communication is the essence of human activity'[5]) and in certain passages devalues alternative communication channels by restricting communication options to communication via ICT, or rather the Internet.[6] It is then of no surprise that he uses this reductionist logic to infer that 'all domains of social life are being modified by the pervasive uses of the Internet'[7] or that economic survival is contingent upon connecting to global networks with an Internet infrastructure.[8] Third, positing information as the prevailing source of productivity growth in an informational society is associated with an orientation towards high-tech, expert knowledge-based global networks of production and distribution as the ultimate opportunities for economic prosperity. This leads to downplaying the economic (and therefore also the human and cultural) role of microenterprises and low-tech industries in the economy.[9] If the technological and economic definition carries the most weight in Castells' information society theory, does this impede upon the context-specific understanding of the effects of ICT and the validity of the entire subsequently constructed argumentation?

As we have seen in Chapter 6, it would be erroneous to interpret the digital divide as a temporary deviation in the development of a social order in which access to the ICT infrastructure is a precondition for participation in society: the digital divide is a structural feature of the informational society. The notion that the deepening of the digital divide has increased 'the gap between the promise of the Information Age and its bleak reality for many people around the world'[10] is therefore a false one: 'the promise of the Information Age' has already produced this bleak reality through its realization. Let us not forget that in a context-based approach to the digital divide, the information society theory is not a universally valid one: the validity of claims such as 'the centrality of the Internet', 'information as the main source of productivity', and the Internet being 'the fabric of our lives' is compelling only in certain socio-technical configurations (i.e., in certain fixed sets of relationships between people and the material environments they have constructed) which are well in line with information society theory, while in other configurations such claims can legitimately be interpreted as ideological manifestations, out of line with the real conditions of social existence. The information society theory thus totalizes certain features of contemporary society, despite occasional reminders calling attention to the endurance of older forms of social organization. Castells later moved away from the totalizing tendency

---

[4] Castells (2001b, p. 2).

[5] Castells (2001b, p. 275).

[6] Cf. Castells (2000b, Chapter 5) and Castells (2001b, Chapter 7).

[7] Castells (2001b, p. 275).

[8] Upon examining the situation in Africa, Castells (1998) reached the conclusion in *End of Millennium* that the only alternative is self-modernization, which must be accompanied by some form of 'de-linking of Africa in its own terms' (p. 128). He saw this scenario as highly unlikely, however, as it would necessitate a revolution in its deep, structural meaning.

[9] See Hirsch-Kreinsen, Jacobson, and Robertson (2006) for a more detailed argument.

[10] Castells (2001b, p. 274).

attached to the term 'information society' by shifting his focus to the 'network society', but this concept is also loaded with totalizing tendencies in the assumption of a universal network and the indispensability of connecting to the ICT infrastructure.[11] Such a reading naturally leads us to the unoriginal but necessary warning against applying theoretical constructions to all facets of social life with a broad stroke. What is more interesting on a scientific scale is the potential of this perspective when considering the validity of social theory as hinging upon certain socio-technical contexts.

It may be of use here to compare Castells' earlier and later works. Earlier Castells focuses on the issue of relationships which exceed the scope of the dominant system (capitalism) and the conflicting relationships that constitute it (e.g., when analysing the capitalization of economies in the context of economic colonization), which effectually confines this system to a limited applicability for identified correlations and causalities. Some of his research methods and findings could then successfully be translated into contextual analyses of social inequality under the conditions of informatization. Such a basic analogy sheds light on the futility of thinking in the binary terms of informational/industrial, an analysis of global informatization as another layer in the system of global dependency, and an interpretation of marginalization as the product of information policies (cf. Chapter 3). Later Castells, in contrast, treated this system (informational capitalism) as the point of departure for his analysis and posited it as a global totality of relationships from which 'there is no escape' (which is, inter alia, out of line with the concept of technological relations as relatively autonomous from the system of production relations). The relationships that remain concealed, then, are those teetering on the brink of this system or those operating in contexts where the system has but limited validity, such as local systems of low-tech production and exchange independent of the global system of production or the option to engage in social participation via alternative communication channels. This is precisely why this system can only be contradicted using its own internal inconsistencies and uneven development and why later Castells sees no other way out than the use of the network logic – and therefore the ICT infrastructure – of the dominant parts of this system. The development of Castells' theory can then be described as a successful escape from the trap of urban endogeneity[12] followed by a plunge into the trap of informatization endogeneity.

If a reworking of the current information society theory were in order, we would have to problematize its universal applicability in all contexts. A contextual approach to the digital divide paves the way for an analysis of informatization as a socially formed process, one 'coming into fruition' as a result of certain debatable decisions and partial power-based influences, and thus not one where the digital divide functions as a present or inevitable future 'state' of society, dissolvable by way of political measures espousing the total informatization of society.

---

[11] See, e.g., Castells (2004a).

[12] The term 'endogeneity trap' was used by Saskia Sassen (2006, p. 4) when explaining the origin and workings of a given phenomenon based only on an analysis of its prototypical traits.

Such a perspective requires a focus on the process of the social formation of ICT as a socio-technical infrastructure, this infrastructure's interaction with what we perceive to be the social structure, and an analysis of the role of the social sciences, based on the presumed necessity of its general applicability. We can find fruitful sources of inspiration here in critical discursive analyses, studies by Saskia Sassen on the embeddedness of the ICT infrastructure in non-digital contexts,[13] and the discussion in *Science and technology studies* on the seamless interweaving of technology and society (hence the term 'socio-technology') and social structures made durable via technological means.[14]

The social responsibility of sociologists and their contribution to the self-production of society is not a novel issue, though its currently pressing nature stems both from the critical role of sociologists in the context of growing societal reflexivity[15] and from the identified legitimizing, ideological function of sociology in the informatization process. A related question, and one which has not yet been answered, is which qualities of sociological texts (covering the sociological theory of social change) resonate with the lay public and thus constitute a part of public discourse and interpretations of reality, thereby contributing to the self-production of society.

We can find several examples in the development of post-industrial or information society. We know, for example, that an analysis by Radovan Richta in *Civilization at the crossroads*[16] played a significant role in political discussions on the socio-technical reconstruction of the socialist system (which is why he had to retract it after the Soviet invasion of Czechoslovakia). Daniel Bell was an active player in official American prognostics, which had the ideological function of rationalizing American technological development as a progressive path towards a new type of society.[17] Bell's thesis on post-industrial society resonated with the Regan administration and the 'Atari Democrats' (Al Gore, Tim Wirth and Gary Hart) as it seemed to provide a scientifically grounded path towards bolstering the American system, which had been weakened by the oil crisis of the 1970s.[18] In a similar vein, European digital divide researchers have laid down the groundwork for European Union activities geared towards a 'digital society for all'. None of these practices paint a picture of scientists sitting atop ivory towers, removed from the social dynamics of the societies they study, even if that is their intention. Similarly, Castells' expertise has not been relegated to the arena of scientific conferences and his purported intention to not put forth any specific

---

[13] For example, Sassen (2002b, 2006).

[14] Bijker, Hughes, and Pinch (1987), Bijker and Law (1992).

[15] David Lyon (2000) employed this argument in response to the absence of an explicit stance towards the studied object in Castells. Similarly, also Elliott (1980) and Waterman (1999).

[16] Richta (1969).

[17] Bell (1999, p. xxvii); Barbrook (2007).

[18] Stevenson (2009, p. 80), also with reference to Harris, M. H., Hannah, S. A., and Harris, P. C. (1998). *Into the Future: The Foundations of Library and Information Services in the Post-Industrial Era* (2nd ed.). Greenwich, Conn: Ablex Pub.

recommendations for future development (see p. 19) is a stark contrast to the declared necessity to acquiesce to global informational capitalism, as advocated by Castells himself during his time as an advisor to the United Nations, Russia, and the European Union and in consultations with high-ranking officials and politicians.[19] Aldeno stated that Castells 'warned South African President Thabo Mbeki that Africa's failure to adapt to the needs of the increasingly networked environment of states, regions and firms meant that it risked being "deleted" from the future world system'[20]. Castells' work became, as in the case of Daniel Bell, a bestseller, read (or at the very least discussed) far beyond the realm of academia.[21] This has resulted in something which can be described as a distinction between the physical Castells and Castells the imaginary. While analyses of the former prove as contradictory as reality itself, explicitly pointing to the ideological and power-based facets behind the formation of a singular version of the information society,[22] Castells the imaginary, embodied in popular interpretations of his work, serves as a testament to the pervasive impact of the Internet and the inexorable logic of history catapulting us into the Information Age. It seems that the latter has wielded the most vital influence.[23]

If information society theory is not to be historically relegated to being merely a symbolic construct, though its historic role has already been fulfilled, it will be of utmost importance to elaborate an approach, one which has been marginalized in contemporary socio-scientific reflections on informatization and which will treat discourse on the impact of ICT on social change predominantly as a socially and culturally embedded performative practice which employs a certain set of tools to interpret, mask and co-construct social reality. The focus here should then be on examining the broader cultural and political contexts responsible for the formation of a certain type of truth, while not resigning ourselves to approximating an ideal of truth as such.

A part of this story has been published by Richard Barbrook in an effort to illustrate the political dimension of the interaction between the development of the IT infrastructure, American social scientists' visions of future societal development, and the formation of popular cyberculture.[24] We can find another piece of the puzzle in *Imaginaire d'internet*, in which Patrice Flichy elaborated the function of a specifically structured 'imaginaire' in the realization of an information society.[25] However, outlining the entire process of the social construction

[19] See, e.g., Castells (1999).
[20] Alden (2003, p. 476), who was paraphrasing information from Southscan, Monthly Regional Bulletin, 2000, November 3.
[21] See, e.g., Zachary (2004).
[22] See, e.g., Castells (2004a).
[23] It is beyond doubt, however, that without the use of attractive language (e.g., the Information Age) and without offering readers a different, more engaged and critical stance, his voice might have gone unheard. This is obviously an internal conflict that every researcher of social change must face and there seems to be no ideal way out of it.
[24] Barbrook (2007).
[25] Flichy (2007).

of the information society would require a comprehensive analysis to map the functions and interactions of the key social players informing the symbolic and material definitions of future societal development, namely the scientific community, the media and influential political and economic players. The resulting picture could then enlighten us about the power with which human society dictates its own future development in both publicly accessible terms and the terms of the social scientists most competent in the matter, all under the umbrella of a non-human historical necessity. This work, in an attempt to shed light on the position of one scientific debate in the informatization process, is only one chapter of the whole story.

Bibliography

Abbate, J. (2000). *Inventing the Internet*. Cambridge, MA: MIT Press.

Abell, P., & Reyniers, D. (2000). On the failure of social theory. *The British Journal of Sociology*, *51*(4), 739–750. Retrieved from https://doi.org/10.1080/00071310020015352

Agarwal, R., Animesh, A., & Prasad, K. (2009). Social interactions and the 'digital divide': Explaining variations in Internet use. *Information Systems Research*, *20*(2), 277–294. Retrieved from https://doi.org/10.1287/isre.1080.0194

Alampay, E. A. (2006). Beyond access to ICTs: Measuring capabilities in the information society. *International Journal of Education and Development Using Information and Communication Technology*, *2*(3), 4–22.

Ala-Mutka, K. (2011). *Mapping digital competence: Toward a conceptual understanding*. Luxembourg: Publications Office of the European Union. Retrieved from http://ftp.jrc.es/EURdoc/JRC67075_TN.pdf

Albert, F., Dávid, B., & Molnár, S. (2008). Links between the diffusion of Internet usage and social network characteristics in contemporary Hungarian society: A longitudinal analysis. *Review of Sociology*, *14*(1), 45–66. Retrieved from https://doi.org/10.1556/RevSoc.14.2008.3

Alden, C. (2003). Let them eat cyberspace: Africa, the G8 and the digital divide. *Millennium*, *32*(3), 457–476. Retrieved from https://doi.org/10.1177/03058298030320030601

Alvarez, A. S. (2003). Behavioral and environmental correlates of digital inequality. *IT&Society*, *1*(5), 97–140.

Amichai-Hamburger, Y., Wainapel, G., & Fox, S. (2002). 'On the Internet no one knows I'm an introvert': Extroversion, neuroticism, and Internet interaction. *CyberPsychology & Behavior*, *5*(2), 125–128. Retrieved from https://doi.org/10.1089/109493102753770507

Anderson, J. Q. (2005). *Imagining the Internet: Personalities, predictions, perspectives*. Lanham, MD: Rowman & Littlefield.

Anderson, R. H., Bikson, T. K., Law, S. A., & Mitchell, B. M. (1995). *Universal access to e-mail: Feasibility and societal implications*. Santa Monica, CA: RAND.

Andrés, L. D., Cuberes, D., Diouf, M., & Serebrisky, T. (2010). Diffusion of the Internet: A cross-country analysis. *Telecommunications Policy*, *34*(5–6), 323–340. Retrieved from https://doi.org/10.1016/j.telpol.2010.01.003

Aron, R. (1967). *The industrial society: Three essays on ideology and development*. London: Weidenfeld & Nicolson (Original work published in 1963).

Avgerou, C. (1998). How can IT enable economic growth in developing countries? *Information Technology for Development*, *8*(1), 15–28.

Bakardjieva, M. (2005). *Internet society: The Internet in everyday life*. London: Sage.

Baker, L. R., & Oswald, D. L. (2010). Shyness and online social networking services. *Journal of Social and Personal Relationships*, *27*(7), 873–889. Retrieved from https://doi.org/10.1177/0265407510375261

Barabási, A.-L. (2002). *Linked: The new science of networks*. Cambridge, MA: Perseus.

Barbrook, R. (2007). *Imaginary futures: From thinking machines to the global village*. London: Pluto Press.

Bawden, D. (2008). Origins and concepts of digital literacy. In C. Lankshear & M. Knobel (Eds.), *Digital literacies: Concepts, policies and practices* (pp. 17–32). New York, NY: Peter Lang.

Beck, U. (1997). *The reinvention of politics: Rethinking modernity in the global social order*. (M. Ritter, Trans.). Cambridge: Polity Press (Original work published in 1996).

Beck, U. (2000). *What is globalization?* (P. Camiller, Trans.). Malden, MA: Polity Press (Original work published in 1997).

Beckers, J., Schmidt, H., & Wicherts, J. (2008). Computer anxiety in daily life: Old history? In E. Loos, L. Haddon & E. A. Mante-Meijer (Eds.), *The social dynamics of information and communication technology* (pp. 13–24). New York, NY: Routledge.

Belinfante, A. (2009). *Telephone penetration report (through March 2009)*. Washington, DC: Industry Analysis and Technology, Division Wireline Competition Bureau, Federal Communications Commission. Retrieved from https://apps.fcc.gov/edocs_public/attachmatch/DOC-297986A1.pdf

Bell, D. (1973). *The coming of post-industrial society: A venture in social forecasting.* New York, NY: Basic Books.

Bell, D. (1979). Communications technology: For better or for worse. *Harvard Business Review, 57*(3), 20–42.

Bell, D. (1999). The axial edge of technology foreword 1999. In *The coming of post-industrial society: A venture in social forecasting* (Special anniversary ed., pp. ix–lxxxvi). New York, NY: Basic Books.

Bell, P., Reddy, P., & Rainie, L. (2004). *Rural areas and the Internet.* Washington, DC: Pew Internet & American Life Project. Retrieved from http://www.pewinternet.org/2004/02/17/rural-areas-and-the-internet/

Beniger, J. R. (1986). *The control revolution technological and economic origins of the information society.* Cambridge, MA: Harvard University Press.

Bennett, S., Maton, K., & Kervin, L. (2008). The 'digital natives' debate: A critical review of the evidence. *British Journal of Educational, 39*(5), 775–786. Retrieved from https://doi.org/10.1111/j.1467-8535.2007.00793.x

Bijker, W. E., Hughes, T. P., & Pinch, T. (Eds.). (1987). *The social construction of technological systems: New directions in the sociology and history of technology.* Cambridge, MA: MIT Press.

Bijker, W. E., & Law, J. (Eds.). (1992). *Shaping technology/building society: Studies in sociotechnical change.* Cambridge, MA: MIT Press.

Bikson, T. K., & Panis, C. W. A. (1999). *Citizens, computers, and connectivity: Review of trends.* Santa Monica, CA: RAND.

Billon, M., Lera-Lopez, F., & Marco, R. (2010). Differences in digitalization levels: A multivariate analysis studying the global digital divide. *Review of World Economics, 146*(1), 39–73. Retrieved from https://doi.org/10.1007/s10290-009-0045-y

Bimber, B. (2000). Measuring the gender gap on the Internet. *Social Science Quarterly, 81*(3), 868–876.

Blank, G. (2013). Who creates content? *Information, Communication & Society, 16*(4), 590–612. Retrieved from https://doi.org/10.1080/1369118X.2013.777758

Blank, G., & Groselj, D. (2014). Dimensions of Internet use: Amount, variety, and types. *Information, Communication & Society, 17*(4), 417–435. Retrieved from https://doi.org/10.1080/1369118X.2014.889189

Boase, J. (2010). The consequences of personal networks for Internet use in rural areas. *American Behavioral Scientist, 53*(9), 1257–1267. Retrieved from https://doi.org/10.1177/0002764210361681

Boase, J., Horrigan, J. B., Wellman, B., & Rainie, L. (2006). *The strength of Internet ties.* Washington, DC: Pew Internet & American Life Project. Retrieved from http://www.pewinternet.org/2006/01/25/the-strength-of-internet-ties/

Boase, J., & Wellman, B. (2006). Personal relationships: On and off the Internet. In A. L. Vangelisti & D. Perlman (Eds.), *The Cambridge handbook of personal relationships* (pp. 709–723). Cambridge, MA: Cambridge University Press.

Bonfadelli, H. (2002). The Internet and knowledge gaps: A theoretical and empirical Investigation. *European Journal of Communication, 17*(1), 65–84. Retrieved from https://doi.org/10.1177/0267323102017001607

Boonaert, T., & Vettenburg, N. (2011). Young people's internet use: Divided or diversified? *Childhood, 18*(1), 54–66. Retrieved from https://doi.org/10.1177/0907568210367524

Bourdieu, P. (2001). *Masculine domination*. Stanford, CA: Stanford University Press.

Brandtweiner, R., Donat, E., & Kerschbaum. J. (2010). Toward a unified media-user-typology (MUT): A meta-analysis and review of the research literature on media-user typologies. *Computers in Human Behavior, 26*(5), 940–956. Retrieved from https://doi.org/10.1016/j.chb.2010.02.008

Brandtzæg, P. B. (2010). Towards a unified media-user typology (MUT): A meta-analysis and review of the research literature on media-user typologies. *Computers in Human Behavior, 26*(5), 940–956. Retrieved from https://doi.org/10.1016/j.chb.2010.02.008

Brandtzæg, P. B., Heima, J., & Karahasanovi⊠a, A. (2011). Understanding the new digital divide: A typology of Internet users in Europe. *International Journal of Human-Computer Studies, 69*(3), 123–138. Retrieved from https://doi.org/10.1016/j.ijhcs.2010.11.004

Brown, K., Campbell, S. W., & Ling, L. (2011). Mobile phones bridging the digital divide for teens in the US? *Future Internet, 3*(2), 144–158. Retrieved from https://doi.org/10.3390/fi3020144

Brown, S. A., & Venkatesh, V. (2003). Bringing non-adopters along: The challenge facing the PC industry. *Communications of the ACM, 46*(4), 76–80. Retrieved from https://dx.doi.org/doi:10.1145/641205.641208

Brown, S. A., Venkatesh, V., & Bala, H. (2006). Household technology use: Integrating household life cycle and the model of adoption of technology in households. *The Information Society, 22*(4), 205–218. Retrieved from https://doi.org/10.1080/01972240600791333

Bruno, G., Esposito, E., Genovese, A., & Gwebu, K. L. (2010). A critical analysis of current indexes for digital divide measurement. *The Information Society, 27*(1), 16–28. Retrieved from https://doi.org/10.1080/01972243.2010.534364

Büchi, M., Just, N., & Latzer, M. (2016). Modeling the second-level digital divide: A five-country study of social differences in Internet use. *New Media & Society, 18*(11), 2703–2722. Retrieved from https://doi.org/10.1177/1461444815604154

Bucy, E. P., & Newhagen, J. E. (2004). Preface: The new thinking about media access. In E. P. Bucy & J. E. Newhagen (Eds.), *Media access: Social and psychological dimensions of new technology use* (pp. IX.–XIX.). Mahwah, NJ: Lawrence Erlbaum Associates.

Bunz, U. (2004). The computer-email-web (CEW) fluency scale-development and validation. *International Journal of Human-Computer Interaction, 17*(4), 479–506. Retrieved from https://doi.org/10.1207/s15327590ijhc1704_3

Bure, C. E. (2005). Digital inclusion without social inclusion: The consumption of information and communication technologies (ICTs) within homeless subculture in Scotland. *The Journal of Community Informatics, 1*(2), 116–133.

Burning Glass Technologies. (2015). Crunched by the numbers: The Digital Skills gap in the workforce. Burning Glass Technologies. Retrieved from http://burning-glass.com/wp-content/uploads/2015/06/Digital_Skills_Gap.pdf

Cairncross, F. (1997). *The death of distance: How the communications revolution will change our lives*. Boston, MA: Harvard Business School Press.

Calhoun, C. (2000). Resisting globalization or shaping it? *Prometheus, 3*, 29–47.

Callinicos, A. (2004). Myths of the 'new economy'. In F. Webster & B. Dimitriou (Eds.), *Manuel Castells* (Vol. III, pp. 207–218). London: Sage.

Campbell, D. (2001). Can the digital divide be contained? *International Labour Review, 140*(2), 119–141. Retrieved from https://doi.org/10.1111/j.1564-913X.2001.tb00217.x

Campbell, S. W., & Park, Y. J. (2008). Social implications of mobile telephony: The rise of personal communication society. *Sociology Compass, 2*(2), 371–387. Retrieved from https://doi.org/10.1111/j.1751-9020.2007.00080.x

Campos-Castillo, C. (2015). Revisiting the first-level digital divide in the United States: Gender and race/ethnicity patterns, 2007–2012. *Social Science Computer Review, 33*(4), 423–439. Retrieved from https://doi.org/10.1177/0894439314547617

Caplan, S. E. (2007). Relations among loneliness, social anxiety, and problematic Internet use. *CyberPsychology & Behavior*, *10*(2), 234–242. Retrieved from https://doi.org/10.1089/cpb.2006.9963

Carpentier, N. (2003). Access and participation in the discourse of the digital divide: The European perspective at/on the WSIS. In J. Servaes (Ed.), *The European information society: A reality check* (pp. 99–120). Bristol: Intellect Books.

Castells, M. (1977). *The urban question: A Marxist approach*. (A. Sheridan, Trans.). London, Edward Arnold (Original work published in 1972).

Castells, M. (1978). *City, class, and power*. London: MacMillan.

Castells, M. (1983). *The city and the grassroots: A cross-cultural theory of urban social movements*. Los Angeles, CA: University of California Press.

Castells, M. (1989). *The informational city: Information technology, economic restructuring, and the urban-regional process*. Oxford: Blackwell.

Castells, M. (1998). *End of millennium* (1st ed., Vol. III). Malden, MA: Blackwell.

Castells, M. (1999). Information Technology, Globalization and Social Development. Presented at the UNRISD conference on Information Technologies and Social Development, Geneva: The United Nations Research Institute for Social Development (UNRISD).

Castells, M. (2000a). Materials for an exploratory theory of the network society. *The British Journal of Sociology*, *51*(1), 5–24. Retrieved from https://doi.org/10.1111/j.1468-4446.2000.00005.x

Castells, M. (2000b). *The rise of the network society* (2nd ed., Vols. I). Chichester: Blackwell.

Castells, M. (2001a). A rejoinder to Abell and Reyniers' 'failure of social theory'. *The British Journal of Sociology*, *52*(3), 541–546. Retrieved from https://doi.org/10.1080/00071310120071179

Castells, M. (2001b). *The Internet Galaxy: Reflections on the Internet, business, and society*. Oxford: Oxford University Press.

Castells, M. (2004a). Informationalism, networks, and the network society: A theoretical blueprint. In M. Castells (Ed.), *The network society: A cross-cultural perspective* (pp. 3–45). Cheltenham: Edward Elgar.

Castells, M. (2004b). *The power of identity* (2nd ed., Vols. II). Malden, MA: Blackwell.

Castells, M. (2007). Communication, power and counter-power in the network society. *International Journal of Communication*, *1*, 238–266.

Castells, M. (2009). *Communication power*. Oxford: Oxford University Press.

Castells, M. (2012). *Relative ranking of a selected pool of leading scholars in the social sciences by number of citations in the social science citation index, 2000–2010*. Retrieved from http://www.manuelcastells.info/en

Castells, M. (2015). *Networks of outrage and hope: Social movements in the Internet age* (2nd ed.). Malden, MA: Polity Press.

Castells, M. (2017). *Relative ranking of a selected pool of leading scholars in the social sciences by number of citations in the social science citation index, 2000–2015*. Retrieved from http://www.manuelcastells.info/en

Castells, M., Fernández-Ardevol, M., Qui, J. L., & Sey, A. (2007). *Mobile communication and society: A global perspective*. Cambridge, MA: MIT Press.

Castells, M., & Ince, M. (2003). *Conversations with Manuel Castells*. Cambridge: Polity Press.

Cattagni, A., & Farris, E. (2001). *Internet access in U.S. public schools and classrooms, 1994–2000*. Washington, DC: Department of Education, National Centre for Education Statistics. Retrieved from https://nces.ed.gov/pubs2001/2001071.pdf

Cawkell, A. E. (1986). The real information society: Present situation and some forecasts. *Journal of Information Science Information Scientist*, *12*(3), 87–95. Retrieved from https://doi.org/10.1177/016555158601200301

Chapela, J. G. (2016). Disentangling income and price effects in the demand for time online. Information Economics and Policy, 35, 65–75. https://doi.org/10.1016/j.infoecopol.2015.10.004

Chigona, W., Pollock, M., & Roode, J. D. (2010). South Africa's socio-techno divide: A critical discourse analysis of government speeches. *South African Computer Journal, 44*, 3–20. Retrieved from https://doi.org/10.18489/sacj.v44i0.19

Chinn, M. D., & Fairlie, R. W. (2007). The determinants of the global digital divide: A cross-country analysis of computer and internet penetration. *Oxford Economic Papers, 59*(1), 16–44. Retrieved from https://doi.org/10.1093/oep/gpl024

Chinn, M. D., & Fairlie, R. W. (2010). ICT use in the developing world: An analysis of differences in computer and internet penetration. *Review of International Economics, 18*(1), 153–167. Retrieved from https://doi.org/10.1111/j.1467-9396.2009.00861.x

Chowdhur, N. (2000). *Information and communications technologies and IFPRI's mandate: A conceptual framework (draft)*. Washington, DC: International Food Policy Research Institute (IFPRI). Retrieved from http://citeseerx.ist.psu.edu/viewdoc/download?doi=10.1.1.58.3096&rep=rep1&type=pdf

Clement, A., & Shade, L. R. (1996). What do we mean by 'universal access?': Social perspectives in a Canadian context. *Proceedings of INET '96 (The Internet Society)*, Montreal. Retrieved from http://libguides.scu.edu.au/c.php?g=356657&p=2408473

Compaine, B. M. (2001). Information gaps: Myth or reality? In B. M. Compaine (Ed.), *The digital divide: Facing a crisis or creating a myth?* (pp. 105–118). Cambridge, MA: MIT Press.

Compaine, B. M., & Weinraub, J. (2001). Universal access to online services: An examination of the issue. In B. M. Compaine (Ed.), *The digital divide: Facing a crisis or creating a myth?* (pp. 147–178). Cambridge, MA: MIT Press.

Cooper, M., & Kimmelman, G. (2001). The digital divide confronts the Telecommunications Act of 1996: Economic reality versus public policy. In B. M. Compaine (Ed.), *The digital divide: Facing a crisis or creating a myth?* (pp. 199–211). Cambridge, MA: MIT Press.

Cooper, J., & Weaver, K. D. (2003). *Gender and computers: Understanding the digital divide*. Mahwah, NJ: Lawrence Erlbaum Associates.

Correa, T. (2014). Bottom-up technology transmission within families: Exploring how youths influence their parents' digital media use with dyadic data. *Journal of Communication, 64*(1), 103–124. Retrieved from https://doi.org/10.1111/jcom.12067

Correa, T. (2016). Acquiring a new technology at home: A parent-child study about youths' influence on digital media adoption in a family. *Journal of Broadcasting & Electronic Media, 60*(1), 123–139. Retrieved from https://doi.org/10.1080/08838151.2015.1127238

Correa, T., Straubhaar, J. D., Chen, W., & Spence, J. (2013). Brokering new technologies: The role of children in their parents' usage of the internet. *New Media & Society, 17*(4), 483–500. Retrieved from https://doi.org/10.1177/1461444813506975

Couldry, N. (2003). Digital divide or discursive design? On the emerging ethics of information space. *Ethics and Information Technology, 5*(2), 89–97. Retrieved from https://doi.org/10.1023/A:1024916618904

Courage, M. L., Bakhtiar, A., Fitzpatrick, C., Kenny, S., & Brandeau, K. (2015). Growing up multitasking: The costs and benefits for cognitive development. *Developmental Review, 35*, 5–41. Retrieved from https://doi.org/10.1016/j.dr.2014.12.002

Courtois, C., & Verdegen, P. (2016). With a little help from my friends: An analysis of the role of social support in digital inequalities. *New Media & Society, 18*(8), 1508–1527. Retrieved from https://doi.org/10.1177/1461444814562162

Crawford, S. (1983). The origin and development of a concept: The information society. *Bulletin of the Medical Library Association, 71*(4), 380–385.

Crothers, C., Smith, P., Urale, P. W. B., & Bell, A. (2016). *World Internet Project New Zealand: The Internet in New Zealand 2015*. Auckland: Institute of Culture, Discourse & Communication, Auckland University of Technology. Retrieved from https://workresearch.aut.ac.nz/__data/assets/pdf_file/0003/71328/WIPNZ-Report-060515.pdf

de Lanerolle, I. (2012). *The New Wave report*. University of Witwatersrand. Retrieved from http://networksociety.co.za

de Miranda, A. (2009). Technological determinism and ideology: Questioning the 'information society' and the 'digital divide'. In J. Burnett, P. Senker & K. Walker (Eds.), *The myths of technology: Innovation and inequality* (pp. 23–38). New York, NY: Peter Lang.

DeMunter, C. (2006). *How skilled are Europeans in using computers and the Internet? (No. 17).* Luxembourg: Statistics in focus, Eurostat. Retrieved from http://ec.europa.eu/eurostat/documents/3433488/5439785/KS-NP-06-017-EN.PDF/436995e1-4034-4c04-bac5-5ba1eea36d65

Dervin, B. (2003). Users as research inventions: How research categories perpetuate inequities. In B. Dervin, L. Foreman-Wernet & E. Lauterbach (Eds.), *Sense-making methodology reader: Selected writings of Brenda Dervin* (pp. 47–60). Cresskill, NJ: Hampton Press.

Descombes, V. (1980). *Modern French philosophy*. New York, NY: Cambridge University Press (Original work published in 1979)

De Souza e Silva, A., Sutko, D. M., Salis, F. A., & de Souza e Silva, C. (2011). Mobile phone appropriation in the *favelas* of Rio de Janeiro, Brazil. *New Media & Society, 13*(3), 411–426. Retrieved from https://doi.org/10.1177/1461444810393901

Dewan, S., & Riggins, F. J. (2005). The digital divide: Current and future research directions. *Journal of the Association for Information Systems, 6*(2), 298–337.

DiMaggio, P., & Hargittai, E. (2001). *From the 'digital divide' to 'digital inequality': Studying internet use as penetration increase.* Working Paper Series Number #15. Princeton University Center for Arts and Cultural Policy Studies. Retrieved from https://www.princeton.edu/~artspol/workpap/WP15%20-%20DiMaggio%2BHargittai.pdf

DiMaggio, P., Hargittai, E., Celeste, E., & Shafer, S. (2004). Digital inequality: From unequal access to differentiated use. In K. M. Neckermann (Ed.), *Social Inequality* (pp. 355–400). New York, NY: Russell Sage Foundation.

DiMaggio, P., Hargittai, E., Neuman, W. R., & Robinson, J. P. (2001). Social implications of the Internet. *Annual Review of Sociology, 27*(1), 307–336. Retrieved from https://doi.org/10.1146/annurev.soc.27.1.307

Dobransky, K., & Hargittai, E. (2012). Inquiring minds acquiring wellness: Uses of online and offline sources for health information. *Health Communication, 27*(4), 331–343. Retrieved from https://doi.org/10.1080/10410236.2011.585451

Donner, J. (2008). Shrinking fourth world? Mobile, development, and inclusion. In J. E. Katz (Ed.), *Handbook of mobile communication studies* (pp. 29–42). Cambridge, MA: MIT Press.

Dowling, M. (2001). *Mapping a future for digital connections: A study of the digital divide in San Diego county.* San Diego, CA: San Diego Regional Technology Alliance. Retrieved from https://files.eric.ed.gov/fulltext/ED463391.pdf

Drucker, P. F. (1968). *The age of discontinuity: Guidelines to our changing society.* London: Routledge.

Duff, A. S. (2000). *Information society studies.* London: Routledge.

Duff, A. S. (2001). On the present state of information society studies. *Education for Information, 19*(3), 231–244. Retrieved from https://doi.org/10.3233/EFI-2001-19304

Duff, A. S., Craig, D., & McNeill, D. A. (1996). A note on the origins of the 'information society'. *Journal of Information Science, 22*(2), 117–122. Retrieved from https://doi.org/10.1177/016555159602200204

Duncombe, R., & Heeks, R. (2002). Enterprise across the digital divide: Information systems and rural microenterprise in Botswana. *Journal of International Development, 14*(1), 61–74. Retrieved from https://doi.org/10.1002/jid.869

Dutton, W. H., Blank, G., & Groselj, D. (2013). *Cultures of the Internet: The Internet in Britain.* Oxford: Oxford Internet Institute, University of Oxford. Retrieved from http://oxis.oii.ox.ac.uk/wp-content/uploads/2014/11/OxIS-2013.pdf

Dutton, W. H., Helsper, E. J., & Gerber, M. M. (2009). *The Internet in Britain 2009.* Oxford: Oxford Internet Institute, University of Oxford. Retrieved from http://oxis.oii.ox.ac.uk/wp-content/uploads/sites/43/2014/11/oxis2009-report.pdf

Dutton, W. H., Rogers, E. M., & Jun, S.-H. (1987). Diffusion and social impacts of personal computers. *Communication Research, 14*(2), 219–250. Retrieved from https://doi.org/10.1177/009365087014002005

Edwards, P. N. (1995). From 'impact' to social process: Computers in society and culture. In S. Jasanoff (Ed.), *Handbook of science and technology studies* (pp. 257–285). Thousand Oaks, CA: Sage.

Elliott, B. (1980). Manuel Castells and the new urban sociology. *The British Journal of Sociology, 31*(1), 151. Retrieved from https://doi.org/10.2307/590099

Eshet-Alkalai, Y., & Amichai-Hamburger, Y. (2004). Experiments in digital literacy. *CyberPsychology & Behavior, 7*(4), 421–429. Retrieved from https://doi.org/10.1089/cpb.2004.7.421

Eshet-Alkalai, Y., & Chajut, E. (2009). Changes over time in digital literacy. *CyberPsychology & Behavior, 12*(6), 713–715. Retrieved from https://doi.org/10.1089/cpb.2008.0264

European Commission. (2010). *Communication from the Commission to the European Parliament, the Council, the European Economic and Social Committee and the Committee of the Regions: A Digital Agenda for Europe*. Brusel. Retrieved from http://eur-lex.europa.eu/LexUriServ/LexUriServ.do?uri=COM:2010:0245:FIN:ENG:PDF

European Council. (2000). *Lisbon European council, 23 and 24 March 2000, presidency conclusions*. Brusel: European Parliament. Retrieved from http://www.europarl.europa.eu/summits/lis1_en.htm#

Eurostat. (2017). *Digital economy and society database*. Retrieved from http://ec.europa.eu/eurostat/web/digital-economy-and-society/data/database

Eynon, R. (2009). Mapping the digital divide in Britain: Implications for learning and education. *Learning, Media and Technology, 34*(4), 277–290. Retrieved from https://doi.org/10.1080/17439880903345874

Eynon, R., & Geniets, A. (2016). The digital skills paradox: How do digitally excluded youth develop skills to use the internet? *Learning, Media and Technology, 41*(3), 463–479. Retrieved from https://doi.org/10.1080/17439884.2014.1002845

Eynon, R., & Helsper, E. J. (2015). Family dynamics and Internet use in Britain: What role do children play in adults' engagement with the Internet? *Information, Communication & Society, 18*(2), 156–171. Retrieved from https://doi.org/10.1080/1369118X.2014.942344

Fafchamps, M., & Minten, B. (2012). Impact of SMS-based agricultural information on Indian farmers. *The World Bank Economic Review, 26*(3), 383–414. Retrieved from https://doi.org/10.1093/wber/lhr056

Fairclough, N. (2003). Analysing discourse: textual analysis for social research. London ; New York: Routledge.

Fairlie, R. W. (2004). Race and the digital divide. *The B.E. Journal of Economic Analysis & Policy, 3*(1), 1–38. Retrieved from https://doi.org/10.2202/1538-0645.1263

Fairlie, R. W. (2005). The effects of home computers on school enrolment. *Economics of Education Review, 24*(5), 533–547. Retrieved from https://doi.org/10.1016/j.econedurev.2004.08.008

Fairlie, R. W. (2007). Explaining differences in access to home computers and the Internet: A comparison of Latino groups to other ethnic and racial groups. *Electronic Commerce Research, 7*(3–4), 265–291. Retrieved from https://doi.org/10.1007/s10660-007-9006-5

Fallows, D. (2005). *How women and men use the Internet*. Washington, DC: Pew Internet & American Life Project. Retrieved from http://www.pewinternet.org/2005/12/28/how-women-and-men-use-the-internet/

Feenberg, A. (2002). *Transforming technology: A critical theory revisited*. New York, NY: Oxford University Press.

Ferras, C., Garcia, Y., & Pose, M. (2013). Can we get around rural isolation? Adolescents and mobile telephones in rural areas: A case study in Galicia. *International Journal of Communication, 7*, 23, 2586–2608.

Fieseler, C., Meckel, M., & Müller, S. (2014). With a little help of my peers. The supportive role of online contacts for the unemployed. *Computers in Human Behavior, 41*, 164–176. Retrieved from https://doi.org/10.1016/j.chb.2014.09.017

Findahl, O. (2008). *The Internet in Sweden 2007*. Hudiksvall: World Internet Institute. Retrieved from http://iis.se/docs/the_internet_in_sweden_2007.pdf

Findahl, O. (2012). *Swedes and the Internet 2012*. Stockholm: SE – The Internet infrastructure foundation. Retrieved from https://www.iis.se/docs/Swedes-and-the-Internet-2012.pdf

Findahl, O. (2014). *The Swedes and the Internet 2014*. Stockholm: SE – The Internet infrastructure foundation. Retrieved from http://en.soi2014.se

Finn, S., & Korukonda, A. R. (2004). Avoiding computers: Does personality play a role? In E. P. Bucy & J. E. Newhagen (Eds.), *Media access: Social and psychological dimensions of new technology use* (pp. 73–90). Mahwah, NJ: Lawrence Erlbaum Associate.

Fischer, J. (1999). Manuel Castells' brave new world. Retrieved from http://www.acturban. org/biennial/DOC_planners/castells_article9904.pdf

Fishman, R. (1986). The city and the grassroots: A cross-cultural theory of urban social movements by Manuel Castells. *American Historical Journal*, *91*(5), 1163–1164. Retrieved from http://dx.doi.org/10.2307/1864387

Flichy, P. (2007). *The Internet imaginaire*. Cambridge, MA: MIT Press.

Foucault, M. (1976). *Histoire de la sexualité I: La volonté de savoir* [The history of sexuality I: The will to knowledge]. Paris: Gallimard.

Foucault, M. (1981). The order of discourse. In R. Young (Ed.), *Untying the text: A post-structuralist reader* (pp. 51–78). London: Routledge.

Fountain, C. (2005). Finding a job in the Internet age. *Social Forces*, *83*(3), 1235–1262.

Fox, S. (2005). *Digital divisions*. Washington, DC: Pew Internet & American Life Project. Retrieved from http://www.pewinternet.org/2005/10/05/digital-divisions/

Fox, S., & Duggan, M. (2013). *Health online 2013*. Washington, DC: Pew Internet & American Life Project. Retrieved from http://www.pewinternet.org/2013/01/15/health-online-2013/

Freeden, M. (2003). *Ideology: A very short introduction*. Oxford: Oxford University Press.

Friemel, T. N. (2016). The digital divide has grown old: Determinants of a digital divide among seniors. *New Media & Society*, *18*(2), 313–331. Retrieved from https://doi. org/10.1177/1461444814538648

Fuchs, C. (2008). *Internet and society: Social theory in the information age*. London: Routledge.

Fuchs, C. (2009). The role of income inequality in a multivariate cross-national analysis of the digital divide. *Social Science Computer Review*, *27*(1), 41–58. Retrieved from https:// doi.org/10.1177/0894439308321628

García, D. L. (2002). The architecture of global networking technologies. In S. Sassen (Ed.), *Global networks, linked cities* (pp. 39–69). London: Routledge.

Garnham, N. (2000). 'Information society' as theory or ideology: A critical perspective on technology, education and employment in the information age. *Information, Communication & Society*, *3*(2), 139–152. Retrieved from https://doi.org/10.1080/ 13691180050123677

Garnham, N. (2004). Information society theory as ideology. In F. Webster & R. Blom (Eds.), *The information society reader* (pp. 165–183). London: Routledge.

Gaziano, C. (1983). The knowledge gap: An analytical review of media effects. *Communication Research*, *10*(4), 447–486. Retrieved from https://doi.org/10.1177/009365083010004003

Gaziano, C. (1995). A twenty-five-year review of knowledge gap research. Presented at the 50th annual conference of the American Association for Public Opinion Research, Fort Lauderdale, FL. Retrieved from http://eric.ed.gov/PDFS/ED383009.pdf

Gaziano, C., & Gaziano, E. (2009). Theories and methods in knowledge gap research. In D. W. Stacks & M. B. Salwen (Eds.), *Integrated approach to communication theory and research communication series*. (2nd ed., pp. 122–136). London: Routledge.

Gibson, C. (2016, September 6). The disconnected: Teen lives and futures depend on the Internet. What happens when they can't afford it? *The Washington Post*. Retrieved from http://www.washingtonpost.com/sf/style/2016/09/06/teen-lives-depend-on-the-internet-what-happens-when-they-cant-afford-it/?utm_term=.8fb11e65f79d

Giddens, A. (1990). *The consequences of modernity*. Stanford, CA: Stanford University Press.

Giddens, A., & Sutton, P. W. (2009). *Sociology* (6th ed.). Malden, MA: Polity Press.

Goldfarb, A. (2006). The (teaching) role of universities in the diffusion of the Internet. *International Journal of Industrial Organization*, *24*(2), 203–225. Retrieved from https://doi.org/10.1016/j.ijindorg.2005.11.004

Goldfarb, A., & Prince, J. (2008). Internet adoption and usage patterns are different: Implications for the digital divide. *Information Economics and Policy*, *20*(1), 2–15. Retrieved from https://doi.org/10.1016/j.infoecopol.2007.05.001

Gonzales, A. L. (2014). Health benefits and barriers to cell phone use in low-income urban U.S. neighborhoods: Indications of technology maintenance. *Mobile Media & Communication*, *2*(3), 233–248. Retrieved from https://doi.org/10.1177/2050157914530297

Gonzales, A. (2016). The contemporary US digital divide: From initial access to technology maintenance. *Information, Communication & Society*, *19*(2), 234–248. Retrieved from https://doi.org/10.1080/1369118X.2015.1050438

Gonzales, A. L., Ems, L., & Suri, V. R. (2016). Cell phone disconnection disrupts access to healthcare and health resources: A technology maintenance perspective. *New Media & Society*, *18*(8), 1422–1438. Retrieved from https://doi.org/10.1177/1461444814558670

Gordo, B. (2003). Overcoming digital deprivation. *IT&Society*, *1*(5), 166–180.

Gourova, E., Hermann, C., Leijten, J., & Clements, B. (2001). *The digital divide – a research perspective: A report to the G8 Opportunities Task Force* (No. EUR 19913 EN). (n.p.): European Commission, Joint Research Centre.

Graham, M. (2011). Time machines and virtual portals: The spatialities of the digital divide. *Progress in Development Studies*, *11*(3), 211–227. Retrieved from https://doi.org/10.1177/146499341001100303

Greenberg, B. S., Eastin, M. S., Skalski, P., Cooper, L., Levy, M., & Lachlan, K. (2005). Comparing survey and diary measures of internet and traditional media use. *Communication Reports*, *18*(1–2), 1–8. Retrieved from https://doi.org/10.1080/08934210500084164

Greenbrook-Held, J., & Morrison, P. S. (2011). The domestic divide: Access to the Internet in New Zealand. *New Zealand Geographer*, *67*(1), 25–38. Retrieved from https://doi.org/10.1111/j.1745-7939.2011.01195.x

Greenstein, S., & Prince, J. (2009). Internet diffusion and the geography of the digital divide in the United States. In R. Mansell, C. Avgerou, D. Quah & R. Silverstone (Eds.), *The Oxford handbook of information and communication technologies* (pp. 168–195). New York, NY: Oxford University Press. Retrieved from https://doi.org/10.1093/oxfordhb/9780199548798.003.0007

Gross, E. F. (2004). Adolescent Internet use: What we expect, what teens report. *Journal of Applied Developmental Psychology*, *25*(6), 633–649. Retrieved from https://doi.org/10.1016/j.appdev.2004.09.005

Guillén, M. F., & Suárez, S. L. (2005). Explaining the global digital divide: Economic, political and sociological drivers of cross-national Internet use. *Social Forces*, *84*(2), 681–708. Retrieved from https://doi.org/10.1353/sof.2006.0015

Gunkel, D. J. (2003). Second thoughts: Toward a critique of the digital divide. *New Media & Society*, *5*(4), 499–522. Retrieved from https://doi.org/10.1177/146144480354003

Haddon, L. (2004). *Information and communication technologies in everyday life: A concise introduction and research guide* (Eng.). Oxford: Berg.

Hafner, K., & Lyon, M. (1996). *Where wizards stay up late: The origins of the Internet*. New York, NY: Touchstone.

Haight, M., Quan-Haase, A., & Corbett, B. A. (2014). Revisiting the digital divide in Canada: The impact of demographic factors on access to the internet, level of online activity, and social networking site usage. *Information, Communication & Society*, *17*(4), 503–519. Retrieved from https://doi.org/10.1080/1369118X.2014.891633

Hale, T. M., Cotten, S. R., Drentea, P., & Goldner, M. (2010). Rural-urban differences in general and health-related Internet use. *American Behavioral Scientist*, *53*(9), 1304–1325. Retrieved from https://doi.org/10.1177/0002764210361685

Hampton, K. N. (2010). Internet use and the concentration of disadvantage: Globalization and the urban underclass. *American Behavioral Scientist, 53*(8), 1111–1132. Retrieved from https://doi.org/10.1177/0002764209356244

Hampton, K., Sessions, L. F., Her, E. J., & Raine, L. (2009). *Social isolation and new technology*. Washington, DC: Pew Internet & American Life Project. Retrieved from http://www.pewinternet.org/2009/11/04/social-isolation-and-new-technology/

Hampton, K. N., & Ling, R. (2013). Explaining communication displacement and large-scale social change in core networks: A cross-national comparison of why bigger is not better and less can mean more. *Information, Communication & Society, 16*(4), 561–589. Retrieved from https://doi.org/10.1080/1369118X.2013.777760

Hampton, K. N., & Wellman, B. (2002). The not so global village of Neville. In B. Wellman & C. A. Haythornthwaite (Eds.), *The Internet in everyday life* (pp. 345–371). Malden, MA: Blackwell.

Hanafizadeh, M. R., Saghaei, A., & Hanafizadeh, P. (2009). An index for cross-country analysis of ICT infrastructure and access. *Telecommunications Policy, 33*(7), 385–405. Retrieved from https://doi.org/10.1016/j.telpol.2009.03.008

Hargittai, E. (2002). Second level digital divide: Difference in people's online skills. *First Monday, 7*(4), 1–16. Retrieved from http://dx.doi.org/10.5210/fm.v7i4.942

Hargittai, E. (2005). Survey measures of Web-oriented digital literacy. *Social Science Computer Review, 23*(3), pp. 371–379. Retrieved from https://doi.org/10.1177/0894439305275911

Hargittai, E. (2009). An update on survey measures of Web-oriented digital literacy. *Social Science Computer Review, 27*(1), 130–137. Retrieved from https://doi.org/10.1177/0894439308318213

Hargittai, E. (2010). Digital na(t)ives? Variation in Internet skills and uses among members of the 'Net Generation'. *Sociological Inquiry, 80*(1), 92–113. Retrieved from https://doi.org/10.1111/j.1475-682X.2009.00317.x

Hargittai, E., & Hinnant, A. (2008). Digital inequality: Differences in young adults' use of the internet. *Communication Research, 35*(5), 602–621. Retrieved from https://doi.org/10.1177/0093650208321782

Hargittai, E., & Shafer, S. (2006). Differences in actual and perceived online skills: The role of gender. *Social Science Quarterly, 87*(2), 432–448. Retrieved from https://doi.org/10.1111/j.1540-6237.2006.00389.x

Hargittai, E., & Walejko, G. (2008). The participation divide: Content creation and sharing in the digital age. *Information, Communication & Society, 11*(2), 239–256. Retrieved from https://doi.org/10.1080/13691180801946150

Harzing, A., & van der Wal, R. (2008). Google Scholar as a new source for citation analysis. *Ethics in Science and Environmental Politics, 8*, 61–73. Retrieved from https://doi.org/10.3354/esep00076

Hatlevik, O. E., Guðmundsdóttir, G. B., & Loi, M. (2015). Digital diversity among upper secondary students: A multilevel analysis of the relationship between cultural capital, self-efficacy, strategic use of information and digital competence. *Computers & Education, 81*, 345–353. Retrieved from https://doi.org/10.1016/j.compedu.2014.10.019

Hauben, M., & Hauben, R. (1997). *Netizens: On the history and impact of Usenet and the Internet*. Los Alamitos, CA: IEEE Computer Society Press.

Haythornthwaite, C. A., & Wellman, B. (2002). The Internet in everyday life: An introduction. In B. Wellman & C. A. Haythornthwaite (Eds.), *The Internet in everyday life* (pp. 3–41). Malden, MA: Blackwell.

Heeks, R. (1999). *Information and communication technologies, poverty and development*. Manchester: Institute for Development Policy and Management, University of Manchester.

Heeks, R. (2010). Do information and communication technologies (ICTs) contribute to development? *Journal of International Development, 22*(5), 625–640. Retrieved from https://doi.org/10.1002/jid.1716

Helsper, E. J. (2008). *Digital inclusion: An analysis of social disadvantage and the information society.* London: Department for Communities and Local Government. Retrieved from http://eprints.lse.ac.uk/26938/1/__libfile_REPOSITORY_Content_Helsper%2C%20E_Digital%20inclusion_Helsper_Digital%20inclusion_2013.pdf

Helsper, E. J. (2012). A corresponding fields model for the links between social and digital exclusion: A corresponding fields model for digital exclusion. *Communication Theory, 22*(4), 403–426. Retrieved from https://doi.org/10.1111/j.1468-2885.2012.01416.x

Helsper, E. J. (2017a). A socio-digital ecology approach to understanding digital inequalities among young people. *Journal of Children and Media, 11*(2), 256–260. Retrieved from https://doi.org/10.1080/17482798.2017.1306370

Helsper, E. J. (2017b). The social relativity of digital exclusion: Applying relative deprivation theory to digital inequalities. *Communication Theory, 27*(3), 223–242. Retrieved from https://doi.org/10.1111/comt.12110

Helsper, E. J., & Deursen, A. J. A. M. van. (2017). Do the rich get digitally richer? Quantity and quality of support for digital engagement. *Information, Communication & Society, 20*(5), 700–714. Retrieved from https://doi.org/10.1080/1369118X.2016.1203454

Helsper, E. J., & Eynon, R. (2010). Digital natives: Where is the evidence? *British Education Research Journal, 36*(3), 503–520. Retrieved from https://doi.org/10.1080/01411920902989227

Helsper, E. J., & Eynon, R. (2013). Distinct skill pathways to digital engagement. *European Journal of Communication, 28*(6), 696–713. Retrieved from https://doi.org/10.1177/0267323113499113

Helsper, E. J., & Gerber, M. M. (2012). The plausibility of cross-national comparisons of Internet use types. *The Information Society: An International Journal, 28*(2), 83–98. Retrieved from https://doi.org/10.1080/01972243.2011.650294

Helsper, E. J., & Reisdorf, B. C. (2013). A quantitative examination of explanations for reasons for internet nonuse. *Cyberpsychology, Behavior, and Social Networking, 16*(2), 94–99. Retrieved from https://doi.org/10.1089/cyber.2012.0257

Helsper, E. J., & Reisdorf, B. C. (2017). The emergence of a 'digital underclass' in Great Britain and Sweden: Changing reasons for digital exclusion. *New Media & Society, 19*(8), 1253–1270. Retrieved from https://doi.org/10.1177/1461444816634676

Helsper, E. J., & van Deursen, A. J. A. M. (2015). Digital skills in Europe: Research and policy. In K. Andreasson (Ed.), *Digital divides: The new challenges and opportunities of e-inclusion* (pp. 125–146). London: CRC Press.

Helsper, E. J., van Deursen, A. J. A. M., & Eynon, R. (2015). *Tangible outcomes of internet use: From digital skills to tangible outcomes project report.* Oxford Internet Institute, University of Twente and London School of Economics and Political Science. Retrieved from www.oii.ox.ac.uk/research/projects/?id=112

Hess, F. M., & Leal, D. L. (2001). A shrinking 'digital divide'? The provision of classroom computers across urban school systems. *Social Science Quarterly, 82*(4), 765–778. Retrieved from http://dx.doi.org/10.1111/0038-4941.00058

Hilbert, M. (2016). The bad news is that the digital access divide is here to stay: Domestically installed bandwidths among 172 countries for 1986–2014. *Telecommunications Policy, 40*(6), 567–581. Retrieved from https://doi.org/10.1016/j.telpol.2016.01.006

Hindman, D. B. (2000). The rural-urban digital divide. *Journalism & Mass Communication Quarterly, 77*(3), 549–560. Retrieved from https://doi.org/10.1177/107769900007700306

Hindman, M. S. (2008). *The myth of digital democracy.* Princeton, NJ: Princeton University Press.

Hirsch-Kreinsen, H., Jacobson, D., & Robertson, P. L. (2006). 'Low-tech' industries: Innovativeness and development perspectives – A summary of a European research project. *Prometheus, 24*(1), 3–21. Retrieved from https://doi.org/10.1080/08109020600563762

Hoffman, D. L. (2012). Internet indispensability, online social capital, and consumer well-being. In D. G. Mick, S. Pettigrew, C. Pechmann & J. L. Ozanne (Eds.), *Transformative consumer research for personal and collective well-being* (pp. 193–204). New York, NY: Routledge.

Hoffman, D. L., & Novak, T. P. (1998). *Bridging the digital divide: The impact of race on computer access and internet use.* Nashville: Vanderbilt University.

Hoffman, D., Novak, T., & Schlosser, A. E. (2001). The evolution of the digital divide: Examining the relationship of race to Internet access and usage over time. In B. M. Compaine (Ed.), *The digital divide: Facing a crisis or creating a myth?* (pp. 47–97). Cambridge, MA: MIT Press.

Hoffman, D. L., Novak, T. P., & Venkatesh, A. (2004). Has the internet become indispensable? Empirical findings and model development. *Communications of the ACM, 47*(7), 37–42.

Holloway, D. (2005). The digital divide in Sydney: A sociospatial analysis. *Information, Communication & Society, 8*(2), 168–193. Retrieved from https://doi.org/10.1080/13691180500146276

Horrigan, J. B. (2006). *Home broadband adoption 2006.* Washington, DC: Pew Internet & American Life Project. Retrieved from http://www.pewinternet.org/2006/05/28/home-broadband-adoption-2006/

Horrigan, J. B. (2007). *A typology of information and communication technology users.* Washington, DC: Pew Internet & American Life Project. Retrieved from http://www.pewinternet.org/2007/05/06/a-typology-of-information-and-communication-technology-users/

Horrigan, J. B. (2008). *Mobile access to data and information.* Washington, DC: Pew Internet & American Life Project. Retrieved from http://www.pewinternet.org/2008/03/05/mobile-access-to-data-and-information-2/

Horrigan, J. B. (2010). *Broadband adoption and use in America: OBI working paper series No. 1.* Federal Communication Commissions. Retrieved from http://hraunfoss.fcc.gov/edocs_public/attachmatch/DOC-296442A1.pdf

Horrigan, J. B. (2011). What are the consequences of being disconnected in a broadband-connected world? *Daedalus, 140*(4), 17–31. Retrieved from https://doi.org/10.1162/DAED_a_00112

Horrigan, J. B., & Duggan, M. (2015). *Home broadband 2015.* Washington, DC: Pew Research Center. Retrieved from http://www.pewinternet.org/2015/12/21/home-broadband-2015/

Horrigan, J. B., & Rainie, L. (2002). *The broadband difference: How online Americans' behavior changes with high-speed Internet connections at home.* Washington, DC: Pew Internet & American Life Project. Retrieved from http://www.pewinternet.org/2002/06/23/the-broadband-difference-how-online-behavior-changes-with-high-speed-internet-connections/

Horrigan, J. B., & Rainie, L. (2006). *The Internet's growing role in life's major moments.* Washington, DC: Pew Internet & American Life Project. Retrieved from http://www.pewinternet.org/2006/04/19/the-internets-growing-role-in-lifes-major-moments/

Houston, R. D., & Erdelez, S. (2002). The digital divide: Who really benefits from the proposed solutions for closing the gap. *Proceedings of the American Society for Information Science and Technology, 39*(1), 99–106. Retrieved from https://doi.org/10.1002/meet.1450390111

Howard, P. E. N., Rainie, L., & Jones. S. (2002). Days and nights on the Internet. In B. Wellman & C. Haythornthwaite (Eds.), *The Internet in everyday life* (pp. 45–73). Malden, MA: Blackwell.

Hwang, J. (2006). *Deconstructing the discourse of the global digital divide in the age of neo-liberal global economy.* Unpublished Ph.D. thesis, The Pennsylvania State University. Retrieved from https://etda.libraries.psu.edu/files/final_submissions/3156

International Telecommunication Union (ITU). (2010). *Measuring the information society 2010.* Geneva. Retrieved from https://www.itu.int/en/ITU-D/Statistics/Documents/publications/mis2010/MIS_2010_without_annex_4-e.pdf

International Telecommunication Union (ITU). (2016). *Measuring the information society report 2016*. Geneva. Retrieved from https://www.itu.int/en/ITU-D/Statisti cs/Documents/publications/misr2016/MISR2016-w4.pdf

Jackson, L. A., Barbatsis, G., Biocca, F. A., von Eye, A., Zhao, Y., & Fitzgerald, H. E. (2004). Home Internet use in low-income families: Is access enough to eliminate the digital divide? In E. P. Bucy & J. E. Newhagen (Eds.), *Media access: Social and psychological dimensions of new technology use* (pp. 155–184). Nahwan, NJ: Lawrence Erlbaum Associates.

Jagun, A., Heeks, R., & Whalley, J. L. (2008). The impact of mobile telephony on developing country micro-enterprises: A Nigerian case study. *Informational Technology and International Development*, *4*(4), 47–65. Retrieved from https://strathprints.strath.ac.uk/id/eprint/15425

James, J. (2005). The global digital divide in the Internet: Developed countries constructs and Third World realities. *Journal of Information Science*, *31*(2), 114–123. Retrieved from https://doi.org/10.1177/0165551505050788

James, J. (2007). From origins to implications: Key aspects in the debate over the digital divide. *Journal of Information Technology*, *22*(3), 284–295. Retrieved from https://doi.org/10.1057/palgrave.jit.2000097

James, J. (2008a). Digital divide complacency: Misconceptions and dangers. *The Information Society: An International Journal*, *24*(1), 54–61. Retrieved from https://doi.org/10.1080/01972240701774790

James, J. (2008b). Re-estimating the difficulty of closing the digital divide. *Journal of the American Society for Information Science and Technology*, *59*(12), 2024–2032. Retrieved from https://doi.org/10.1002/asi.20897

James, J. (2011). Sharing mobile phones in developing countries: Implications for the digital divide. *Technological Forecasting and Social Change*, *78*(4), 729–735. Retrieved from https://doi.org/10.1016/j.techfore.2010.11.008

Jansen, J. (2010). *Use of the internet in higher-income household*. Washington, DC: Pew Internet & American Life Project. Retrieved from http://www.pewinternet.org/2010/11/24/use-of-the-internet-in-higher-income-households/

Jones, C., Ramanau, R., Cross, S., & Healing, G. (2010). Net generation or digital natives: Is there a distinct new generation entering university? *Computers and Education*, *54*(3), 722–732. Retrieved from https://doi.org/10.1016/j.compedu.2009.09.022

Jensen, R. (2007). The digital provide: Information (technology), market performance, and welfare in the South Indian fisheries sector. *The Quarterly Journal of Economics*, *122*(3), 879–924. https://doi.org/10.1162/qjec.122.3.879

Karvalics, L. Z. (2008). Information society: What is it exactly? (The meaning, history and conceptual framework of an expression). In P. Róbert & K. Attila (Eds.), *Information society: From theory to political practice* (pp. 27–46). Budapest: Gondolat: Új Mandátum. Retrieved from http://www.lincompany.kz/pdf/Hungary/NETIS_Course_Book_English2008.pdf

Katz, J., & Aspden, P. (1997). Motives, hurdles, and dropouts. *Communications of the ACM*, 40(4), 97–102. Retrieved from http://dx.doi.org/10.1145/248448.248464

Katz, J. E., & Rice, R. E. (2002). *Social consequences of internet use: Access, involvement, and interaction*. Cambridge, MA: MIT Press.

Kennedy, T. L. M., Smith, A., Wells, A. T., & Wellman, B. (2008). *Networked families*. Pew Internet & American Life. Retrieved from http://www.pewinternet.org/2008/10/19/networked-families/

Kidane, Y. H., & Gloor, P. A. (2007). Correlating temporal communication patterns of the Eclipse open source community with performance and creativity. *Computational and Mathematical Organization Theory*, *13*(1), 17–27.

Kim, B.-K. (2005). *Internationalising the Internet: The co-evolution of influence and technology*. Northampton, MA: Edward Elgar.

Kim, J., LaRose, R., & Peng, W. (2009). Loneliness as the cause and the effect of problematic Internet use: The relationship between internet use and psychological well-being. *CyberPsychology & Behavior, 12*(4), 451–455. Retrieved from https://doi.org/10.1089/cpb.2008.0327

Kim, M.-C., & Kim, J.-K. (2001). Digital divide: Conceptual discussions and prospect. In *The human society and the internet Internet-related socio-economic issues* (pp. 78–91). Springer, Berlin, Heidelberg. Retrieved from https://doi.org/10.1007/3-540-47749-7_6

Kim, S. (2011). The diffusion of the Internet: Trend and causes. *Social Science Research, 40*(2), 602–613. Retrieved from https://doi.org/10.1016/j.ssresearch.2010.07.005

Kohut, A., & Bowman, C. (1994). *Technology in the American household.* Los Angeles, CA: Times Mirror Center for The People & The Press. Retrieved from http://www.people-press.org/1994/05/24/technology-in-the-american-household/#summary-of-findings

Korte, W. B., & Hüsing, T. (2006). *Benchmarking access and use of ICT in European schools 2006: Final report from Head Teacher and Classroom Teacher Survey in 27 European countries.* Bonn: Empirica Gesellschaft für Kommunikations und Technologieforschung. Retrieved from https://publications.europa.eu/en/publication-detail/-/publication/74067431-ecd4-11e5-8a81-01aa75ed71a1/language-en/format-PDF

Kral, I. (2014). Shifting perceptions, shifting identities: Communication technologies and the altered social, cultural and linguistic ecology in a remote indigenous context. The Australian Journal of Anthropology, 25(2), 171–189. https://doi.org/10.1111/taja.12087

Korupp, S. E., & Szydlik, M. (2005). Causes and trends of the digital divide. *European Sociological Review, 21*(4), 409–422. Retrieved from https://doi.org/10.1093/esr/jci030

Kraut, R., Kieslar, S., Boneva, B., Cummings, J., Helgeson, V., & Crawford, A. (2002). Internet paradox revisited. *Journal of Social Issues, 58*(1), pp. 49–74. Retrieved from https://doi.org/10.1111/1540-4560.00248

Kraut, R. E., Patterson, M., Lundmark, V., Kiesler, S., Mukopadhyay, T., & Scherlis, W. L. (1998). Internet paradox: A social technology that reduces social involvement and psychological well-being? *American Psychologist, 53*(9), 1017–1031.

Kuhn, T. S. (1970). *The structure of scientific revolutions* (2nd ed.). Chicago, IL: University of Chicago Press.

Kvasny, L. (2005). The role of the habitus in shaping discourses about the digital divide. *Journal of Computer-Mediated Communication, 10*(2). Retrieved from https://doi.org/10.1111/j.1083-6101.2005.tb00242.x

Kvasny, L. (2006). Cultural (re)production of digital inequality in a US community technology initiative. *Information, Communication & Society, 9*(2), 160–181. Retrieved from https://doi.org/10.1080/13691180600630740

Kvasny, L., & Trauth, E. M. (2003). The digital divide at work and home: The discourse about power and underrepresented groups in the information society. In E. H. Wynn, E. A. Whitley, M. D. Myers, & J. I. DeGross (Eds.), *Global and organizational discourse about information technology* (pp. 273–291). Boston, MA: Kluwer Academic Publishers.

Kvasny, L., & Truex, D. (2001). Defining away the digital divide: A content analysis of institutional influences on popular representations of technology. In N. L. Russo, B. Fitzgerald, & J. I. DeGross (Eds.), *Realigning research and practice in information systems development: The social and organizational perspective* (pp. 399–414). New York, NY: Kluwer Academic Publishers.

Kwak, N. (1999). Revisiting the knowledge gap hypothesis: Education, motivation, and media use. *Communication Research, 26*(4), 385–414. Retrieved from https://doi.org/10.1177/009365099026004002

Labaton, S. (2001, February 7). New F.C.C. chief would curb Agency reach. *The New York Times.* Retrieved from http://www.nytimes.com/2001/02/07/business/new-fcc-chief-would-curb-agency-reach.html

Lee, S. J. (2009). Online communication and adolescent social ties: Who benefits more from Internet use? *Journal of Computer-Mediated Communication, 14*(3), 509–531. Retrieved from https://doi.org/10.1111/j.1083-6101.2009.01451.x

Lefort, R. (1999). Talking to…Manuel Castells: The citizen versus the machine. *UNESCO Courier, 52*(10), 46–50.

Lei, W., Gibbs, M. R., & Chang, S. (2008). Rethinking the digital divide. In A. Mills & S. Huff (Eds.), *Creating the future transforming research into practice: Proceeding of the 19th Australasian Conference on Information Systems, 3–5 December 2008*. Christchurch: University of Canterbury.

Lenhart, A. (2000). *Who's not online*. Washington, DC: Pew Internet & American Life Project. Retrieved from http://www.pewinternet.org/2000/09/21/whos-not-online/

Lenhart, A., & Horrigan, J. B. (2003). Re-visualizing the digital divide as a digital spectrum. *IT&Society, 1*(5), 23–39.

Lenhart, A., Horrigan, J. B., Rainie, L., Allen, K., Boyce, A., Madden, M., & O'Grady, E. (2003) *The ever-shifting Internet population: A new look at Internet access and the digital divide*. Washington, DC: Pew Internet & American Life Project. Retrieved from http://www.pewinternet.org/2003/04/16/the-ever-shifting-internet-population-a-new-look-at-internet-access-and-the-digital-divide/

Lenhart, A., Madden, M., & Hitlin, P. (2005). *Teens and technology*. Pew Internet & American Life. Retrieved from http://www.pewinternet.org/2005/07/27/teens-and-technology/

Leslie Steeves, H., & Kwami, J. (2017). Interrogating gender divides in technology for education and development: The case of the One Laptop per Child Project in Ghana. *Studies in Comparative International Development, 52*(2), 174–192. Retrieved from https://doi.org/10.1007/s12116-017-9245-y

Lévi-Strauss, C. (1963). *Structural anthropology*. New York, NY: Basic Books.

Leye, V. (2007). UNESCO, ICT corporations and the passion of ICT for development: Modernization resurrected. *Media, Culture & Society, 29*(6), 972–993. Retrieved from https://doi.org/10.1177/0163443707081711

Liu, D., & Yang, C. (2016). Media niche of electronic communication channels in friendship: A meta-analysis. *Journal of Computer-Mediated Communication, 21*(6), 451–466. Retrieved from https://doi.org/10.1111/jcc4.12175

Livingston, G., Parker, K., & Fox, S. (2009). *Latinos online, 2006–2008: Narrowing the gap*. Washington, DC: Pew Hispanic Center, Pew Internet & American Life Project. Retrieved from http://www.pewhispanic.org/2009/12/22/latinos-online-2006-2008-narrowing-the-gap/

Livingstone, S., & Helsper, E. (2007). Gradations in digital inclusion: Children, young people and the digital divide. *New Media & Society, 9*(4), 671–696. Retrieved from https://doi.org/10.1177/1461444807080335

Loges, W. E., & Jung, J.-Y. (2001). Exploring the digital divide: Internet connectedness and age. *Communication Research, 28*(4), 536–562. Retrieved from https://doi.org/10.1177/009365001028004007

Lüders, M., & Gjevjon, E. R. (2017). Being old in an always-on culture: Older people's perceptions and experiences of online communication. *The Information Society: An International Journal, 33*(2), 64–75. Retrieved from https://doi.org/10.1080/01972243.2016.1271070

Luhmann, N. (2012). *Love as passion: The codification of intimacy*. (J. Gaines & D. L. Jones, Trans.). Cambridge, MA: Polity Press; Harvard University Press. (Original work published 1982.)

Lupač, P. (2011). Building up critical theory of the information society. *Masaryk University Journal of Law and Technology, 3*(2), 339–344.

Lupač, P., Chrobáková, A., & Sládek, J. (2015). *The Internet in the Czech Republic 2014*. Retrieved from http://www.worldinternetproject.com/api/file/filemanage/56/Reports/20171009/files/da66af1b8b5d24151bc530393e1dec3b.pdf

Lyon, D. (2000). The net, the self and the future. *Prometheus, 3*, 56–68.

Macek, J., Macková, A., & Kotišová, J. (2015). Participation or new media use first? Reconsidering the role of new media in civic practices in the Czech Republic. *Medijske Studije, 6*(11), 68–83.

Macionis, J. J. (2016). *Sociology* (16th ed.). Hoboken, NJ: Pearson Education.

MacKenzie, D. (1984). Marx and the machine. *Technology and culture, 25*(3), 473. Retrieved from https://doi.org/10.2307/3104202

Madden, K. (2006). *Internet penetration and Impact.* Washington, DC: Pew Internet & American Life Project. Retrieved from http://www.pewinternet.org/2006/04/26/internet-penetration-and-impact/

Madden, M., Lenhart, A., Duggan, M., Cortesi, S., & Gasser, U. (2013). *Teens and technology 2013.* Washington, DC: Pew Research Center's Internet & American Life Project. Retrieved from http://www.pewinternet.org/2013/03/13/teens-and-technology-2013/

Mahajan, V., & Peterson, R. A. (1985). *Models for innovation diffusion.* Beverly Hills, CA: Sage.

Markus, M. L. (1987). Toward a 'critical mass' theory of interactive media: Universal access, interdependence and diffusion. *Communication Research, 14*(5), 491–511. Retrieved from https://doi.org/10.1177/009365087014005003

Martin, S. P. (2003). Is the digital divide really closing? A critique of inequality measurement in a nation online. *IT&Society, 1*(4), 1–13.

Martin, S. P., & Robinson, J. P. (2004). The income digital divide: An international perspective. *IT&Society, 1*(7), 1–20.

Martin, S. P., & Robinson, J. P. (2007). The income digital divide: Trends and predictions for levels of Internet use. *Social Problems, 54*(1), 1–22. Retrieved from https://doi.org/10.1525/sp.2007.54.1.1

Martínez-Santos, P., Cerván, J., Cano, B., & Díaz-Alcaide, S. (2017). Water versus wireless coverage in rural Mali: Links and paradoxes. *Water, 9*(6), 375. Retrieved from https://doi.org/10.3390/w9060375

Mason, S. M., & Hacker, K. L. (2003). Applying communication theory to digital divide research. *It&Society, 1*(5), 40–55.

Masuda, Y. (1980). *The information society as post-industrial society.* Washington, DC: World Future Society.

Matei, S., & Ball-Rokeach, S. J. (2002). Belonging in geographic, ethnic, and Internet spaces. In B. Wellman & C. A. Haythornthwaite (Eds.), *The Internet in everyday life* (pp. 404–427). Malden, MA: Blackwell.

May, C. (2002). *The information society: A sceptical view.* Malden, MA: Polity Press.

Mayberry, L. S., Kripalani, S., Rothman, R. L., & Osborn, C. Y. (2011). Bridging the digital divide in diabetes: Family support and implications for health literacy. *Diabetes Technology & Therapeutics, 13*(10), 1005–1012. Retrieved from https://doi.org/10.1089/dia.2011.0055

McChesney, R. W. (2013). *Digital disconnect: How capitalism is turning the Internet against democracy.* New York, NY: The New Press.

McKenzie, K. (2007). Digital divides: The implications for social inclusion. *Learning Disability Practice, 10*(6), 16–21. Retrieved from https://doi.org/10.7748/ldp2007.07.10.6.16.c4272

McLuhan, M. (1995). *Essential McLuhan.* (E. McLuhan & F. Zingrone, Eds.). New York, NY: BasicBooks.

McQuail, D. (1994). *Mass communication theory: An introduction* (3rd ed.). London: Sage.

Menou, M. J. (2001a). *Digital and social equity? Opportunities and threats on the road to empowerment.* Presented at the LIDA 2001 Annual Course and Conference, Libraries in the Digital Age, Dubrovnik, Croatia. Retrieved from http://www.ffzg.hr/infoz/lida/lida2001/present/menou.rtf

Menou, M. J. (2001b). The global digital divide; Beyond hICTeria. *Aslib Proceedings, 53*(4), 112–114. Retrieved from https://doi.org/10.1108/EUM0000000007045

Mesch, G., & Talmud, I. (2008). Culture differences in communication technology use: Adolescent Jews and Arabs in Israel. In J. E. Katz (Ed.), *Handbook of mobile communication studies* (pp. 313–324). Cambridge, MA: MIT Press.

Meza-Cordero, J. A. (2017). Learn to play and play to learn: Evaluation of the One Laptop per Child Program in Costa Rica. *Journal of International Development*, *29*(1), 3–31. Retrieved from https://doi.org/10.1002/jid.3267

Michaels, G., Natraj, A., & Van Reenen, J. (2014). Has ICT polarized skill demand? Evidence from eleven countries over twenty-five years. *Review of Economics and Statistics*, *96*(1), 60–77. Retrieved from https://doi.org/10.1162/REST_a_00366

Mitchell, W. J. (1996). *City of bits: Space, place, and the Infobahn*. London; Cambridge, MA: MIT Press.

Moodley, G. (2005). *Critical analysis of the post-apartheid South African government's discourse on information and communication technologies (ICTs), poverty and development*. Unpublished Ph.D. thesis, University of Stellenbosch, the School of Public Management and Planning, Stellenbosch.

Morahan-Martin, J., & Schumacher, P. (2003). Loneliness and social uses of the Internet. *Computers in Human Behavior*, *19*(6), 659–671. Retrieved from https://doi.org/10.1016/S0747-5632(03)00040-2

Mossberger, K., Tolbert, C. J., & Anderson, C. (2017). The mobile Internet and digital citizenship in African-American and Latino communities. *Information, Communication & Society*, *20*(10), 1587–1606. Retrieved from https://doi.org/10.1080/1369118X.2016.1243142

Mossberger, K., Tolbert, C. J., & McNeal, R. S. (2008). *Digital citizenship: The internet, society, and participation*. London, Cambridge, MA: MIT Press.

Mossberger, K., Tolbert, C. J., & Stansbury, M. (2003). *Virtual inequality: Beyond the digital divide*. Washington, DC: Georgetown University Press.

Murdock, D. (2000). *Digital divide? What digital divide?* Washington, DC: Cato Institute. Retrieved from https://www.cato.org/publications/commentary/digital-divide-what-digital-divide

National Telecommunications and Information Administration (NTIA). (1995). *Falling through the net: A survey of the 'have nots' in rural and urban America*. Washington, DC: US Department of Commerce. Retrieved from http://www.ntia.doc.gov/ntiahome/fallingthru.html

National Telecommunications and Information Administration (NTIA). (1998). *Falling through the net: New data on the digital divide*. Washington, DC: US Department of Commerce. Retrieved from http://www.ntia.doc.gov/ntiahome/fallingthru.html

National Telecommunications and Information Administration (NTIA). (1999). *Falling through the net: Defining the digital divide*. Washington, DC: US Department of Commerce. Retrieved from https://www.ntia.doc.gov/report/1999/falling-through-net-defining-digital-divide

National Telecommunications and Information Administration (NTIA). (2000). *Falling through the Net: Toward digital inclusion*. Washington, DC: US Department of Commerce. Retrieved from https://www.ntia.doc.gov/report/2000/falling-through-net-toward-digital-inclusion

National Telecommunications and Information Administration (NTIA). (2002). *A nation online: How Americans are expanding their use of the Internet*. Washington, DC: US Department of Commerce. Retrieved from https://www.ntia.doc.gov/legacy/ntiahome/dn/anationonline2.pdf

Negroponte, N. (1995). *Being digital*. New York, NY: Knopf.

Newhagen, J. E., & Bucy, E. P. (2004). Routes to media access. In E. P. Bucy & J. E. Newhagen (Eds.), *Media access: Social and psychological dimensions of new technology use* (pp. 3–23). Nahwan, NJ: Lawrence Erlbaum Associates.

Nguyen, A., & Western, M. (2007). Socio-structural correlates of online news and information adoption/use: Implications for the digital divide. *Journal of Sociology*, *43*(2), 167–185. Retrieved from https://doi.org/10.1177/1440783307076894

Nie, N. H. (2001). Sociability, interpersonal relations, and the internet: Reconciling conflicting findings. *American Behavioral Scientist*, *45*(3), 420–435. Retrieved from https://doi.org/10.1177/00027640121957277

Nie, N. H., & Hillygus, D. S. (2002). The impact of Internet use on sociability: Time-diary findings. *The American Behavioral Scientist, 45*(3), 420–435.

Nie, N. H., Hillygus, D. S., & Ebring, L. (2002). Internet use, interpersonal relations, and sociability: A time diary study. In B. Wellman & C. A. Haythornthwaite (Eds.), *The Internet in everyday life* (pp. 216–243). Malden, MA: Blackwell.

Noce, A. A., & McKeown, L. (2008). A new benchmark for Internet use: A logistic modeling of factors influencing Internet use in Canada, 2005. *Government Information Quarterly, 25*(3), 462–476. Retrieved from https://doi.org/10.1016/j.giq.2007.04.006

Norris, P. (2001). *Digital divide: Civic engagement, information poverty, and the Internet worldwide*. Cambridge; New York, NY: Cambridge University Press.

O'Hara, K., & Stevens, D. (2006). *inequality.com: Power, poverty and the digital divide*. Oxford: Oneworld.

OECD, ISOC & UNESCO. (2013). *The relationship between local content, Internet development and access prices* (OECD Digital Economy Papers No. 217). Retrieved from https://doi.org/10.1787/5k4c1rq2bqvk-en

Ono, H., & Zavodny, M. (2003). Gender and the Internet. *Social Science Quarterly, 84*(1), 111–121. Retrieved from https://doi.org/10.1111/1540-6237.t01-1-8401007

Overå, R. (2008). Mobile traders and mobile phones in Ghana. In J. E. Katz (Ed.), *Handbook of mobile communication studies* (pp. 43–54). Cambridge, MA: MIT Press.

Pantea, S., & Martens, B. (2014). Has the digital divide been reversed? Evidence from five EU countries. *International Journal of Time Use Research, 11*(1), 13–42. Retrieved from https://doi.org/10.13085/eIJTUR.11.1.13-42

Park, S. R., Choi, D. Y., & Hong, P. (2015). Club convergence and factors of digital divide across countries. *Technological Forecasting and Social Change, 96*, 92–100. Retrieved from https://doi.org/10.1016/j.techfore.2015.02.011

Pearce, K. E., & Rice, R. E. (2014). The language divide: The persistence of English proficiency as a gateway to the Internet: The cases of Armenia, Azerbaijan, and Georgia. *International Journal of Communication, 8*, 2834–2859.

Pellizzari, M., Biagi, F., & Brecko, B. (2015). *E-skills mismatch: Evidence from international assessment of adult competencies (PIAAC)*. Institute for Prospective Technological Studies Digital Economy Working Paper 2015/10. Retrieved from https://ec.europa.eu/jrc/sites/jrcsh/files/JRC98228.pdf

Peng, G. (2010). Critical mass, diffusion channels, and digital divide. *Journal of Computer Information Systems, 50*(3), 63–71. Retrieved from https://doi.org/10.1080/08874417.2010.11645408

Peng, G. (2017). Do computer skills affect worker employment? An empirical study from CPS surveys. *Computers in Human Behavior, 74*, 26–34. Retrieved from https://doi.org/10.1016/j.chb.2017.04.013

Peng, T.-Q., Zhu, J. J. H., Tong, J.-J., & Jiang, S.-J. (2012). Predicting Internet non-users' adoption intention and adoption behavior. *Information, Communication & Society, 15*(8), 1236–1257. Retrieved from https://doi.org/10.1080/1369118X.2011.614628

Perkins, R., & Neumayer, E. (2011). Is the Internet really new after all? The determinants of telecommunications diffusion in historical perspective. *The Professional Geographer, 63*(1), 55–72. Retrieved from https://doi.org/10.1080/00330124.2010.500994

Perrin, A., & Duggan, M. (2015). *Americans' Internet access: 2000–2015*. Washington, DC: Pew Research Center. Retrieved from http://www.pewinternet.org/2015/06/26/americans-internet-access-2000-2015/

Pick, J. B., & Sarkar, A. (2015). *The global digital divides*. Berlin, Germany: Springer. Retrieved from https://doi.org/10.1007/978-3-662-46602-5

Pintér, R. (2008). Towards getting to know information society. In P. Róbert & K. Attila (Eds.), *Information society: From theory to political practice* (pp. 11–28). Budapest: Gondolat: Új Mandátum. Retrieved from http://www.lincompany.kz/pdf/Hungary/NETIS_Course_Book_English2008.pdf

Pitkow, J. E., & Kehoe, C. M. (1995). Results from the third WWW user survey. *The World Wide Web Journal, 1*(1). Retrieved from https://smartech.gatech.edu/bitstream/handle/1853/3494/96-08.pdf?sequence=1&isAllowed=y

Pitkow, J. E., & Recker, M. (1995). Using the Web as a survey tool: Results from the second WWW user survey. *Journal of Computer Networks and ISDN Systems, 27*(6), 809–822. Retrieved from https://doi.org/10.1016/0169-7552(95)00018-3

Porat, M. U. (1977). *The information economy: Definition and measurement (No. OT-SP-77-12 (1))*. Washington, DC: Office of Telecommunications (DOC). Retrieved from https://eric.ed.gov/?id=ED142205

Poster, M. (1990). *The mode of information: Poststructuralism and social context*. Chicago, IL: University of Chicago Press.

Poushter, J., Bell, J., & Oates, R. (2015). *Internet seen as positive influence on education but negative on morality in emerging and developing nations*. Washington, DC: Pew Research Center. Retrieved from http://www.pewglobal.org/2015/03/19/internet-seen-as-positive-influence-on-education-but-negative-influence-on-morality-in-emerging-and-developing-nations/

Prensky, M. (2001). Digital natives, digital immigrants. *On the Horizon, 9*(5), 1–6. Retrieved from https://doi.org/10.1108/10748120110424816

Prescott, M. B., & Conger, S. A. (1995). Information technology innovations: A classification by IT locus of impact and research approach. *ACM SIGMIS Database, 26*(2–3), 20–41. Retrieved from https://doi.org/10.1145/217278.217284

Prior, M. (2005). News vs. entertainment: How increasing media choice widens gaps in political knowledge and turnout. *American Journal of Political Science, 49*(3), 577–592. Retrieved from https://doi.org/10.1111/j.1540-5907.2005.00143.x

Punj, G. (2012). Income effects on relative importance of two online purchase goals: Saving time versus saving money? *Journal of Business Research, 65*(5), 634–640. Retrieved from https://doi.org/10.1016/j.jbusres.2011.03.003

Purcell, K. (2011). *Search and email still top the list of most popular online activities*. Washington, DC: Pew Internet & American Life Project. Retrieved from http://www.pewinternet.org/2011/08/09/search-and-email-still-top-the-list-of-most-popular-online-activities/

Putnam, R. D. (2000). *Bowling alone: The collapse and revival of American community*. New York, NY: Simon & Schuster.

Quan-Haase, A., Wellman, B., Witte, J. C., & Hampton, K. N. (2002). Capitalizing on the net: Social contact, civic engagement, and sense of community. In B. Wellman & C. A. Haythornthwaite (Eds.), *The Internet in everyday life* (pp. 291–324). Malden, MA: Blackwell.

Raban, D. R., Gordon, A., & Geifman, D. (2011). The information society: The development of a scientific specialty. *Information, Communication & Society, 14*(3), 375–399. Retrieved from https://doi.org/10.1080/1369118X.2010.542824

Rainie, L., Lenhart, A., Fox, S., Spooner, T., & Horrigan, J. B. (2000). *Tracking online life*. Washington, DC: Pew Internet & American Life Project. Retrieved from http://www.pewinternet.org/2000/05/10/tracking-online-life/

Rainie, L., & Wellman, B. (2012). *Networked: The new social operating system*. Cambridge, MA: MIT Press.

Rath, B. N. (2016). Does the digital divide across countries lead to convergence? New international evidence. *Economic Modelling, 58*, 75–82. Retrieved from https://doi.org/10.1016/j.econmod.2016.05.020

Reddick, A., Boucher, C., & Groseillier, M. (2000). *The dual digital divide: The information highway in Canada*. Ottawa, ON: Public Interest Advocacy Centre.

Reisdorf, B. C. (2011). Non-adoption of the Internet in Great Britain and Sweden: A cross-national comparison. *Information, Communication & Society, 14*(3), 400–420. Retrieved from https://doi.org/10.1080/1369118X.2010.543141

Reisdorf, B. C., & Groselj, D. (2017). Internet (non-)use types and motivational access: Implications for digital inequalities research. *New Media & Society*, *19*(8), 1157–1176. Retrieved from https://doi.org/10.1177/1461444815621539

Rheingold, H. (2000). The virtual community: Homesteading on the electronic frontier. Cambridge: MIT Press.

Rice, R. E., & Katz, J. E. (2003). Comparing internet and mobile phone usage: Digital divides of usage, adoption, and dropouts. *Telecommunications Policy*, *27*(8–9), 597–623. Retrieved from https://doi.org/10.1016/S0308-5961(03)00068-5

Richta, R. (1969). *Civilization at the crossroads : Social and human implications of the scientific and technological revolution*. (M. Šlingová, Trans.). White Plains, NY: International Arts and Sciences Press. (Original work published 1966.)

Roberts, J. (1999). Theory, technology and cultural power: An interview with Manuel Castells. *Angelaki: Journal of the Theoretical Humanities*, *4*(2), 33–39. Retrieved from https://doi.org/10.1080/09697259908572031

Robinson, J. P., & de Haan, J. (2006). Information technology and family time displacement. In R. E. Kraut, M. Brynin, & S. Kiesler (Eds.), *Computers, phones, and the Internet: Domesticating information technology* (pp. 51–69). New York, NY: Oxford University Press.

Robinson, J. P., DiMaggio, P., & Hargittai, E. (2003). New Social Survey perspectives on the digital divide. *IT&Society*, *1*(5), 1–22.

Robinson, L. (2009). A taste for the necessary: A Bourdieuian approach to digital inequality. *Information, Communication & Society*, *12*(4), 488–507. Retrieved from https://doi.org/10.1080/13691180902857678

Rogers, E. M. (1958). Categorizing adopters of agricultural practices. *Rural Sociology*, *23*(4), 345–354.

Rogers, E. M. (1986). *Communication technology: The new media in society*. New York, NY: The Free Press.

Rogers, E. M. (2001). The digital divide. *Convergence: The International Journal of Research into New Media Technologies*, *7*(4), 96–111. Retrieved from https://doi.org/10.1177/135485650100700406

Rogers, E. M. (2003). *Diffusion of innovations* (5th ed.). New York, NY: Free Press.

Rojas, V., Straubhaar, J. D., Roychowdhury, D., & Okur, O. (2004). Communities, cultural capital, and the digital divide. In E. P. Bucy & J. E. Newhagen (Eds.), *Media access: Social and psychological dimensions of new technology use* (pp. 107–130). Mahwah, NJ: Lawrence Erlbaum Associate.

Roszak, T. (1994). *The cult of information: A neo-luddite treatise on high-tech, artificial intelligence, and the true art of thinking* (2nd ed.). Berkeley, CA: University of California Press.

Salvaggio, J. L., & Steinfield, C. (1989). Toward a definition of the information society. In J. L. Salvaggio (Ed.), *The information society: Economic, social, and structural issues* (pp. 1–14). Hillsdale, NJ: Lawrence Erlbaum Associates.

Samuelson, R., J. (2002, March 24). Debunking the digital divide. *Newsweek*. Retrieved from http://www.newsweek.com/debunking-digital-divide-141675

Sassen, S. (1991). *The global city: New York, London, Tokyo*. Princeton, NJ: Princeton University Press.

Sassen, S. (1998a). *Globalization and its discontents: Essays on the new mobility of people and money*. New York, NY: New Press.

Sassen, S. (1998b). The topoi of e-space: Global cities and global value chains. *Built Environment*, *24*(2–3), 134–141.

Sassen, S. (2002a). Locating cities on global circuits. *Environment and Urbanization*, *14*(1), 13–30. Retrieved from https://doi.org/10.1177/095624780201400102

Sassen, S. (2002b). Towards a sociology of information technology. *Current Sociology*, *50*(3), 365–388. Retrieved from https://doi.org/10.1177/0011392102050003005

Sassen, S. (2006). *Territory, authority, rights: From medieval to global assemblages*. Princeton, NJ: Princeton University Press.

Sassen, S. (2014). Expulsions: Brutality and complexity in the global economy. Cambridge, Massachusetts: The Belknap Press of Harvard University Press.

Satchell, C., & Dourish, P. (2009). Beyond the user: Use and non-Use in HCI. In Association for Computing Machinery & ACM Digital Library (Eds.), *Proceedings of the 21st Annual Conference of the Australian Computer-Human Interaction Special Interest Group Design Open 247* (pp. 9–16). New York, NY: ACM. Retrieved from http://dl.acm.org/citation.cfm?id=1738826

Saunders, P. (2004). The urban as a spatial unit of collective consumption. In F. Webster & B. Dimitriou (Eds.), *Manuel castells* (Vol. I, pp. 82–114). Thousand Oaks, CA: Sage.

Scheerder, A., van Deursen, A. J. A. M., & van Dijk, J. A. G. M. (2017). Determinants of Internet skills, uses and outcomes. A systematic review of the second- and third-level digital divide. *Telematics and Informatics, 34*(8), 1607–1624. Retrieved from https://doi.org/10.1016/j.tele.2017.07.007

Schement, J. R. (2001). Of gaps by which democracy we measure. In B. M. Compaine (Ed.), *The digital divide: Facing a crisis or creating a myth?* (pp. 303–307). Cambridge, MA: MIT Press.

Schiller, H. I. (1996). *Information inequality: The deepening social crisis in America.* New York, NY: Routledge.

Schleife, K. (2010). What really matters: Regional versus individual determinants of the digital divide in Germany. *Research Policy, 39*(1), 173–185. Retrieved from https://doi.org/10.1016/j.respol.2009.11.003

Schneir, R. J., & Xiong, Y. (2016). A cost study of fixed broadband access networks for rural areas. *Telecommunications Policy, 40*(8), 755–773. Retrieved from https://doi.org/10.1016/j.telpol.2016.04.002

Sciadas, G. (2002). *Unveiling the digital divide.* Ottawa, ON: Science, Innovation and Electronic Information Division, Statistics Canada.

Selwyn, N. (2003). Apart from technology: Understanding people's non-use of information and communication technologies in everyday life. *Technology in Society, 25*(1), 99–116. Retrieved from https://doi.org/10.1016/S0160-791X(02)00062-3

Selwyn, N. (2004). Reconsidering political and popular understanding of the digital divide. *New Media and Society, 6*(3), pp. 341–362. Retrieved from https://doi.org/10.1177/1461444804042519

Selwyn, N. (2006). Digital division or digital decision? A study of non-users and low-users of computers. *Poetics, 34*(4–5), 273–292. Retrieved from https://doi.org/10.1016/j.poetic.2006.05.003

Selwyn, N. (2009). The digital native: Myth and reality. *Aslib Proceedings, 61*(4), 364–379. Retrieved from https://doi.org/10.1108/00012530910973776

Selwyn, N., Gorard, S., & Furlong, J. (2005). Whose Internet is it anyway? Exploring adults' (non)use of the internet in everyday life. *European Journal of Communication, 20*(1), 5–26. Retrieved from https://doi.org/10.1177/0267323105049631

Servon, L. J. (2002). *Bridging digital divide: Technology, community and public policy.* Malden, MA: Blackwell.

Shim, M. (2008). Connecting Internet use with gaps in cancer knowledge. *Health Communication, 23*(5), 448–461. Retrieved from https://doi.org/10.1080/10410230802342143

Shneiderman, B. (2004). Universal usability: Pushing human-computer interaction research to empower every citizen. In E. P. Bucy & J. E. Newhagen (Eds.), *Media access: Social and psychological dimensions of new technology use* (pp. 255–266). Mahwah, NJ: Lawrence Erlbaum Associate.

Simons, J. (2001). Cheap computers bridge digital divide. In B. M. Compaine (Ed.). *The digital divide: Facing a crisis or creating a myth?* (pp. 289–292). Cambridge, MA: MIT Press.

Sims, C. (2013). Is it time to rethink 'digital inequality' (again)? *AoIR selected papers of Internet Research, 14.* Retrieved from https://spir.aoir.org/index.php/spir/article/view/834/pdf

Skaletsky, M., Galliers, R. D., Haughton, D., & Soremekun, O. (2016). Exploring the predictors of the international digital divide. *Journal of Global Information Technology Management*, *19*(1), 44–67. Retrieved from https://doi.org/10.1080/10971 98X.2016.1134171

Sklair, L. (1994) Capitalism and development in global perspective. In L. Sklair (Ed.), *Capitalism & Development* (pp. 165–185). New York, NY: Routledge.

Smith, A. (2010a). *Home broadband 2010*. Washington, DC: Pew Internet & American Life. Retrieved from http://www.pewinternet.org/2010/08/11/home-broadband-2010/

Smith, A. (2010b). *Mobile access 2010*. Washington, DC: Pew Internet & American Life. Retrieved from http://www.pewinternet.org/2010/07/07/mobile-access-2010/

Standage, T. (1998). *The Victorian Internet: The remarkable story of the telegraph and the nineteenth century's on-line pioneers*. New York, NY: Walker and Co.

Statistics Bureau, Ministry of Internal Affairs and Communications, Statistics Japan. (2017). *The statistical handbook of Japan 2017*. Tokyo. Retrieved from http://www.stat.go.jp/english/data/handbook/index.htm

Stehr, N. (2000). Deciphering information technologies. Modern societies as networks. *European Journal of Social Theory*, *3*(1), 83–94. Retrieved from https://doi.org/10.1177/13684310022224697

Stepanikova, I., Nie, N. H., & He, X. (2010). Time on the Internet at home, loneliness, and life satisfaction: Evidence from panel time-diary data. *Computers in Human Behavior*, *26*(3), 329–338. Retrieved from https://doi.org/10.1016/j.chb.2009.11.002

Stevenson, S. (2009). Digital divide: A discursive move away from the real inequities. *The Information Society: An International Journal*, *25*(1), 1–22. Retrieved from https://doi.org/10.1080/01972240802587539

Steyaert, J. (2002). Inequality and the digital divide: Myths and realities. In S. Hick & J. G. McNutt (Eds.), *Advocacy, activism, and the internet: Community organization and social policy* (pp. 199–211). Chicago, IL: Lycecum Books.

Sujarwoto, S., & Tampubolon, G. (2016). Spatial inequality and the Internet divide in Indonesia 2010–2012. *Telecommunications Policy*, *40*(7), 602–616. Retrieved from https://doi.org/10.1016/j.telpol.2015.08.008

Tapia, A. H., Kvasny, L., & Ortiz, J. A. (2011). A critical discourse analysis of three US municipal wireless network initiatives for enhancing social inclusion. *Telematics and Informatics*, *28*(3), 215–226. Retrieved from https://doi.org/10.1016/j.tele.2010.07.002

Tapscott, D. (1998). *Growing up digital: The rise of the Net Generation*. New York, NY: McGraw-Hill.

The Broadband Commission for Digital Development. (2003). *Planning for progress: Why national broadband plans matter*. Geneva. Retrieved from http://www.broadbandcommission.org/documents/reportNBP2013.pdf

The Center for the Digital Future at USC Annenberg. (2004). *The digital future report, surveying the digital future, Year four*. Los Angeles, CA. Retrieved from http://www.digitalcenter.org/wp-content/uploads/2013/02/2004_digital_future_report-year4.pdf

The Center for the Digital Future at USC Annenberg. (2009). *World internet project: International report 2009*. Los Angeles, CA. Retrieved from http://www.digitalcenter.org/wp-content/uploads/2013/02/WIP-report-2009-final.pdf

The Center for the Digital Future at USC Annenberg. (2010). *World internet project: International report 2010* (2nd ed.). Los Angeles, CA. Retrieved from http://www.digitalcenter.org/wp-content/uploads/2012/12/2010wip_report.pdf

The Center for the Digital Future at USC Annenberg. (2012). *The world internet project: International report* (4th ed.). Los Angeles, CA. Retrieved from http://www.digitalcenter.org/wp-content/uploads/2013/01/2012wip_report4th_ed.pdf

The Center for the Digital Future at USC Annenberg. (2013). *The world internet project: International report* (5th ed.). Los Angeles, CA. Retrieved from http://www.digitalcenter.org/wp-content/uploads/2013/12/2013worldinternetreport.pdf

The Center for the Digital Future at USC Annenberg. (2014). *The 2014 digital future report, surveying the digital future, year twelve.* Los Angeles, CA. Retrieved from http://www.digitalcenter.org/wp-content/uploads/2014/01/2014-Digital-Future-Report.pdf

The Center for the Digital Future at USC Annenberg. (2016). *The world internet project: International report* (6th ed.). Los Angeles, CA. Retrieved from http://www.digitalcenter.org/wp-content/uploads/2017/12/2015-World-Internet-Project-Report.pdf

The racial digital divide just won't go away. (2004). *Journal of Blacks in Higher Education,* (46), 36–37. Retrieved from https://doi.org/10.2307/4133665

The White House, Office of the Press Secretary. (2000). *A national call to action to close the digital divide.* Washington, DC. Retrieved from https://clintonwhitehouse4.archives.gov/WH/New/html/20000404.html

Thierer, A. (2000, April 20). *How free computers are filling the digital divide.* Heritage Foundation Backgrounder. Retrieved from https://www.heritage.org/technology/report/how-free-computers-are-filling-the-digital-divide

Thomas, F. (2003). Internet dropouts – an essay in cultural diversity: The good, the bad and the irrelevant [SlideShare]. Retrieved from https://www.slideshare.net/ftr_/thomas-internet-dropouts

Thompson, M. (2004). Discourse, 'development' & the 'digital divide': ICT & the World Bank. *Review of African Political Economy, 31*(99), 103–123.

Thompson, W. E., & Hickey, J. V. (2012). *Society in focus: An introduction to sociology* (7th ed.). Boston, MA: Allyn & Bacon.

Tichenor, P. J., Donohue, G. A., & Olien, C. N. (1970). Mass media flow and differential growth in knowledge. *Public Opinion Quarterly, 34*(2), 159–170.

Tickamyer, A. R. (2000). Space matters! Spatial inequality in future sociology. *Contemporary Sociology, 29*(6), 805–813. Retrieved from https://doi.org/10.2307/2654088

Tilly, C. (1985). Review. *British Journal of Sociology, 36*(2), 294–295.

Toffler, A. (1980). *The third wave.* New York, NY: Bantam Books.

Tongia, R., & Wilson, E. J. (2011). The flip side of Metcalfe's Law: Multiple and growing costs of network exclusion. *International Journal of Communication, 5,* 665–681.

Touraine, A. (1971). *The post-industrial society. Tomorrow's social history: Classes, conflicts and culture in the programmed society.* (L. F. X. Mayhew, Trans.). New York, NY: Random House. (Original work published 1969.)

Touraine, A. (1981). *The voice and the eye: An analysis of social movements.* (A. Duff, Trans.). New York, NY: Cambridge University Press. (Original work published 1978)

Tuomi, I. (2000, July 11). *Beyond the digital divide.* Retrieved from http://citeseerx.ist.psu.edu/viewdoc/download?doi=10.1.1.488.6459&rep=rep1&type=pdf

Turkle, S. (2011). *Alone together: Why we expect more from technology and less from each other.* New York, NY: Basic Books.

UNDP. (1999). *Human development report 1999.* United Nations Development Programme. Retrieved from https://doi.org/10.18356/b0af4460-en

United Nations (UN). (2006). *The digital divide report: ICT Diffusion Index 2005.* New York, NY: United Nations.

Valadez, J. R., & Duran, R. (2007). Redefining the digital divide: Beyond access to computers and the Internet. *High School Journal, 90*(3), 31–44.

Valentine, G., Holloway, S., & Bingham, N. (2002). The digital generation? Children, ICT and the everyday nature of social exclusion. *Antipode, 34*(2), 296–315. Retrieved from https://doi.org/10.1111/1467-8330.00239

van Ark, B., Gupta, A., & Erumban, A. A. (2011). Measuring the contribution of ICT to economic growth. In B. van Ark & A. Gupta (Eds.), *The linked world: How ICT is transforming societies, cultures, and economies* (pp. 5–8). New York, NY: Conference Board.

van Deursen, A. J. A. M., Courtois, C., & van Dijk, J. A. G. M. (2014). Internet skills, sources of support, and benefiting from internet use. *International Journal of Human-Computer Interaction, 30*(4), 278–290. Retrieved from https://doi.org/10.1080/10447318.2013.858458

van Deursen, A. J. A. M., & van Diepen, S. (2013). Information and strategic Internet skills of secondary students: A performance test. *Computers & Education, 63*, 218–226. Retrieved from https://doi.org/10.1016/j.compedu.2012.12.007

van Deursen, A. J. A. M., & van Dijk, J. A. G. M. (2009). Using the Internet: Skill related problem in users' online behavior. *Interacting with Computers, 21*(5–6), 393–402. doi:doi.org/10.1016/j.intcom.2009.06.005

van Deursen, A. J. A. M., & van Dijk, J. A. G. M. (2010). Measuring Internet skills. *International Journal of Human-Computer Interaction, 26*(10), 891–916. Retrieved from https://doi.org/10.1080/10447318.2010.496338

van Deursen, A. J. A. M., & van Dijk, J. A. G. M. (2014). The digital divide shifts to differences in usage. *New Media & Society, 16*(3), 507–526 Retrieved from http://dx.doi.org/10.1177/1461444813487959

Van Deursen, A. J. A. M. & Van Dijk, J. A. G. M. (2012). Productiviteitsverlies door ICT-problemen en ontoereikende digitale vaardigheden. Enschede: Universiteit Twente.

van Deursen, A. J. A. M., van Dijk, J. A. G. M., & ten Klooster, P. M. (2015). Increasing inequalities in what we do online: A longitudinal cross sectional analysis of Internet activities among the Dutch population (2010 to 2013) over gender, age, education, and income. *Telematics and Informatics, 32*(2), 259–272. Retrieved from https://doi.org/10.1016/j.tele.2014.09.003

van Deursen, A. J. A. M., van Dijk, J. A. G. M., & Peters, O. (2011). Rethinking Internet skills: The contribution of gender, age, education, Internet experience, and hours online to medium- and content-related Internet skills. *Poetics, 39*(2), 125–144. Retrieved from https://doi.org/10.1016/j.poetic.2011.02.001

van Deursen, A. J. A. M., & Helsper, E. J. (2015). A nuanced understanding of Internet use and non-use among the elderly. *European Journal of Communication, 30*(2), 171–187. Retrieved from https://doi.org/10.1177/0267323115578059

van Deursen, A. J. A. M., & Helsper, E. J. (2017). Collateral benefits of Internet use: Explaining the diverse outcomes of engaging with the Internet. *New Media & Society.* Retrieved from https://doi.org/10.1177/1461444817715282

van Deursen, A. J. A. M., Helsper, E. J., & Eynon, R. (2014, October 7). *Measuring digital skills: From digital skills to tangible outcomes project report.* Retrieved from https://www.oii.ox.ac.uk/research/projects/measures-and-models-of-internet-use

van Deursen, A. J. A. M., Helsper, E., Eynon, R., & van Dijk, J. A. G. M. (2017). The compoundness and sequentiality of digital inequality. *International Journal of Communication, 11*(0), 22.

van Dijk, J. A. G. M. (1999). The one-dimensional network society of Manuel Castells. *New Media & Society, 1*(1), 127–138. Retrieved from https://doi.org/10.1177/1461444899001001015

van Dijk, J. A. G. M. (2000). Widening information gaps and policies of prevention. In J. A. G. M. van Dijk & K. L. Hacker (Eds.), *Digital democracy, issues of theory and practice* (pp. 166–183). Thousand Oaks, CA: Sage.

van Dijk, J. A. G. M. (2005). *The deepening divide: Inequality in the information society.* Thousand Oaks, CA: Sage.

van Dijk, J. A. G. M. (2006a). Digital divide research, achievements and shortcomings. *Poetics, 34*(4–5), 221–235. Retrieved from https://doi.org/10.1016/j.poetic.2006.05.004

van Dijk, J. A. G. M. (2006b). *The network society: Social aspects of new media* (2nd ed.). London: Sage.

van Dijk, J. A. G. M. (2009). One Europe, digitally divided. In A. Chadwick & P. N. Howard (Eds.), *Routledge handbook of internet politics* (pp. 288–304). New York, NY: Routledge.

van Dijk, J. A. G. M., & van Deursen, A. J. A. M. (2014). *Digital skills: Unlocking the information society.* New York, NY: Palgrave Macmillan.

van Dijk, J. A. G. M., & Hacker, K. (2003). The digital divide as a complex and dynamic phenomenon. *The Information Society: An International Journal, 19*(4), 315–326. Retrieved from https://doi.org/10.1080/01972240309487

Vehovar, V., Sicherl, P., Hüsing, T., & Dolnicar, V. (2006). Methodological challenges of digital divide measurements. *The Information Society: An International Journal, 22*(5), 279–290. Retrieved from https://doi.org/10.1080/01972240600904076

Venkatesh, V., & Brown, S. A. (2001). A longitudinal investigation of personal computers in homes: Adoption determinants and emerging challenges. *MIS Quarterly, 25*(1), 71–102.

Verdegem, P., & Verhoest, P. (2009). Profiling the non-user: Rethinking policy initiatives stimulating ICT acceptance. *Telecommunications Policy, 33*(10–11), 642–652. Retrieved from https://doi.org/10.1016/j.telpol.2009.08.009

Vicente, M. R., & López, A. J. (2011). Assessing the regional digital divide across the European Union-27. *Telecommunication Policy, 35*(3), 220–237. Retrieved from https://doi.org/10.1016/j.telpol.2010.12.013

Vinaja, R. (2003). The economic and social impact of electronic commerce in developing countries. In S. Lubbe & J. M. van Heerden (Eds.), *The economic and social impacts of e-commerce* (pp. 22–32). Hershey, PA: Idea Group.

Wang, H., & Wellman, B. (2010). Social connectivity in America: Changes in adult friendship network size from 2002 to 2007. *American Behavioral Scientist, 53*(8), 1148–1169. Retrieved from https://doi.org/10.1177/0002764209356247

Warf, B. (2001). Segueways into cyberspace: Multiple geographies of the digital divide. *Environment and Planning B: Planning and Design, 28*(1), 3–19. Retrieved from https://doi.org/10.1068/b2691

Warschauer, M. (2002). Reconceptualizing the digital divide. *First Monday, 7*(7). Retrieved from https://doi.org/10.5210/fm.v7i7.967

Warschauer, M. (2003). *Technology and social inclusion: Rethinking the digital divide* Cambridge, MA: MIT Press.

Warschauer, M., & Matuchniak, T. (2010). New technology and digital worlds: Analyzing evidence of equity in access, use, and outcomes. *Review of Research in Education, 34*(1), 179–225. Retrieved from https://doi.org/10.3102/0091732X09349791

Washington, J. (2011, January 10). For minorities, new 'digital divide' seen. *USA Today.* Retrieved from https://usatoday.com/tech/news/2011-01-10-minorities-online_N.htm#

Waterman, P. (1999). Review article: The brave new world of Manuel Castells: What on Earth (or in the Ether) is going on? *Development and Change, 30*(2), 357–380. Retrieved from https://doi.org/10.1111/1467-7660.00121

Weaver, C. K., Zorn, T., & Richardson, M. (2010). Goods not wanted: Older people's narratives of computer use rejection. *Information, Communication & Society, 13*(5), 696–721. Retrieved from https://doi.org/10.1080/13691180903410535

Webster, F. (1995). *Theories of the information society*. New York, NY: Routledge.

Webster, F. (2002). *Theories of the information society* (2nd ed.). New York, NY: Routledge.

Webster, F. (2006). *Theories of the information society* (3rd ed.). New York, NY: Routledge.

Wei, L., & Hindman, D. B. (2011). Does the digital divide matter more? Comparing the effects of new media and old media use on the education-based knowledge gap. *Mass Communication and Society, 14*(2), 216–235. Retrieved from https://doi.org/10.1080/15205431003642707

Weidman, A. C., Fernandez, K. C., Levinson, C. A., Augustine, A. A., Larsen, R. J., & Rodebaugh, T. L. (2012). Compensatory Internet use among individuals higher in social anxiety and its implications for well-being. *Personality and Individual Differences, 53*(3), 191–195. Retrieved from https://doi.org/10.1016/j.paid.2012.03.003

Wellman, B. (1988). Structural analysis: From method and metaphor to theory and substance. In B. Wellman & S. D. Berkowitz (Eds.), Social structures: A network approach (pp. 19–61). Cambridge: Cambridge University Press.

Wellman, B., Haase, A. Q., Witte, J., & Hampton, K. (2001). Does the Internet increase, decrease, or supplement social capital? Social networks, participation, and community commitment. *American Behavioral Scientist, 45*(3), 436–455. Retrieved from https://doi.org/10.1177/00027640121957286

Wentrup, R., Ström, P., & Nakamura, H. R. (2016). Digital oases and digital deserts in Sub-Saharan Africa. *Journal of Science and Technology Policy Management, 7*(1), 77–100. Retrieved from https://doi.org/10.1108/JSTPM-03-2015-0013

Whitacre, B. E. (2010). The diffusion of internet technologies to rural communities: A portrait of broadband supply and demand. *American Behavioral Scientist, 53*(9), 1283–1303. Retrieved from https://doi.org/10.1177/0002764210361684

Willis, S., & Tranter, B. (2006). Beyond the 'digital divide': Internet diffusion and inequality in Australia. *Journal of Sociology, 42*(1), 43–59. Retrieved from https://doi.org/10.1177/1440783306061352

Wilson, M. (2002). Understanding the international ICT and development discourse: Assumptions and implications. *The African Journal of Information and Communication, 2002*(3), 80–93.

Wilson, K. R., Wallin, J. S., & Reiser, C. (2003). Social stratification and the digital divide. *Social Science Computer Review, 21*(2), 133–143. Retrieved from https://doi.org/10.1177/0894439303021002001

Wirth, L. (1938). Urbanism as a way of life. *American Journal of Sociology, 44*(1), 1–24.

World Internet Project Poland. (2011). *World internet project Poland 2010*. Warsaw: Agora S. A. & TP Group

World Summit on the Information Society (WSIS). (2005). *Tunis agenda for the information society*. Retrieved from https://www.itu.int/net/wsis/docs2/tunis/off/6rev1.html#fui

Wu, Y.-H., Ware, C., Damnée, S., Kerhervé, H., & Rigaud, A.-S. (2015). Bridging the digital divide in older adults: A study from an initiative to inform older adults about new technologies. *Clinical Interventions in Aging, 10*, 193–201. Retrieved from https://doi.org/10.2147/CIA.S72399

Wyatt, S., Thomas, G., & Terranova, T. (2002). They came, they surfed, they went back to the beach: Conceptualizing use and non-use of the internet. In S. Woolgar (Ed.), *Virtual society? Technology, cyberbole, reality* (pp. 23–40). New York, NY: Oxford University Press.

Yu, L. (2006). Understanding information inequality: Making sense of the literature of the information and digital divides. *Journal of Librarianship and Information Science, 38*(4), 229–252. Retrieved from https://doi.org/10.1177/0961000606070600

Zachary, P. G. (2004). A philosopher of the web is a hit in silicon valley. In F. Webster & B. Dimitriou (Eds.), *Manuel castells* (Vol. I, pp. 301–304). Thousand Oaks, CA: Sage.

Zhao, F., Collier, A., & Deng, H. (2014). A multidimensional and integrative approach to study global digital divide and e-government development. *Information Technology & People, 27*(1), 38–62. Retrieved from https://doi.org/10.1108/ITP-01-2013-0022

Zhao, S. (2006). Do Internet users have more social ties? A call for differentiated analyses of internet use. *Journal of Computer-Mediated Communication, 11*(3), 844–862. Retrieved from https://doi.org/10.1111/j.1083-6101.2006.00038.x

Zickuhr, K. (2013). *Who's not online and why*. Washington, DC: Pew Research Center. Retrieved from http://www.pewinternet.org/2013/09/25/whos-not-online-and-why/

Zillien, N., & Hargittai, E. (2009). Digital distinction: Status-specific types of Internet usage. *Social Science Quarterly, 90*(2), 274–291. Retrieved from https://doi.org/10.1111/j.1540-6237.2009.00617.x

Zook, M. A. (2005). *The geography of the internet industry: Venture capital, dot-coms, and local knowledge*. Malden, MA: Blackwell.

Zuboff, S. (1988). *In the age of the smart machine: The future of work and power*. New York, NY: Basic Books.

Index

Note: Page numbers followed by "*n*" with numbers indicate notes.

Adopters, 56–57, 74, 83, 85, 155
Age, 41, 53, 57, 60–63, 66, 68–71, 100,
    102, 109–110, 113, 115–118,
    121, 123, 127, 129–130, 153,
    164
Anti-globalization movement, 39
Automaton, 29*n*46, 34

Broadband divide, 85
Broadband Internet (*see also*
    Speed—of Internet
    connection), 85

Capital-enhancing online activities, 123
Capitalism, 9, 12–13, 16, 18, 20,
    22–26, 28, 30, 177
  global informational, 34
  industrial, 29, 34
  informational, 29*n*46, 34, 40,
    177, 179
  and Internet, 40*n*84
  recapitalization, 30
  restructuring, 32
Communication
  channel, 2, 55, 81, 135–136, 144, 151,
    161, 163–165, 176, 177
  skills, 106–107, 115, 172–173
  structure, 34
Community technology center
    project, 51
Comparative analysis, 21, 63, 77*n*115,
    122–123, 141
Composition of household, 63–64
Computer skills, 104–105, 139
Consumption, 21–22, 27, 49, 69, 78
  information, 136
  of luxury goods, 74
Content creation skills, 107

Content-related skills, 105–106
Cyberapartheid, 36
Cultural movements, 38
Deepening divide (*see also* Digital
    divide research), 90, 114
  thesis, 114
Demand-side economies of scale
    (*see* Network effect)
Democratization, 49
Diffusion of innovations theory
    (DOI), 55, 80–90
  critique, 82–84
  curves and categorization of
    adopters, 56
  disconnection with and digital
    divide research, 80–82
  fundamental model of (basic model
    of) 82–84
  normalization model, 88–90
  stratification model,
    5, 88–90, 155
Digital
  generation, 116–117
  immigrants, 116–117
  inclusion, 170
  media, 111
  natives, 116
  skills (*see* Skills, digital)
Digital Agenda for Europe 2020
    strategy, 114
Digital divide, 94–98
  bridging, 40–42, 59–75, 154–157
  contextual approach to, 5, 162,
    165–173, 177
  cultural reproduction of, 148
  dual, 99
  gaps in internet usage, 118–131
  global, 75–80, 145–146

gravity of, 2, 5, 75–76, 80, 88, 113, 124, 131, 137, 154
key argument, 95–96, 104 paradox of the digital divide, 164
organically closing digital divide argument, 55–58
perpetual resurgence of, 84–87
Digital divide research, 1, 45, 58, 176
adaptation to technological change, 135
early research, 48–51
matrix of digital divide dimensions, 92–93
Digital divide thesis, 4–5, 47–48, 87, 96, 98, 103, 111, 123, 135–136, 140, 148, 151, 157, 167–170
assumptions, 84, 133–157
validity, 47, 84, 101, 130–131, 133–134, 147, 154, 164, 166
Digitization (*see also* Informatization), 161
Discursive analysis, 166, 170
Displacement hypothesis, 141–143
Dropouts, 99, 101, 102
Dual digital divide, 99

E-future, 53
Economy
development, 138, 147
neoliberalism, 171
segmentation of, 33
Education, 68–69, 78, 89, 98, 102, 109–110, 121–122, 124, 127, 139, 150, 164
Employment, 71, 68, 97, 99, 140n30
reemployment, 139
structure, 11–12, 26
unemployment, 33–34, 72, 102
Endogeneity trap, 177n12
Equipment
functional (*see also* technology maintenance), 120
ICT, 67, 80
Etatism, 24, 28, 29

Ethnicity, 41, 53, 59, 60, 65, 67–68, 75, 95, 102
Euro-American cultural sphere, 15, 75
European Union (EU), 52, 172, 178, 179
Ex-users (*see* Dropouts)
Exclusion, 33–34, 160

Facebook, 108, 162, 164, 171, 173
Financial resources, insufficient, 103, 153
Formal learning, 114
Functional equipment, 120

Gender, 41, 53, 66, 75, 95
local gender dynamics, 66
Geographic mobility, 166
Geography of the Internet, 73
Gini coefficient, 53, 60, 76
Global digital divide, 75–80, 145–146
Global geometry of new economy, 33–34
Global informational capitalism, 34
Global institutions, 76
Globalization, 20, 30–31, 41
technological dimension, 49
Google, 171
Gravity of digital divide, 2, 5, 75–76, 80, 88, 113, 124, 131, 137, 154

HomeNet study, 141–142
Household, composition of, 63–64

Ideology, information society as, 7, 168
Increase hypothesis, 141–142, 144–145
Indispensability, 160
Individual learning, 114
Individual-blame bias, 150–153, 167
Industrial Age, 8, 28
Industrial mode of development, 27
Industrial society, 35
Inequality, 1, 45
categorical, 95–96
digital, 91
ethnic or racial, 67–68

global, 75, 87, 171
income, 53, 70, 78, 138
local, 87
social, 3, 41, 51, 54, 57–58, 71,
    75, 80–81, 94–96, 100, 115,
    131, 150, 154–156, 167–168,
    173, 177
source of, 97, 115, 160
spatial, 71–72
structural, 104, 124
Information, 27
critique of, 11
economy, 9
policies, 52, 75, 86, 114, 140, 150,
    164–165, 167–173, 177
skills, 105–106, 110, 113
society, 134, 137, 170
Information Age, 10, 13, 17, 39, 45,
    49, 99, 172, 176, 179
Information and communication
    technology (ICT), 1, 2, 57, 85
diffusion, 155
infrastructure, 137
non-exceptionality of ICT
    argument, 53–55
reduction of, 134–136
skills (*see* Skills)
Information society theory, 2, 3, 10,
    147, 164–165, 167, 175–180
arguments and versions, 10–16
comparison of Webster and Duff's
    typology, 15
milestones in development of, 8–10
Information technology, 134
paradigm, 28
revolution, 28
Informational capitalism, 29n46, 34,
    40, 177, 179
Informational democracy, 42
Informational mode of development, 27
Informationalism, 27, 28, 31, 39, 40
Informatization, 14, 171, 175, 180
inevitability of, 153–154
presupposed inevitability, 153–154
Innovativeness, 55, 57, 61, 72, 85, 166
Intermittent users, 99

Internet, 1, 79, 134–136, 139, 159, 162
access, 148–149, 159
diffusion, 161
geography, 73
infrastructure, 176
Internet-mediated communication, 142
universal necessity assumption,
    147–150
Internet Galaxy, 34
Joho Shakai, 13

Knowledge
gap, 124, 127–128, 136
industry, 8
knowledge-based economy, 9
society, 3
worker, 8
Knowledgeability, 128, 145, 160, 166

Labour market, 66, 68–69, 72, 74, 106,
    138–140, 161, 164–165
Lapsed users (*see* Dropouts)
Learning
in communities, 114, 130
formal, 114
individual, 114
informal, 114
LinkedIn, 162

Machlup, Fitz, 8–9, 13n29
Marxism, 18, 19, 25, 168
Mass media, 3, 8, 35–36, 69, 82, 124,
    126–127
Mass communication, transformation
    of, 35–36
Mass self-communication, 35
Matthew effect (*see* Rich-get-richer
    hypothesis), 125, 126–128
Metcalfe's law, 61n52, 162
Microelectronics, 28
Microsoft, 171
Mobile phone, 85–87, 135, 162
Smartphones, 67
SMS communication, 135–136
Mode of production, 20, 24, 26
capitalist, 18, 22–23, 26

Modernization, 12, 22, 27, 126, 171
Myspace (social networking
    platforms), 162

N-Gen, 116
National economies, 33
National Telecommunications and
    Information Administration
    (NTIA), 46, 48, 49
Net Evaders, 101
Network enterprise, 31, 32
Network effect, 61n52
Network externality (*see* Network effect)
Network society, 24, 29, 177
Networked individualism, 37
New economy
    formation, 30–31
    global geometry, 33–34
Non-users, 98, 99
    proxy use, 153
    psychologization, 149
    typology of, 99

Online activities, 5, 50, 58, 86, 106,
    108, 112, 115, 118, 122–130,
    134, 137, 143
Operational skills, 105
Organization(al)
    change, 30–31, 32
    contemporary forms of, 32
    network enterprise, 32
    transformations, 32
Outcomes of Internet use, 91, 107,
    111–113, 129–130
    digital factors of, 146
    proportional, positive and constant
    outcomes, 136–147

Paradox of the digital divide, 164
Post-industrial society, 3, 9–10
Post-modern society, 3
Pro-innovation bias, 153–154
Production, 21, 24
    late-capitalist, 20
    mode of, 20, 24, 26

Proxy use, 153
Psychologization, 149
Public transport infrastructure, 163

Race, 53, 59, 60, 67, 68
Reflexive modernization theory, 12
Reproduction
    cultural of digital divide, 148
    intergenerational, 41
    social, 126
Resistance, transformation of, 38–40
Rich-get-richer hypothesis, 145–146

S-curve of adoption, 55–57, 69, 88,
    89, 153
Science and technology studies, 178
Self-efficacy, 109n240
Skills, digital
    communication skills, 106, 107,
    115, 172–173
    computer skills, 104–105, 139
    content creation skills, 107
    content-related skills, 105–106
    formal skills, 105–106, 109–110
    information skills, 105–106, 110, 113
    medium-related skills, 105, 109
    operational skills, 105
    performance tests, 110
    strategic skills, 105–106, 111
    typology of, 105–106
Sociability, 37n72, 65, 166
    displacement hypothesis, 141–143
    increase hypothesis, 141–142,
    144–145
    rich-get-richer hypothesis,
    145–146
    social-compensation hypothesis, 145
    supplement hypothesis, 141
    transformation of, 36–38
Social
    change, 3, 8, 11–12, 14–17, 19,
    21, 23, 25, 28, 38, 40, 43,
    155, 178
    distribution of knowledge, 156
    engagement, 166

environment, 150
formations, 18
participation via alternative
    routes, 137
responsibility of sociologists, 178
Social capital, 141–142
Social construction of information
    society, 3
Social networks, 29–30, 160, 161
peer effects, 65
Social structure, 3, 9, 18, 20, 22, 24,
    25, 27, 33, 39, 40, 125–126,
    128, 175, 178
Social support, 38
in Internet use, 65, 123, 151–153,
    160–161
Society
information, 2, 4, 10–13, 16,
    27, 84, 90, 125, 134, 137,
    154, 170–171, 175, 178, 180
informational, 14, 27n40,
    101, 176
interactive, 36
postindustrial, 10
two-speed, 88
Socio-technical infrastructure, 178
Solaris, 33
Soviet socialism, 26
Space
social, 55 , 73
socially structured, 71
subnational, 71, 73–74
urban, 17, 20, 21, 24, 31
Spatial inequality on national
    level, 71
Speed
of economic processes, 138
of innovation diffusion, 55
of Internet connection, 74, 76,
    84–86
Sporadic use, 100
Strategic skills, 105–106, 111
Stratification model, 88–90
Structuralism, 20

Subnational spaces, 71, 73–74
Supplement hypothesis, 141
Techno-economic structure, 9
Technology (*see also* Information and
    communication technology
    (ICT))
maintenance, 100
spheres, 28
Technology Opportunities Program, 51
Telecommunications, 28, 162
Telephone, 50, 79, 143–144, 155
Theory of information society (TIS),
    2, 7–16, 125, 134, 157, 164
as ideology, 173
critiques of, 168
Japanese, 14
universal applicability of, 177
validity of, 131, 147, 176
Threshold hypothesis, 143, 147
Total inclusion principle, 164–165
Totalizing tendency of theory, 175,
    175n3, 176–177
Touraine, Alain, 17
'Truly unconnected', 99, 101, 102

Unemployment, 33–34, 72, 102
United Nations Development
    Programme, 76
Universal
dispensability, 159
modernization, 27
Urbanization, 22–23, 78
dependent, 22–23
forms of, 20
indicators, 22
mass, 41
Usage gap, 124–125
growing usage gap thesis, 126

Volatility, economic, 33, 41, 138

World Summit on Information
    Society, 76
World Wide Web (www), 45